Mac OS X for Windows Users

A Switchers' Guide

David Coursey

Peachpit Press • Berkeley, California

Mac OS X for Windows Users: A Switchers' Guide

David Coursey

Peachpit Press

1249 Eighth Street
Berkeley, CA 94710
510/524-2178
800/283-9444
510/524-2221 (fax)
Find us on the World Wide Web at: http://www.peachpit.com
Peachpit Press is a division of Pearson Education.

Copyright © 2003 by David Coursey

Editor: Clifford Colby
Production Coordinator: Connie Jeung-Mills
Copyeditors: Lisa Halliday and Elissa Rabellino
Compositor: Owen Wolfson
Indexer: Joy Dean Lee
Cover Design: David Brier

Apple "Switcher" photography by Mark Lipson

ISBN 0-321-16889-5

9 8 7 6 5 4 3 2 1

Acknowledgments

This book grew out of a fight between Natalie Sequeira and myself. Nat works for Apple PR and is, fight aside, a sweetheart. I should have fights that turn into books more often, I suppose. The Apple PR staff has a tough job—and it's not just dealing with me.

There are a zillion other people to thank at Apple, but I want to mention here one person by name—Keri Walker—who runs the editorial loan program that keeps the Macintosh in front of the media. Keri has done as much as any single person I know, save Steve Jobs, to promote Apple's cause.

I want to thank my sweetheart, Elionora Bjuhr, for putting up with me during the months it took to get this book together. She and my two children, Larry and Mo Coursey, were most understanding during the times I was somewhat less than pleasant while trying to kick out another chapter. I feel much better now that this book is done.

Thank you to my AnchorDesk colleagues—Pat, Dan, Sylvia, and Candy—for their tolerance of a columnist turned first-time author. Also to Brian and Christy and the rest of the CNET Radio crew.

Cliff Colby has been a most patient editor. Much more than a disorganized author could hope for. He made important contributions to this book. Thanks also to Connie Jeung-Mills, who handled the production of this book and created something really nice out of a zillion Word documents. If you are thinking about writing a computer book, Peachpit is a great group of folks to work with. It's always nice to call around and find out that the very first offer was more than fair. Those are people you go out of your way to work with.

Thanks also to Lisa Halliday, Ernie Mariette, and Ron Johnson for their help along the way. And to Tiffany, Jody Wickett, Rhonda Holland, David Pogue, Deb McAlister, Rob Enderle, Tim Bajarin, Michael J. Miller, Jim Louderback, Jim Strothman, Jim Casella, Stewart Alsop, Lois Breedlove, Ben Harold, Doug Michels, Philippe Kahn, Ed Ring, Chris Hayes, Allan Coursey, Russ Van Kirk, Shannon O'Brien, Theresa Vernon, Fred Varian, Kimberly Brown, and Sally Atkins. If you are not on this short list, it doesn't mean you aren't important to me—just that I am past deadline. As usual.

Special thanks to Dr. George Reed, without whom this book would not have been possible.

And finally, thanks to Apple's Lindsey Chow and Jerry Hsu and to the Apple Switchers who gave so generously of their time to help me write a book that future Switchers will hopefully find useful.

David Coursey

david@coursey.com

January 2003

Table of Contents

Chapter 7 Software Questions   125

Chapter 8 Getting Connected   167

Chapter 9 Viruses, Hackers, Backups, and Dealing with Emergencies 199

Chapter 10 My Annotated Top 10 Reasons to Switch 219

Switcher or Adder?

Thank you for buying my book (or for merely thumbing through it if you're not past the cash register yet). I appreciate the opportunity to have a conversation with you that I've always wanted to have but that a lack of time has usually prevented.

It's the conversation I've had—always in a much more limited form—with dozens, perhaps hundreds, of people who wanted to know if a Macintosh was the right computer for them. Some made a pro-Mac decision and some didn't, but I felt all had at least given thought to which computer would be best for them.

With this book, I hope to expand the conversation both in the number of people I can have it with and in quality. The contents of this book would make a long conversation in person, but as computer books go, this is actually quite a small one. You can read as much (or as little) as meets your needs.

This is a book written by a veteran Microsoft Windows user for other Windows users. This is also a book by a guy who used to use a Mac all the time and after five Windows-only years has recently started using a Mac again every day. My office is arranged so that turning one way I face Mac OS X and turning the other I am squarely in front of Windows XP.

I like it this way because I have the two best operating systems I have ever seen surrounding me at all times. OK, that sounds a little weird, but I write about technology and that means writing about Microsoft. I also love technology, so my interest naturally extends to Apple as well.

By Apple's standards this makes me a *Switcher*—someone who has moved from Windows to Macintosh. I realize that, strictly speaking, I haven't switched so much as added a Mac back into my life. But the geniuses behind Apple's advertising, searching around for a replacement for the grammatically incorrect "Think Different" and willing at long last to take a swipe at Microsoft, decided that turning Windows users into "Switchers" was sexier than urging them to become mere "Adders." And since a family of deadly serpents already had the trademark on *adder,* the choice was made.

In preparing this book, I have spoken—traded emails mostly—with hundreds of Switchers. Many of them are folks like me who use a Windows machine for some tasks and a Mac for others. Some use a Windows machine at work and a Mac at home. Others bought a Mac rather than upgrade their Windows computer but kept the old machine around should they ever need it. And some, the hard core, bought a Mac and then sold their PC on eBay or somewhere.

I am writing this book for people who have Windows experience and have either just purchased their first Macintosh or are considering joining the Switchers of the world. Ideally, this book would start with a discussion of the reasons why people switch and help you make the buy/no-buy decision.

But Cliff and David, who are editing this masterpiece and know a lot more about the book business than I do (an easy accomplishment, I should add), expect that you've just bought a Mac and, having developed some sort of psychic connection with the book, added it to your purchase on the way out of the store.

I am not one to argue with the guys who decide whether I get the book advance payment or not. Also, having written five or six false starts at a first chapter that began, "To switch or not to switch, that ...," I've decided to go along with the experts. So if you haven't already purchased a Mac, read on. If you are already a Mac owner, feel free to skip ahead to Chapter 3 and read the rest of this chapter later.

Hopefully, you saw the nice rebate we're offering on Detto's Move2Mac software, bought a copy of it with your new Mac, and will get the rebate—making this book an exceptionally good value, if I may say so myself. Move2Mac is covered extensively in Chapter 3, and if you haven't already moved your files from the PC to your new Mac, I'd recommend that you buy the software because it sure beats moving the files manually, described in Chapter 4.

One of the things that surprised me about the Switchers I met was how long many had been using Windows—and that many of them were obviously very competent Windows users. Some of this is doubtlessly because the Switchers were largely self-selected, responding either to Apple's request for Switcher stories or to mine on ZDNet AnchorDesk. I am not sure how many people who felt they had miserably failed learning Windows—which is really Windows' failing them—would have responded.

In this book, I will presume at least some Windows familiarity but won't overdo it. If you feel competent editing your Windows Registry, you don't have to feel embarrassed about it any longer: Macs don't have anything remotely like a Registry, which to me proves the existence of a higher power who loves Mac users. But if you are a Windows expert, parts of this book will definitely be below your level. Get over it and be happy for all the times your new Mac won't suffer a problem that seems to have no cause and that Bill Gates himself couldn't diagnose.

Since I am not sure precisely what you've done already, I am going to start right after you've unpacked the Mac, and I will figure you did just fine setting it up and plugging it in. After that, the book takes a mostly chronological tour of getting your Mac running, applications loaded, information moved from your Windows machine, a network set up, and your Mac connected to any other computers you own.

And of course, we'll get your printer working and talk about some fun things you can do with your Mac, compare the look and feel of Mac OS and Windows, and decide whether you really need to invest in a copy of Microsoft Office for your new Mac. (If you can get it cheap with the new Mac, through a promotion that's running as I write this, go ahead and pay the $200. But over $400? Well, read and see.)

Finally, as an answer to the question asked by that guy who wondered why we all can't just get along, I'll show you how and why to run Windows on your Macintosh.

Along the way, I will also propagandize you on the Mac way of doing things and even explain why the Mac is the way it is. And why we love it.

But there is one thing I will not do: I will not tell you Windows XP is a bad operating system. To be absolutely honest, I actually like Windows XP, but don't get me started on that brain-damaged Windows Me. Anything negative I say about Windows is independent of my feelings toward Macintosh.

"So what are those feelings?" you may ask, though hopefully not in the tone of a father quizzing his teenage daughter's new boyfriend. It's a reasonable question, and the answers explain why I've written this book and my approach in doing so.

1. I believe that many people would be better off with a Mac as their primary computer, yet few of those people ever consider buying one. It's my hope that some of those people will read this book and make the best decision for them.

2. I believe that the Mac approach to computing is better than the Windows approach. At the same time, the success of Macintosh is dependent upon a level of control over operating system, hardware, and applications that Microsoft will never enjoy. This is one of the things that allow Apple the freedom to innovate that it enjoys. Mac OS X is a great operating system in large part because it doesn't carry the burden of being everybody's operating system.

3. I find the Mac almost to be a noncomputer, at least compared with Windows—and that's not said in a pejorative way. When using a Mac I don't spend very much time thinking about the computer. This frees

me to pay more attention to the work—which could be why so many creative people have adopted the Mac as their primary computer.

4. I am pro-Mac, but I am pro-Windows, too. I am as excited by the improvement Apple made with Mac OS X as I am by what Microsoft accomplished with Windows XP. I think Mac OS X is the more perfect operating system, but Microsoft has to deal with many issues Apple never faces. So the two companies should be judged on different standards—but the most important is what's best for a particular customer.

Now that I have bared my computing soul, I'll do what a stand-up guy does: change the subject to something I am much more comfortable talking about—me.

Who Is David Coursey?

As I write this (and hope to be long after I finish), I am the executive editor of ZDNet AnchorDesk (www.anchordesk.com). That's a fancy title that means ZDNet pays me way too much to just call me a columnist, which is closer to what I really am. I am also a host of a daily hour on CNET Radio (www. cnetradio.com) and do video segments for CNET.com and News.com. (CNET owns ZDNet.)

I have spent the last 20 years involved in personal computing— that's half my life and the full lifetimes of both the PC and the Macintosh. For the past decade, I've been a commentator and analyst, which some companies I've written about have shortened to "all-pro pain in the ass." I've hosted important conferences, helped introduce products such as the original Palm Pilot, and even been called a "computer expert" by Bill Gates. Steve Jobs, meanwhile, came pretty close to calling me a bozo when I didn't immediately appreciate the wonders of iPhoto. I'd like to think Bill was right and am embarrassed that Steve was.

I have lots of friends at both Apple and Microsoft as well as at many other companies in personal technology, the Internet, and consumer electronics. My bet is that this book will piss them off about equally—but they will get over it because even if they don't agree, they give me credit for having been around long enough and correct often enough to have earned the right to an opinion.

You are welcome to send comments about this book to this special email address: book@coursey.com. (Catchy, huh?) I cannot promise to respond to your comments and really won't promise to answer questions, but everything you send will help improve future versions of this book.

It Gets Out of the Way

This book grew out of a series of columns I wrote for AnchorDesk during early 2002. Having been away from the Mac for about five years, I thought the arrival of the new iMacs and Mac OS X seemed a good time to revisit my old friend. The question these columns sought to answer was this: Can a Windows user find happiness with a Mac? Or, put another way, does it pay to be a Switcher?

In short, yes. Not for every Windows user, but I've been quite happy using the Mac for a wide variety of tasks and could probably live without a Windows machine if I had to. Of course, what I'd actually do would be to keep a Windows box around, just in case. And if you have access to a Windows box, you'll be able to appreciate—over and over—what makes a Mac so nice.

Even if I didn't like Mac OS X and my iMac so much, I'd still keep one around. Why? Because at any given moment my Mac is more likely to be working flawlessly than my Windows machine. And if I am in a rush and don't want to mess with a computer, the Mac is always ready for me.

At the end of my series of AnchorDesk Switcher columns, I spent a lot of time thinking about what it was that I liked so much about the Macintosh. I thought about a simple user interface, great graphics, and tight integration between the hardware, applications, and operating system. But even the sum of these things didn't add up to the good feeling so many people report having toward their Macs.

Eventually, I settled on a simple phrase that explained how I felt but that I wasn't sure anyone else would understand. I summed up what I like about "the Macintosh experience" by saying that I liked having a computer that just got out of the way. And after a year of daily Mac use, I still feel the same way, though I can now elaborate just a bit.

When I'm using Windows, the fact that I'm using a computer is never far from my mind. Typically, there is some undiagnosable oddness going on—such as the PC that won't save passwords, the one with no sound, or the copy of Outlook that's having trouble connecting

(I have one of each right now). Because of this, I am never very far from thinking about Windows. Even if everything is working fine, Windows is always on my mind.

Now, when I first wrote this—the "Mac gets out of the way" thing—I felt as if I had taken the easy way out, that I'd simply been unable to capture something that should have been easy to explain. So I was very happy when I talked to Switchers who, in some cases, used those exact words to describe what they liked most about using a Mac.

Again, I like Windows a whole lot, and while I could have written this book in Word for Windows, it was much easier on the Mac. That's because when I'm using a Mac—whether for writing, editing video, correcting digital photographs, or even doing something like trading instant messages—I'm much more connected to the creative process. Why? I think it's because Macintosh, well, just gets out of the way, so I spend more time thinking about what I am creating and less time worrying about the computer itself.

Looking back at what I've just written, I feel as if I should be submitting this to *New Age Journal* rather than putting in into a computer book. But I really do feel connected to my Mac in a way that I have never felt connected to Windows. Where Windows is sometimes my enemy, or at least a challenger in a war of wits to make something work, Macintosh just seems to work.

You can intellectualize that any way you want, but what I—and a number of Switchers I've talked to—like most about the Macintosh is *the way it makes us feel*.

A Special Welcome to Linux and Unix Users

Yes, I know some of the people who are buying Macs these days are doing so because Mac OS X is a Unix-based operating system. The way I look at it, a Macintosh is the perfect machine for someone who wants the benefits of Unix but also wants to live in the real world where Microsoft Office rules Corporate America.

With a Mac, you get all this and more, including the ability to run Office and Windows atop Mac OS X without giving up access to the command line; plus, you get effortless portability and wireless networking—prized abilities in the Unix world.

So while I welcome you, I can't dedicate my life to helping you. If you're conversant with Unix, a quick skim of this book will tell you all you need to know about Mac OS X. I won't even try to delve into the Unix aspects of Mac OS X, as I'd be well beyond my depth.

For that information, let me refer you to two of Peachpit's books on Unix—*Unix: Visual QuickStart Guide* and *Unix for Mac OS X: Visual QuickPro Guide*.

"My PC wasn't Plug-n-Play.
It was Plug-n-Get-Mad."

apple.com/switch

Switcher Diary: JANIE PORCHE

Throughout this book I will be introducing you to people who have switched (or added) a Mac to their lives. Some of these will be people from the Apple ads (I call them "celebrity Switchers"), and the others will be people who responded to Apple's request for Switcher stories—but didn't get into the ads—or to a request I put out on ZDNet AnchorDesk.

Janie Porche, the woman who used a Mac to "save Christmas," is a Texan, just like me. She grew up there and is also attending college in the Lone Star state. None of this I would have guessed from the commercial, but I am proud of her, the way all Texans are proud of somebody who's "done good."

Janie does not, for the record, watch television, though she says she had a blast at the commercial shoot in Los Angeles. You can find out just a little more about her by visiting janieporche.com.

In our email interview, I asked her about how the commercial has affected her life.

Janie: The experience with the commercial has been really positive—I truly never thought that sending in an email to a "Feedback" link would lead to all this! There are a few "fans" out there who are a little too eager to contact me—they have posted my address on the Internet, started Stalking Janie Porche Web sites, etc. etc. This motivated me to make an email address where people can contact me, at dontbecreepy@janieporche.com.

But, creepy people aside, everyone who has contacted me has been friendly and curious—they want to know how I got chosen, whether the story is true, and so on. I cannot respond to all of their emails, but I generally read them all and at least share them with my roommates. I have received job offers, scripts to read, and comments from Apple and Microsoft employees. However, I am a busy student … so for the most part, I ignore what is going on and stay out of the way of the "15 minutes of fame" phenomenon.

David: Although Janie "saved Christmas" by using her Mac to download some pictures when Windows balked, that wasn't enough to convince her dad to switch, even if the story was all over national television.

Janie: I am still trying to get my parents to make "the switch"—I am convinced that if my dad bought a Mac for the family for Christmas, that would be the ultimate follow-up commercial. But, he insists that while the ol' PC is still working, there's no need for a new one. (PC users, bah.)

David: How do you rate your Windows skills?

Janie: My Windows skills are above average. I have spent hours upon hours with my father, building and rebuilding our home computers from parts. I have had to deal with every sort of hardware problem and its resolution. Many of the schools that I attended used primarily Windows machines, which increased my comfort level even more. While I am not any sort of certified technician or Windows expert by any means, I definitely feel comfortable in the Windows environment.

Switcher Diary: JANIE PORCHE

David: Do you still use Windows? If so, please explain.

Janie: My university has several Power Macs, but primarily it is a Windows campus. Whenever I do any work at school, I am forced to work on a Dell machine running Windows 2000. The technology director for the video and audio editing labs agrees that Macs are the better choice, but it would appear that we are locked into a Dell contract that puts PCs on every desk.

David: How did you become a Mac user?

Janie: First, the frivolous reason—I saw a commercial for the PowerBook G4 and nearly cried. It has been out for—what?—over a year now and still remains the best-looking laptop on the market. My Titanium lust was urged on by the fact that I had just moved away to college and was having ridiculous problems with my PC. Video cards weren't compatible, Windows was locking up, I was prone to viruses and bugs, software was constantly crashing, I never felt that my PC was fast enough, and on and on and on. I knew that I was interested in the world of digital design, and there is no substitute for a Mac in that field. I did a lot of research online, spoke with Mac users on campus, and started saving the money, and, in August of 2001, logged on to the Internet and bought a PowerBook from Apple for $2500.

David: What do you consider to be the most important differences between using a Mac and using a PC?

Janie: With the integration of software packages such as Microsoft Office and the cross-platform ease of Adobe and Macromedia products, I hardly notice a functional difference between Windows and Mac—with the ever important exception of stability.

David: What was the most confusing part of using Mac OS?

Janie: Remembering to close the window in the top-left corner and not the top-right. That's about it.

David: What do you wish you had known before switching? And what were your biggest concerns?

Janie: I wish I had known before just how many people use Macs—there are way more Mac users out there than people would believe. They form a community unlike any other, offering tech support, buying advice, software conflict resolution, or upgrade opinions. These people form a valuable network—almost a club—that I wish I had known about earlier.

David: What Mac applications do you use?

Janie: Office, Photoshop, GoLive, Flash, Final Cut Pro, Premiere, iTunes, iCal, InDesign, Reason, and my favorite, Stickies.

David: What do you do with your Mac and where do you do it?

Janie: I'm a college student—so I write papers, do research, check email, and download music with my PowerBook. But I am also a designer, which means that I use my PowerBook for Web applications, imaging, and video and music editing. It is my only computer, and I am on it constantly. It travels to the school library, to grad school interviews, to friends' houses, and to commercial shoots (ha!).

Why People Switch

I had planned to write this book from the perspective of a potential Switcher, offering guidance on the benefits and challenges one faces after trading in a PC for a Mac.

Better judgment prevailed at the publisher, however, so the book begins at the point where the reader has decided to switch and has just brought the new machine home. Still, I'd like to address the questions that someone who is merely considering switching would have.

I hope that when you're through with this book, you'll share it with people who are thinking about switching and point them to this chapter. Or perhaps you can suggest they actually buy the book and read this part of the chapter first. Either way, I'd be grateful and perhaps we will have both done your friend a favor.

I know that nothing I say in this book can replace your recommendation and the up-close assistance you can offer a potential Switcher, but perhaps having this book to refer to will save you from answering quite so *many* questions.

Recovering from Windows

"Hi. My name is DJ and I am a recovering PC user."

That's how Dwight Joslin began his email to Apple Computer, responding to a request for people to share stories of why they switched from Microsoft Windows to Apple Macintosh.

Here's Dwight's story:

I've used PCs for years. I've upgraded, replaced, then upgraded again but could never stop my PC from locking up for no apparent reason. It was always the Windows OS from 3.1 right up through XP. There I'd be, right in the middle of a project or download, and then the blue screen of death. XP isn't much better. And security has always been an issue with Windows.

I happened to see a picture of the new iMac on the Net, and it caught my eye. Not only was it the most advanced-looking computer I have ever seen but the coolest as well. I had never been a Mac fan, mostly because of the price but also because it seemed Apple couldn't match the performance of a PC.

So I was pleasantly surprised to read the reviews. The price tag was much better than I thought it would be, as well. I took a chance and bought the top-level iMac. I'm pleased to report that I've been very happy with my iMac with Mac OS X. I love Mac OS X and the stability it offers so much that I've decided to sell my Gateway PC and replace it with a dual G4 Mac system.

Some people told Apple that they had switched after discovering Macintosh to be the best tool for their professional life. University professor Joyce Nutta specializes in distance learning but found she couldn't produce instructional materials by herself—at least not until she discovered the Macintosh. And after that, well, let her tell you:

I am constantly developing materials for my classes, and with a PC I had to depend on others to produce videos and multimedia presentations. I went to a faculty training session and saw how easy Macs made video production and editing, as well as organizing and presenting photographs and music. It was liberating to learn that I no longer needed to depend on others to develop my ideas into materials.

Soon thereafter, I got an iBook and an iMac, and then I bought my kids two iBooks. My husband chucked his PC clone and now is the proud owner of an iMac. My kids and I also purchased iPods so that we're tethered to a Mac of some sort at all times. We are now a 100 percent Mac family, and we find that there's something special about folks who are Mac users. We would never go back!

And there is Wesley Underwood, a student who turned an Apple iPod MP3 player into a constant companion.

In March 2002, I gave myself the best birthday present I ever got. The iPod is the greatest invention ever. It's awesome to be able to listen to whatever you want, whenever you want, or to be able to listen to your 50 favorite songs in random order.

All my music is on my computer. I'm 16, and my friends and family joke about how my iPod has become a part of me, and I never go anywhere without my iBook.

The only downside about owning a Mac is all the people who still think their clunky Windows machines are better than my Mac, but I know better. I just smile and nod. Thank you, Apple, for helping me find my passion in my life.

Those are three typical stories selected from among the thousands Apple received from its customers. Some were chosen to appear in a groundbreaking series of television, print, and online advertisements. These especially photogenic people are now enjoying their 15 minutes of fame—some even have Web sites created by their fans.

In preparing this book, I've had exclusive access to hundreds of these stories as well as the original email messages that Apple received. I've also traded email with dozens of Switchers, both those introduced to me by Apple and others I've found through my ZDNet AnchorDesk columns and by referrals from friends and Mac user groups.

Mac Users Are Different

For years, I've believed that if more Windows users were exposed to the Macintosh, many of them would end up buying a Mac. It hardly ever works in reverse: Very few Mac users will ever take a Windows machine as their new "favorite" computer.

There is a fundamental difference between Windows and Macintosh users: Most Windows users are sheep, while most Mac users decided to think for themselves and buy the computer they wanted for themselves.

I know that sounds strong, and perhaps *sheep* isn't the right word, but when you became a Windows user, was it because you actually chose Windows? Or was it because you were forced to use it (such as at work) or just bought what everyone seemed to be buying? After all, you have to go out of your way *not* to buy a Windows-based computer.

While most Windows users became Windows users by default— or because somebody else made the decision for them—every Macintosh user I know made the decision on his or her own. Now that decision is yours.

But it's not a decision you'll have to make by yourself.

About This Book

This is a book for people who want to make their own decisions about the computer that's best for them. It is a book by a Windows user for other Windows users. It is also a book by a Macintosh user for his Windows-using friends. My hope is that this book will be the long conversation I'd like to have with everyone who has seen my Mac and asked the question "Should I buy one, too?"

This book grew out of a series of columns—included here— that I wrote in early 2002, almost immediately after the new iMac came out. The idea was for me to spend a month using a Mac as my primary tool, doing all the things on the Macintosh using Mac OS X that I would normally do in Windows.

My Month-on-a-Mac extended into three months, partly because I had the flu for a month but also because I can be a very slow product reviewer when I'm having a good time.

The iMac turned out to be a much pleasanter computer than I'd expected. The screen really could move into almost any position, making it easy to find a comfortable position at my desk. The screen was also very easy on the eyes, though a bit too small.

AirPort was the easiest wireless network I'd ever set up, and I've been using wireless networks in my home since the beginning. My printer just installed itself and started working, as did my Olympus digital camera, a Canon video camera, and of course, an iPod.

In the interest of full disclosure, this was not my first Mac experience. But about five years ago I was a Switcher of a different kind: I went from using Macs in my small business to using Windows machines—not because I didn't like my Macs but because it didn't seem that we could run my newsletter and conference business on them. Today I might make a different decision, but it was the right thing to do at the time.

So after using Macs for five years as my main computer, I spent the next five years hardly touching them at all. My Month-on-a-Mac was intended to answer the question of whether a confirmed and fairly expert Windows user could find happiness using Mac OS X.

The test went well enough that while I didn't trash my Windows machines, I now use a Mac for most of my writing as well as digital photography and video editing. I love my iPod, but I haven't found a Palm OS device that beats my iPAQ and Pocket PC. So, I've ended up with one foot in the Mac camp and the other still firmly planted in Windows. I don't have any choice; playing with computers—both Windows machines and Macs—is my job.

Peachpit Press approached me about expanding the columns to book length, and you're holding the result. This book is not intended to tell you everything you might want to know about Macintosh. But it will carry you from the "Do I want a Mac?" stage through the purchase, taking it home, installing applications, and moving data over from your PC, and it will introduce you to your Mac as a digital hub for your home and family. Along the way, you'll learn about Mac OS X, setting up networks, sharing files with Windows users, and even how to run Windows on your new Mac.

There are only two questions I am certain this book won't answer: I won't decide for you what computer you should use, and I won't tell you what computer I'd use if I could only use Mac or Windows. That's a question I go out of my way to never seriously consider: I think I'd end up going nuts.

I do not claim to know the answer for every individual. There are many good reasons for someone not to switch from Windows to Mac, and throughout this book you will find them.

But there are also tens of millions of people for whom Macintosh would be a better choice than Windows but who have never had someone around to answer their questions.

If you're one of those folks, I'm at your service.

But first, let me apologize for some of my fellow Mac users, who can be a bit like excited puppies—or perhaps like the most evangelical members of some 12-step program. Or maybe they're at times like those folks who try to get you into their multilevel marketing schemes.

Most Mac users I know fall into the category of "true believers," and they are so excited about their Macs that they want everyone to share their excitement. Windows users can be excused for finding this a bit tiring. Especially since Mac users tend to use one word to describe their computers that I haven't heard used to describe a Windows machine in many years:

Love.

If you get Macintosh users talking about their computer, it won't be very long before either they tell you they love their Mac or their affection for the computer becomes patently obvious. And you may ask yourself a very reasonable question (for a Windows user): Are these people nuts?

Yes and no.

In the good sense of the word, many Mac users really are nuts over their computers. There are, for example, doubtless many more Macs whose owners have given them names than there are Windows computers similarly honored—at least with names that can be shared in polite company.

Mac users, however, also tend to behave a bit like members of a persecuted minority, which can become old pretty fast. It's important to admit that Macintosh isn't all things to all people.

But it could be everything to you.

Another thing that drives Mac users' evangelism is their painful childhoods, by which I refer to the many years some of them spent using Windows machines—often not knowing that computing didn't have to be so terrible. Having switched to a Mac, they have come to see Windows as the enemy and Windows users as the great unwashed.

If only there were more Mac users in the world, they would no doubt send their children off on bicycles, wearing conservative clothing, to go door-to-door to share the good news of a computer that wasn't so difficult to use. You might find articles from *Macworld* magazine, printed on cheap paper, left propped next to the front doors of millions of American households, waiting for the arrival of some poor Windows user, tempting him or her to the better way.

But the better way for whom? Let me say it right here: The Macintosh is not for everyone, just as Windows *shouldn't* be for everyone. This book will discuss why you might not want to make the switch to Mac and why some Mac users (myself included) also still use Windows machines—or even run Windows on their Macs (guilty again).

So if you're expecting a Mac good/Windows bad book, this won't be it. But if you're considering a Mac, I'm sure I can help you make the right choice.

Switchers Defined

Technically speaking, a Switcher is anyone who has used a Windows-based personal computer and who now uses a Macintosh. You can make the definition as complex or simple as you like. To be a "real" Switcher, must you forsake all your Windows machines? Even if it costs you your job?

Probably not.

What about people who are perfectly happy using a Mac for some tasks and a Windows machine for others? Or people who—gasp!—run Windows on their Macs, courtesy of a program called Virtual PC? (It really works, and we discuss it elsewhere in the book.)

And there are those people who buy a portable Mac to use on the road but are still tied to Windows everywhere else.

I choose to be ecumenical about this: If you add a Mac to your computing, you're a Switcher and should be proud of it. Take me, for example—I have no choice but to use a Windows computer in my work, being that it largely involves writing columns and talking on the radio about Windows and the world that revolves around Redmond, Washington, where Microsoft is based.

But I also use a Macintosh, and not just for writing this book. I find the Mac gets out of my way when I am trying to be creative. I never forget the computer when I am using Windows—it won't let me. When I am working on the Mac, however, I am better able to focus on what I am trying to say, rather than the process of saying it.

I also use the Mac for digital photography and making home movies, and I love my iPod, which I've loaded with music, audio books, and my collection of old radio programs (Jack Benny and *Dragnet,* not my own shows). Since my iPod also can carry my contact list and calendar, sometimes it's the only device I really need when I am away from the office.

There is one more thing I like about my Mac: It's reliable. For years I have kept a Mac in the office ready for use when Windows (or more likely a Windows application) gives up the ghost and I've got more important things to do than fix a computer.

Why People Switch

Why do people move from Windows to Macintosh? Having read the stories of hundreds of Switchers and talked to dozens more, I've found the answer to be really simple:

1. Switchers had a bad Windows experience, or perhaps 15 years of bad Windows experiences, and

2. They fell in love with the Macintosh and Mac OS.

It's about as simple as that, although there is usually a Mac user somewhere between steps one and two. Someone had to introduce the potential Switcher to the Mac. I found very few Switchers who were minding their own business when they passed the Apple Store and felt a sudden urge to own one of those cute new iMacs.

Many, in fact, spent weeks or even months thinking about moving to the Mac before making a move. Switcher Danny Cox is one of these:

> *A few months before I bought my iMac, I spent hours on apple.com reading everything I could. The main factor in my choice to buy a Mac was Mac OS X. I was so impressed. I would watch the videos on the Web site over and over again. I couldn't get enough. So I finally bought my Mac and haven't turned back since. I will NEVER, EVER buy a PC again.*

What is it about the Macintosh that makes Danny so happy? It's that using Windows caused him to feel a great deal of stress. That feeling vanished when a Mac arrived in his life.

> *Windows can make even power users like me feel uncertain about some things—not Mac OS X. It's so simple that I'm not afraid to change something. Thank you so much for creating a product that people can actually enjoy using.*

But often it's not so much that people hate Windows as much as they love—there's that word again—things that the Macintosh makes possible for them. Switcher James Grossman considers himself a "skilled PC user" but chose the Macintosh after an event that changed his life.

> *Prior to buying my G4, I hadn't used a Mac in 16 years. I currently manage a technology fund. I use and analyze a lot of technology. I like to think I am a skilled PC user. What brought me back to Mac was when I had my first child.*
>
> *We have thousands of digital pictures, hundreds of hours of digital video, and no way to really organize it all. Then I started to read about this new Unix-based operating system called Mac OS X. Read about Final Cut Pro and iMovie. Spent an entire month on Apple's Web site. I finally configured my dream machine at the Apple Store.*

Bought a G4 Dual 800 MHz, 1 GB of memory, two 80 GB hard drives, and an absolutely gorgeous 22-inch Studio Display. Can't forget the iPod. I was so blown away I needed more. One month later, I bought a PowerBook so I could take my fun on the road. My friends at first thought I might need counseling. Until they saw how really cool my stuff was. Now, they're converting.

I've included in the book interviews with several Switchers, and in the interests of fairness—and because some of the Switcher email surprised me—I need to point out that many of the people you will meet in this book are quite Windows-savvy. These people knew, or could presumably figure out, how to do almost anything they wanted to do on a Windows machine.

So I was more than a bit surprised when these Windows power users switched to the Macintosh to do things I know Windows does pretty well. What was it about Mac that so attracted them?

I think it's the difference between Windows' doing things well and the Mac's doing the same tasks both well and easily—traits you will see demonstrated throughout this book.

Switcher Diary: JIM FEUERSTEIN

"I was no longer going to have technical guys to get my machine running for me when it broke."

Despite using Windows for nearly a decade and becoming a designer and builder of complex database and Lotus Notes applications, Jim Feuerstein never became comfortable with Windows itself. Yet he successfully started and managed a small Windows software business.

But when he sold the business, Feuerstein left the protective cocoon of having Windows technical-support people close at hand, so he selected a computing platform he could fully master himself. And as you'll see, he had very specific reasons for choosing—and falling in love with—Macintosh.

Jim: I was an adept and sophisticated user of applications (including high-level development environments such as Lotus Notes or database tools, where I designed and built apps), but I was at a loss when something went wrong with Windows itself.

David: How did you become a Mac user?

Jim: There were multiple factors. It will be helpful if I start by telling you my situation when I switched. I had just sold my business—a small software company (Windows software, of course)—and was about to leave the company and do other things. I had been management for long enough that my serious technical skills were outdated, and I had been relying for years on the technical-support guys to keep my own PC running.

When I left that environment and wanted to buy a laptop for personal use, this is how I saw my situation:

1. I was no longer going to have technical guys to get my machine running for me when it broke.

2. My computer needs were pretty basic: portability, Web access, email, word processing, and spreadsheets.

And, of course, this was the time when Apple was reviving itself with the iMac and the iBook.

So I figured it was worth a try.

David: What do you consider to be the most important differences between using a Mac and using a PC?

Jim:

1. Stuff just *works*. I plug in a digital video camera, and iMovie says "Camera Connected" and, with the push of a VCR-like control, begins downloading the contents. I plug in a digital camera, and iPhoto captures the images without any setup. I plug in a printer, and I don't

download drivers, I just print. I stick a CD in the CD drive, and iTunes transfers the music from it, getting the track info off the Web. I plug in my iPod and my music syncs up. I plug my AirPort into my cable modem, and it connects (and my TiBook connects).

2. The user experience is so pleasant—this may sound silly (I *know* it sounds silly to my real technical friends), but the look and feel and sense of everything is just really nice.

3. Setup is a snap. I still remember fondly opening up the iBook box (even the packing is pretty and well engineered), plugging in the iBook, hitting the "on" switch, and having it start playing music, spinning some big pretty graphics, and walking me through a couple of simple Internet setup steps. And I was connected.

4. The new Mac OS X is beautiful. I've been using it since the day it was first released, and for the past six or eight months, I've rarely had to use Mac OS 9. Mac OS X is *really* stable—I rarely shut down the machine; usually I just put it to sleep.

David: What do you consider to be the most important differences between Mac OS X and Windows?

Jim: The user-friendliness, by which I mean:

1. Things work intuitively (in fact, at first it was tough to transition from Windows because I kept trying to find obscure ways to do things rather than trying the obvious thing).

2. Things just work.

David: Is there something you would tell people who are concerned about switching?

Jim: There's *tons* of software for the Mac (I've got two word processors, four browsers, two email packages, two spreadsheets, five graphics packages, and so on).

Data exchange is a snap—in fact, most of what I do with my Windows-based friends and clients is exchange

1. Word, Excel, and PowerPoint files by email

2. Photos or movies in standard formats (TIF, JPEG, QuickTime)

3. PDFs (although my Windows friends can't seem to match that capability)

With Mac OS X, you can turn anything into a PDF, which you can share with anybody. (I prefer AppleWorks to MS Word, and when I don't need to exchange editable copies, I prefer to draft in AppleWorks and send a PDF of the document; the same is true with database reports, spreadsheets, and so on.)

My Official Guide to Switching: The Easy Way

A professional educator would probably gag at how I am going to immediately delve into moving your PC data over to your Mac. But I am doing this for two reasons: First, I know this is what you want to do—right now—and I am concerned that if we don't get it out of the way, you will make a mistake, like trying to do it without some software help.

Second, I believe most Windows users can turn on a Mac and find their way around. Chapter 6 is dedicated to the operating system, and from it you can learn some of the nonobvious aspects of Mac OS X 10.2. And since what's obvious to me may not be obvious to you, and vice versa, I'll try to cover most of the obvious aspects of the operating system as well.

Nevertheless, this chapter starts with a brief look at the Macintosh desktop (**Figure 3.1**), presuming that you've already turned your Mac on and gone through the various sign-up and registration routines.

Figure 3.1 On this unnaturally tidy desktop, the Dock is over there on the right. By default it sits down at the bottom of the screen, but you can anchor the Dock to either side of the screen as well.

I'll call this my "60-Second Introduction to Mac OS X 10.2 Jaguar for Windows Users." It almost took longer to write that title than the introduction will take. Here goes:

Look, up at the top: It's a bird, it's a plane—no, it's the menu bar (**Figure 3.2**). Mac OS X only has one of these, at the top, while Windows has one at the top and another at the bottom.

Figure 3.2 This is the menu bar, which is at the top of the screen. Note the Apple icon at the far left. Click it and see what happens.

At the left end of the menu bar is the Apple menu. Click it, and you will see the closest thing the Mac has to a Windows Start menu (**Figure 3.3**). It contains such useful things as shortcuts to your recently used applications and System Preferences, which is what Windows users have learned to call control panels.

Figure 3.3 Here's what happens when you click the Apple menu and then open the Recent Items submenu. It displays a menu of the applications and documents you've used lately, ready to be opened with another mouse click. Very handy.

The menu bar always reflects the application you are using at the time, so the menu choices change based upon the application in use (**Figure 3.4**).

Figure 3.4 In Figure 3.2 I was in the Finder; now I am in Microsoft Word. Note that the menu choices have changed to reflect the new application—it even says *Word* on the menu bar.

The Apple desktop is really an application called the Finder, which allows you to, well, find things (**Figures 3.5** to **3.7**). Like files and other computers.

You will always see the Finder icon at the left end of that funny-looking (to most Windows users) icon bar at the bottom of the screen. You can also get to the Finder by clicking anywhere on the Desktop.

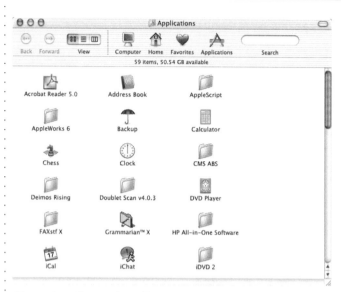

Figure 3.5 The Finder offers you three ways to look at the contents of your drives as well as a handy place to enter a search term (clicking *Search* gets you more options). This is my Applications folder as seen in the icon view. Notice the first View button on the Finder toolbar, which conveniently looks like a window filled with icons. Well, sort of.

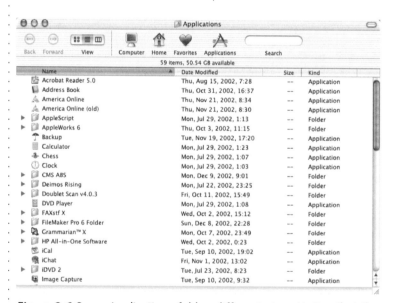

Figure 3.6 Same Applications folder, different view. Notice that the second of the little View buttons in the Finder toolbar is selected; that's what changed us to the list view. And the little button does look like a tiny list window.

Figure 3.7 Last, and perhaps most useful, is the column view, a nice way to navigate when you aren't sure where you are going. It's accessed from the third tiny button, and yes, those are little columns on the button.

That "funny-looking" thing at the bottom of the Desktop is called the Dock (**Figure 3.8**). This is where your most frequently used applications live, as icons, which you can click to start. Do a click-and-hold, and you can quit the application and sometimes even control it (try this in iTunes; see **Figure 3.9**). Applications that are currently running are signified with small black triangles. Some icons change when the application wants your attention, such as telling you how many unread messages are living in your inbox.

Figure 3.8 This is the Dock, where you can open applications, close applications that are running, and even control some applications. You can add and remove application items from the Dock by dragging and dropping. This is the Mac OS X feature that takes Windows users the most getting used to. But it's worth the effort.

Figure 3.9 Clicking and holding an icon in the Dock gets you a menu of application-specific commands, such as these for iTunes. "Dancing Queen," BTW, was voted the No. 1 dance song by VH1 viewers.

At the far right end of the Dock is a folder icon with an *A* on it. This is where your applications live, including all those not in your Dock at a particular moment. Also at the right end is an icon that looks like a house. That is your home folder, and each user on the Mac has one. It contains all your personal files, settings, email, address book entries, and so on. Erase this folder and you are gone from the machine. Copy it to a new one, and you exist on the new machine. OK, it's not quite that simple, but compared with the way things are organized in Windows, where personal information can sometimes be impossible to find, this is quite an advance (**Figure 3.10**).

Figure 3.10 This is my Dock, while I am using the machine. From left to right: The Finder icon with the little triangle that says the Finder is running, as it always is while your Mac is in operation; Mac OS X's Mail, with an alert for 115 unread messages, hope one isn't from you; iChat, a nice client for AOL Instant Messaging discussed later in the book; Address Book; Microsoft Internet Explorer; iTunes; Microsoft Word; iPhoto; iMovie; Sherlock, the search program; iCal, also running and with an extra triangle for the notification program that runs behind the scenes. After the divider that separates applications from places is a house icon, which leads you to my home folder, called David, after my user name; the Applications folder; and the Trash.

OK, that's what a curious person should know about Mac OS X before starting the migration process. While running the automated migration, you will have some time to read the other chapters and learn more about your new Mac before you actually start using it.

As I said earlier, I think most Windows users could find their way around a Mac without my help. But it would take longer and involve more trial and error—error especially—and since you have the book now, let me show you around. But always feel free to explore on your own. As long as you stay away from the Utilities folder (in the Applications folder), there is pretty limited damage you can do. "Go have fun with the OS" is not an idea I'd want to put into the mind of a Windows newbie, but Mac OS X is more bulletproof, and errant changes are easier to undo than in Windows.

So, now on to the important business of becoming a Switcher, not just in word but in deed!

The Easy Way or the Hard Way—You Choose

Moving your files and data from your old PC to your new Mac sounds far worse than it actually is. Many of the popular Mac applications have Windows counterparts, and the files you create in the Windows version of an application usually open easily on the Mac side, and the same is true going from the Mac version to Windows. Microsoft, for example, has done a good job of ensuring that you can open and work with a Word document in either the Windows or Mac edition of the word-processing application. Adobe and Macromedia have taken similar approaches with their cross-platform applications, so files you create on one platform will work just fine on the other.

> **Warning:** *Stop. I am sitting here editing the book, and the first paragraph in this section, written three months ago, is a lie. Well, half a lie. Moving your files and data manually from a PC to your new Mac is a painful process. Yes, I provide step-by-step instructions in Chapter 4, but please use the Move2Mac software and save yourself time and aggravation. I've even gotten you a special rebate on the software, so there's little reason not to take this advice.*

A few Windows applications, however, do not have a Mac equivalent—Microsoft Access, for example—and for those you will have to decide whether to move to a similar Macintosh application or to run Windows-emulation software on your Mac that lets you continue to use the Windows programs you can't live without. (I'll talk more about this in Chapter 7, where I cover applications for your Mac.)

Fortunately, moving your files is something you'll do only once, and there's some new software available that will help make the job almost painless.

You should install the major applications you plan to use on your Mac before you start moving files. That software may just be a copy of Microsoft Office for the Mac, or maybe you don't need to install any software at all, relying on the software that came with your Mac. That's fine, although if iCal and iSync aren't already installed on your Mac, you should download and install them before proceeding, as you may want to use them later. You can find them at www.apple.com/ical and www.apple.com/isync, respectively.

Caution: Please read this entire chapter before beginning the migration process. The more you know about migrating your files and data from your PC to your Mac, the easier it'll be.

Note that during this process we never actually remove files from your PC—we are copying the information rather than moving it. Your information stays intact, in case something goes wrong. You should be fine even if you have to start over, and the worst outcome would be having multiple copies of your files on your Mac. Nevertheless, I recommend that you back up the information on your PC before continuing.

Outlook vs. Outlook Express—night and day

A special note about Microsoft Outlook: The usual assumption is that people who are switching from Windows to Mac are using Microsoft Outlook Express as their PC mail program rather than the full Microsoft Outlook that comes with Microsoft Office. The reason this is assumed is that it's convenient, as moving from Outlook is a pain, while moving from Outlook Express is easy.

If you must use Outlook because you're connected to an Exchange Mail server at work, you may experience some difficulties after switching to the Mac. I recommend talking to your company's mail administrator about using Outlook Web Access (with the built-in Mac OS X 10.2 VPN client or some other firewall client software) to connect to your email.

The problem here is twofold: There is no Exchange client for Mac OS X, and the built-in Apple VPN client may not work with your company's firewall. So if a connection to an Exchange server is vital, switching from a PC to a Mac may be problematic.

This doesn't affect most Switchers, and even Exchange users may find ways to get around it, such as having Exchange email be redirected to another email account or connecting to an Exchange server in POP3 mode. Because there are so many variables, however, a full description of making peace between Mac OS X's Mail application and Microsoft Exchange is a book in itself. If you handle this problem, drop me a note (book@coursey.com) and tell me how you do it, and I'll post these stories on my Web site at www.coursey.com.

I also remain hopeful, if not optimistic, that Microsoft will hear the anguished cries of Exchange users and make Entourage (the Mac Office not-really-equivalent of Outlook) capable of being an Exchange client.

The Easy Way: Detto Technologies' Move2Mac

The real challenge of switching is moving your files from your old PC to your new Macintosh. You have two options: doing it manually or buying a kit that will do the dirty work for you. (A third option is hiring someone knowledgeable to do the dirty work for you.) Although I will explain the hard way of doing things in detail in Chapter 4, I hope to make the method of letting the computers do the work as attractive as possible.

To that end, for purchasers of this book I've arranged a $10 rebate on Move2Mac (www.move2mac.com), a software package that makes the process of moving files and settings from Windows to Mac almost automatic (see the very back of the book for details). The software, which includes a special USB-to-USB cable, sells for $59.95 and is expensive only if you place no value on your personal time and frustration. There is also a version, priced at $69.95, containing a parallel (printer)-to-USB cable for PCs running Microsoft Windows 95 or that lack a USB port. After you purchase Move2Mac—at a retail store or online—send in the coupon to Detto for your rebate.

The Detto people estimate that their product will complete a 500 MB migration in about 15 minutes, compared with hours for some migrations you might do manually. Move2Mac saves you from finding files, burning them to CD, copying those files to your Mac, and setting up your folders on the new machine. With this software, you are able to select what gets moved to the Mac, and your existing folder structure is automatically re-created on the new computer. That means you can move the information you need while leaving potentially gigabytes of useless data behind.

Move2Mac transfers the following types of files:

- Documents
- Spreadsheets
- Photos
- Music
- Files
- Folders
- Internet Explorer Favorites
- Databases
- Graphics
- Dial-up connections
- Address book
- Backgrounds

Here are the limitations: Move2Mac does not move applications or do file conversions. Although most files—those created by Microsoft Office, for example—require no conversion, some do. The most notable of these is Quicken, for which conversion instructions may be found on the Move2Mac CD and on the Quicken Web site (www.quicken.com).

Another limitation: Your email must be prepared for migration, a process I am about to explain. You have two ways of doing this: the first, recommended by Detto, and the second, recommended by Apple. Of the two, I think the Detto method, which requires Netscape 7.0 to be installed on the PC, works better.

System requirements

Move2Mac requires

- A PC with a 486 or faster processor
- Windows 95B, 98, 98 SE, 2000, or XP
- Internet Explorer 4.01 or later
- A keyboard and mouse
- 32 MB of RAM (good luck running Windows with this little memory)
- 30 MB or more free hard-drive space
- A CD-ROM drive
- A USB connection

If you are running a notebook, you will want it connected to AC power, rather than running on battery power, before you move.

Moving your email *(for users of Netscape Communicator, Outlook, Outlook Express, and Eudora)*

> **Important:** *You should complete the following before actually running the Move2Mac program.*

One of the major problems in switching is how difficult Microsoft makes it to move your email and calendar information from your PC to your Mac. Many users will find there is no equivalent mail program on the Mac capable of accepting their mail programs' mailboxes as is. Detto's approach is to transfer your mail to your Mac and then import it into the mail program of your choice. I recommend the Mail application, which is already installed with Mac OS X.

Detto recommends Netscape 7.0 mail installed on your PC as the simplest tool to prepare your email for transfer to the Mac. To do the transfer, you first import your mail into Netscape. Move2Mac transfers the Netscape mail files to your Mac, where you can import them into your Mac mail application.

Although this isn't difficult, you do need to follow instructions. And you'll probably be happy that you only have to do this once.

Important: This process—which requires you to make a copy of all the mail on your PC to have a file your Mac can use—can eat up a bunch of disk space. Ideally, your hard drive has 100 to 200 MB free when you begin this process. Netscape itself is about 25 MB in size, and you need additional space depending on the size of your message files.

1. We begin by installing Netscape 7.0 (which the Detto people have thoughtfully included on the Move2Mac disc) onto the PC. Do this by finding the Netscape setup application on the Detto CD.

   As I write this, the final location of the installer hasn't been set, but a search for NSSetupb.exe will find it.

2. Start the setup program, and choose the Recommended Install option.

3. Once Netscape is installed, run Netscape Mail from the Start menu by choosing Programs > Netscape > Mail and Newsgroups.

4. From the Netscape Mail Menu, choose Tools > Import > Mail. Do not choose address book, since Move2Mac will handle this on its own.

5. Select the mail program you currently use: Communicator, Eudora, Outlook, or Outlook Express (**Figure 3.11**).

   Whoosh! Your email is now imported into Netscape. It will still be available in the original program, however, which is good in case something gets messed up.

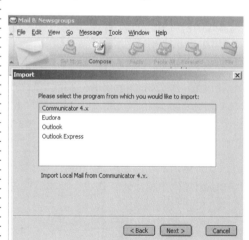

Figure 3.11 Netscape 7.0 provides an easy way to move mail from PC to Mac. It can handle email from many popular email programs, including Communicator 4 and later, Eudora, Outlook, and Outlook Express.

6. You can now run Move2Mac, and it will transfer your email to the Mac.

7. After you have completed running Move2Mac, launch Mac OS X's Mail on your Mac. Choose File > Import Mailboxes. In the Import Mailboxes window that comes up, select Netscape.

8. Mail asks you to navigate to the location of your Netscape mail. It is in your Mac's home folder in the Migrated PC Files folder (**Figure 3.12**).

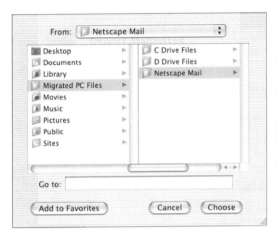

Figure 3.12
Once you have run Move2Mac, you will need to import your mail into the Mac OS X's Mail program. This is what you'll see as you select the mailbox you created in Netscape 7.0 for importing into Mac OS X Mail.

9. Open the Netscape Mail Data folder.

10. Open the Default folder or the folder with your Netscape user name. Click Next, and your mail is imported into Mac Mail.

   If you want to use a different application, such as Communicator, Eudora, or Entourage, the importing process is quite similar.

When you are finished, it's a good idea to uninstall Netscape from the PC. This won't impact your original mail files but will get rid of the files Netscape created, as well as the program itself. You'll also free up a bunch of hard-drive space.

I wish the email-migration process were easier, but it really isn't all that difficult, either. Don't let it scare you.

How Move2Mac works on the PC

Move2Mac works by first scanning the PC registry—something I hope you'll never see for yourself—to find all the registered applications and their associated file types, such as Excel and .xls and .xlc, or Word and .doc files.

Having identified what files go with which application, the program then scans the entire hard drive to find all the files of those file types. This is probably the most valuable thing the program does, since it has infinite patience to find files and then the ability to keep track of their locations. You could spend all day doing this on a really loaded PC.

Move2Mac also searches the PC hard drive for important settings, including those for dial-up connections and POP3 email and other application-configuration settings. At the same time, the program uses an exclusion list that prevents files that might be harmful to the Mac (such as drivers and system files) from being moved over from the PC.

There is also an inclusion list for files created by applications that do not create registry entries. These include Outlook's .pst files, V-card files (.vcf), and Quicken's QIF files. This list ensures that those files get moved as well.

The hard-drive scan can take anywhere from 30 seconds to a couple of minutes, depending on how much information there is to scan. Once the scan is completed, you are presented with the Migrating Your Computer Settings dialog.

In Move2Mac the following settings can be migrated:

- Background settings, so your current desktop background image will become the background on your Mac. Not something I would usually want to do.
- Internet Explorer Favorites, which are a special pain to move manually.
- Netscape settings, but only those necessary to bring over Netscape 7 mail. I'll explain the reason for this in a moment.
- Outlook Express POP3 settings.

- Outlook Express contacts.
- Dial-up connection settings (including your user name and your ISP's dial-in telephone number).

Move2Mac also presents the option of moving all files in your profile to the Mac (**Figure 3.13**). You will probably want to do this; click the Select All button at the bottom of the Select Files to Transfer dialog. If you know exactly what you want to bring over and what you want to leave behind, you can select the file types you don't wish to transfer by using this dialog as follows:

1. Select Desktop Folder Files to bring over files sitting on your PC desktop.

2. Select the folders My Documents, My Pictures, My Music, and My Videos. In most cases this will bring over your work files, although mine sometimes end up scattered in other folders as well.

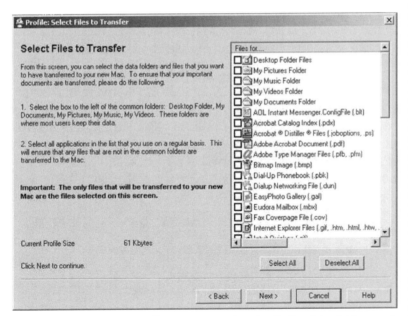

Figure 3.13 Move2Mac allows you to select both the data folders and the types of files it will move to your new Mac. By selecting both folders and types of files, you ensure that even files left in odd locations on your PC will end up on your Mac. This also means that, by not acquiring certain file types, your new Mac can be "cleaner" than the old PC.

3. Look at the list of applications whose files will be brought over to the Mac. Select those you recognize as the ones you use. If you are certain you won't be using a particular type of file on the Mac, don't select it.

4. If you play music on the PC, don't forget to select your music player so that any files formatted for that program will be brought over.

5. If you see names you don't recognize, don't worry. It shouldn't hurt to move them, but if you don't, you can always rerun Move2Mac later.

Remember that although the program is called Move2Mac, it really is a file copier rather than mover. At the end of the process, the files that were on your PC are still there; only copies have been created and placed on your Mac.

Preparing for installation

Move2Mac comes with a special USB cable that can be used only for the PC-to-Mac file transfers. The software is licensed for use on a single PC/single Mac combination, although you may use it as often as the need arises on those machines.

Your copy of Move2Mac will require activation, necessary to keep people from buying one copy of the software and using it on multiple machines. Activation is specific to the PC where the first activation occurs. You'll be asked to enter a license code, and an activation code will be generated using a mathematical formula based on the license code and a PC-specific code. The activation code is then tied to that PC's code and cannot be used on another PC.

Here are the recommended preparation steps on the PC:

1. Run a virus scan (be sure to update your virus descriptions).

2. Close all open applications, including the antivirus software.

3. If possible, connect to the Internet. This makes activation of the Move2Mac software easier, although you may also activate over the phone (**Figure 3.14**). Being connected to the Internet also allows you to automatically download any available Move2Mac updates.

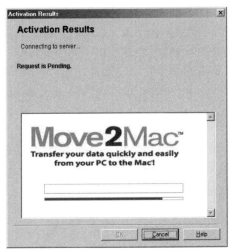

Figure 3.14 Yes, requiring you to activate a program to use it is the sincerest way a software company has of saying it doesn't trust you. But who can really blame it? Lots of PC users happily use pirated software. This activation process means you can use this PC only with this copy of Move2Mac, but you can use it whenever you like.

On the Mac:

1. Install all the software applications you plan to use. For many people, this will only be Microsoft Office for the Mac, if you install any software at all.

2. Run a virus scan.

3. Close all open software applications, including your antivirus software.

Now we're ready to begin transferring.

Note: You don't connect the data-transfer cable until step 11.

1. Install the Move2Mac application on your PC. Following installation, the application starts automatically.

2. Follow the onscreen instructions in Move2Mac's Wizard dialog, and then activate your software.

   If you have an Internet connection, the software activates automatically and then downloads any updates to the program.

   Once done activating, Move2Mac scans your computer for files and data to transfer.

3. By default, all settings and preferences will transfer. You may deselect any you don't want to transfer to the Mac.

4. To choose which files to transfer, you're given a chance to select them. When you've selected what you want to move, click Next. If you miss something, you can rerun the transfer later.

5. When the Waiting for Connection dialog appears, wait for the View/Print report button to become active. Click the button to print the report.

6. Once the report has finished printing, close the report window by choosing File > Exit.

 Important: *Be sure to leave Move2Mac running. Do not click Cancel. Do not shut down your PC.*

7. Remove the Move2Mac disc from your PC.

   Now, over on your new Mac:

8. Insert the Move2Mac CD.

9. Double-click the Move2Mac CD icon on your Desktop, open the Mac folder on the CD, and then open the Move2Mac.pkg file.

   Following installation, the Move2Mac application starts immediately. Note that activation is not required on the Mac—it's already been taken care of on the PC.

10. Read the instructions, and click the Next button at the bottom of the Welcome screen.

11. When the Set Up: Connect the Data Transfer Cable dialog appears, connect the USB cable to the Mac's USB port and to the PC's USB port (**Figure 3.15**). Click Next. Note that if you are using the Move2Mac parallel-to-USB version for Windows 95 or PCs with no USB port, then you'll connect the smaller USB end to the Mac's USB port and the larger parallel end to the PC's parallel port.

12. Move2Mac displays the Migration: Transferring and Integrating Your Profile screen, and you'll see all of your data being moved (**Figure 3.16**). When the migration is complete, click Next.

13. You can now print another migration report, and you'll be asked to click Finish to end the process.

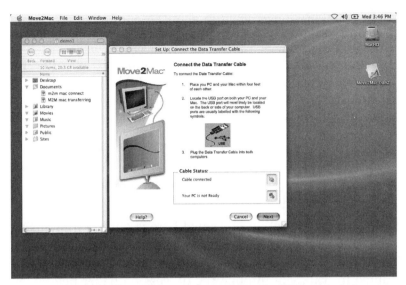

Figure 3.15 Resist the temptation to connect the USB cable between your PC and Mac until you see this screen on the Mac, lest dire consequences ensue. I'm serious, especially if you're an "install the cable and ask questions later" sort of person (like I am).

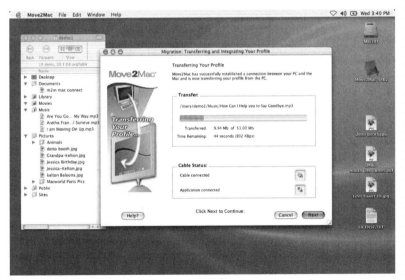

Figure 3.16 Seeing this screen should make you happy—especially after you read the next chapter and discover all the pain you missed by using Move2Mac. This is what the actual transfer of PC files to your Mac looks like from the Mac end of the connection.

Congratulations—your PC files should now be on your Mac! Your files will be located on your Mac as follows:

- The contents of My Documents have been transferred to the Documents folder in your home folder.

- The contents of My Pictures have been transferred to the Pictures folder in your home folder.

- My Music, My Videos—are you seeing a trend here? Think Music and Movies.

- All other folders and files have been moved into the Migrated PC Files folder on the Mac.

Most of the information presented here is based on my using a beta version of the Move2Mac program and documentation. There will doubtless be changes in the final version, but I wanted to walk you through the process on paper before you tried it on your computers. To find the Move2Mac documentation on your PC (once the program is installed), select Start > Programs > Move2Mac > User's Manual.

Rerunning Move2Mac

Here's how to rerun Move2Mac so you can bring more files over, perhaps because there are some you didn't select the first time you ran the program. Or maybe you've been using the PC since the first move and now have a bunch—if it's not a bunch I'd just burn a CD—of new files you want to move to the Mac. Follow these instructions:

1. In the Migrate Your Computer Settings dialog, all settings are normally selected by default. Choose Deselect All, and then select any settings you didn't move previously—or just leave them all unchecked.

2. In the Select Files to Transfer dialog, select the file types you want to bring over, but do not select anything you've selected before or else you'll get duplicate copies of those files on your Mac.

The "Pay Someone Else" Option

I have heard that some Apple retailers, including perhaps even Apple's own stores, offer migration services on either a formal (pay the store) or informal (pay someone who works at the store) basis. Except for the problem of needing to haul your PC in to the Apple dealer, this sounds very convenient. Even more so would be having someone come to your home or office to move files from your PC to your Mac.

Depending on whom you are paying (store or an individual) and whether you bring the machines to them or them to the machines, this service could cost from $100 to $400.

By the way, for a tax-deductible $3,000 donation to my favorite public-safety charity plus travel expenses, I will come to your home or office and migrate your files myself, have a nice lunch with you, and leave an autographed copy of this book as well as a copy of Move2Mac, probably autographed by the Detto people. Interested? Send a note to book@coursey.com.

Switcher Diary: AARON ADAMS

Aaron Adams is a computer professional who agreed to do the commercial for Apple "because I sincerely believe in their product and I'd like to help them promote it however I can." And he admits that perhaps he's become a living Apple commercial himself, even though he still uses Windows machines every day.

Aaron had read the ZDNet columns that led me to write this book and said he found reading about my experiences to be "very gratifying because I went through something very similar not long ago. Seeing a familiar subject such as computing in a new way is exciting stuff."

You can read those columns elsewhere in this book, but let's see how Aaron's experiences as a computer professional who starts using a Mac map to mine as a writer.

Aaron: I started using Windows at version 3.0, which was about 1991. Before that I had used DOS back to version 3.3, and before that I had a TI-99/4a growing up. Until I got my Mac, I had always built my own computers from parts that I would buy. In college, I worked in the operations room and got a chance to become familiar with a number of operating systems, including different flavors of Unix, MVS, VMS, and NetWare.

David: How do you rate your Windows skills?

Aaron: I would rate my Windows skills at 8 out of 10. I haven't had a real chance to dig in to Active Directory yet.

David: What do you like most about Windows?

Aaron: The things I always liked about Windows were the multitasking and the graphical user interface (GUI). At the time, Windows was the only operating system available to me that had both of those features. Yes, Macs had a GUI, but the multitasking wasn't comparable and Macs were viewed as toys among the computer people I associated with. DOS and Unix were command-line operating systems that were harder to use. Unix had X Windows, but its ins and outs were beyond my understanding. Windows was the simplest way to get multitasking and a good GUI.

David: What did/do you like least about Windows?

Aaron: The thing I liked least about Windows was that it seemed something was always wrong with it. People would ask why my machine had so many problems if I knew so much about Windows, but the fact is you can't predict or prevent every problem. Some problems I've encountered come out of left field somewhere. One example I like to use is a case where a corrupted font prevents Microsoft Access from starting because it thinks there's a licensing problem. How does that work? I never would have connected those two items.

Since I knew more about computers than most of my friends, I often got to fix their glitches, too. It always amazes me to see the messes people can make out of their machines. I've often wondered why it was so easy for people to muck up their machines.

Switcher Diary: AARON ADAMS

David: Do you still use Windows? If so, please explain.

Aaron: Yes, I use Windows every day. I administer a LAN for a company in Dayton, Ohio. Right now we run a combination of Windows NT, 2000 Professional, 2000 Server, and 2000 Advanced Server. I have a laptop with Windows 2000 Pro on my desk. At home, however, I'm all Mac. What does that tell you?

David: How did you become a Mac user?

Aaron: I was spending more time at work troubleshooting workstation problems than administering the LAN. Then I would come home to my Windows machine and have to wrestle with it, too. I thought, computing shouldn't be this difficult! I installed Mandrake Linux on another drive, but the learning curve was steeper than I liked. Sure, I could learn Linux, I'm smart enough for that. At home, I wanted to spend my time doing things with my computer rather than doing things to my computer. Additionally, Linux help was questionable. The answers I always seemed to get were, "Figure it out, dimwit!" Linux seems to be very stuck in its own techie bubble. It has come a long way in the past few years, but it still is not a friendly OS for the nontechnical user.

David: Is your Mac a good value? How do you feel about Mac pricing?

Aaron: I've always been a firm believer in the ideal that you get what you pay for. In my PC days, I always told my friends to buy the brand-name stuff they recognized—they'd be glad they did when it came to things like support and updated drivers, and product quality was usually better. I believe the same thing is true with Macs.

It's true that Macs cost a bit more than PCs, but you're buying peace of mind. For instance, I bought an AirPort Base Station at about the same time a friend of mine bought a 3Com router. Every couple of weeks he tells me about the latest problem with his 3Com. I pretty much plugged in my AirPort and forgot about it. That's a good thing! For almost a year now, it has just worked with almost no intervention. That's worth a little extra cash to me.

When you buy your Mac, it'll hurt. You'll look at the number on the cash register and cringe and wonder if you're doing the right thing. But when you get it home and use it, you'll realize exactly what you paid for, and it will be worth every penny. Apple pays attention to the little details.

David: What was the most confusing part of using Mac OS?

Aaron: In the beginning, the most confusing part was Mac plug-and-play. Here's an example: I have an Iomega USB CD drive. When I would plug it into my Windows machine, a little window stating that I had new hardware would pop up, it would grind at the disk for a while, tell me the new hardware had been installed, and put an icon in the system tray. When I wanted to unplug the drive, I had to click the icon, stop the device, wait for the OK, and unplug it.

Switcher Diary: AARON ADAMS

I decided to see if that burner would work with my Mac. I plugged it in and nothing happened—the machine didn't even blink. I thought, great, this drive isn't supported. Just to be sure, I decided to put a CD into the drive. It popped up right on the Desktop. Ahhh, how deceptively simple, plug-and-play the way it should work. No histrionics, just a working drive. And when I was done, I ejected the disc and unplugged the drive—no further action needed.

The reason I describe that as confusing is because I was so used to doing things a different way, and when a simpler and (to me) more logical way was presented, it threw me off. How sad is that? When things work the right way, you're confused :)

David: Are there any applications you used on Windows that you don't use on your Mac?

Aaron: None that I can think of. As I said in my commercial, everything I used to do with my Windows machine, I now do with my Mac. I've found a direct replacement for every single app I used in Windows. I've even started doing things I never did before, like burning DVDs and printing pictures, simply because I can. Invention is the mother of necessity, or something like that. ;)

David: Anything else I should have asked but didn't? Anything you want to tell me?

Aaron: It may sound like I'm a living, breathing Apple commercial, and in many ways perhaps I am. However, professionally, I still deal with Windows. I know a lot about both environments, and there's one I prefer for my personal use. I really have nothing to gain by promoting Apple because my commercial went off the air long ago, and I'm not on their payroll. Heck, I haven't gotten a phone call of any kind from them in months. I'm nobody in the big scheme of things, and Apple doesn't need my endorsement. But I sincerely believe they're doing a lot of things right and that they make great products, and I don't hesitate to recommend Macintoshes to other people.

We've made computing an integral part of everyone's daily life. The ability to effectively use a computer means power—not just hardware power but brain power. It's possible to create things that were only dreamt of 10 years ago. It's possible to overcome geography and communicate instantaneously with anyone. It's possible to obtain information the second it's made available. Why shouldn't the machines that enable us to do these things be understandable, reliable, and beautiful?

My Official Guide to Switching: The Hard Way

I'd like to think you're reading this section for entertainment, to see how much pain you're saving yourself by following the directions in Chapter 3. My hope is that a quick scan of this chapter will convince you that buying and using Detto's Move2Mac is a much better use of your time and money than doing the migration from Windows to the Mac all by yourself.

This is especially true since (in case you missed it earlier) as a purchaser of this book you are entitled to a nice $10 rebate on the Detto application (see the back of the book for details).

This section is based on a guide you'll find on the Apple Web site (www.apple.com/switch/howto/), with comments arising from my own experience and covering things Apple is shy about telling you.

> **Stop:** *Me again, feeling the need to comment while doing the last editing. Just reading this chapter and creating the illustrations for it made me sort of ill. Yes, these instructions should work, Apple says they will work, and I have even tried most of them. But that doesn't mean you should actually use these instructions if you can possibly avoid it.*

What You Need

To do this, you'll need a PC running Windows 95 or later plus one of the following:

- A CD burner
- An external USB hard drive (or FireWire drive if your PC supports it)
- A .Mac account (not available for Windows 95)
- A network that connects to both the PC and the Mac

These instructions concentrate on moving data by burning it to a CD on the Windows machine and then copying the data from the CD onto your Mac. One benefit of doing it this way is that the discs you create are a permanent backup of the files you move.

Most people who have a CD burner have used it, if only to copy music discs. If you haven't, take some time to look at the CD-burning information that came with your PC, or open the CD-burning application that came with it and burn a few discs for fun before the serious work of switching begins.

If, for whatever reason, you don't have CD-burning software, you'll need to acquire some. If this will be the last time you'll use the PC, however, I don't think it makes sense to spend money on CD-burning software when you can buy Detto's Move2Mac for less money. However, if you're going to keep the PC and want CD-burning software, I recommend Roxio's Easy CD Creator ($99.95; www.roxio.com).

Each blank CD can hold about 650 MB of information. You'll probably be able to move all your word-processing and spread-sheet files with one CD, along with your email and settings—typically, the files are fairly small. If you have more than 650 MB of data to move, use multiple CDs. That works as long as no single file is larger than 650 MB. If you have a file bigger than *that,* you can use a network to transfer it.

CD burning can be a slow process, and some burners are notorious for running into problems during the burning process and spitting out the disc in disgust before it's finished. If that happens, the disc is useless, and you have to start over with a new blank disc. I've built a nice collection of silver coasters that way, although I've since learned that the hole in the middle means they won't protect your fine furniture from condensation off a can of Dr Pepper.

Slow CD-burn speeds and potential burning problems are OK if you are only moving a disc or two of information, but if you have a big MP3 collection or a few thousand digital photographs, expect to spend a long time sitting in front of the computer that you just spent a fair amount of money to get rid of. Burning all that data to CD will take time and effort.

Apple recommends that you create a CD with a number of folders to hold your files. It's easiest to do this by creating a folder on your PC, dragging the files into the folder, and then dragging the folder into your CD-burning software.

The gods at Apple recommend that you name this CD "Switch" so you'll always know what it is. However, I recommend that you name it after me, "David," in honor of how boring it was for me to write this part of the book.

But if you must use CDs, here are the Apple-recommended folders you should create on your PC:

- Email Address Book
- Favorites
- Music
- Office Documents
- Palm
- PDF (as if PC users all have a bunch; mine live with my Microsoft Office docs, anyway)
- Pictures
- Quicken (all Mac users seem also to use Quicken to manage their finances, but the migration from Windows is painful if you are a hard-core Quicken user. Directions to ease the pain are on the Quicken Web site at www.intuit.com).

Once you have moved all the appropriate files into these folders on your PC, move the folders into the software that will burn your CD (**Figure 4.1**). Be sure to chant a mystical incantation so the CD will burn successfully.

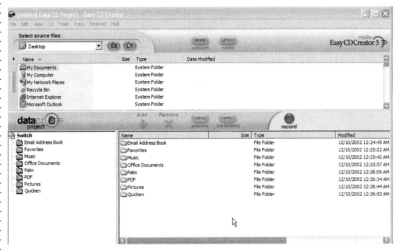

Figure 4.1 This is Roxio's Easy CD Creator, with the folders I describe in the text. Dragging your files into the proper folders will make them easier to migrate over to your new Mac.

As a reminder, even if the CD dies, you're still OK, since the disc-burning software uses copies of your files, not the original files themselves. Still, it used to really bother me when only one out of three CDs would burn properly. This is less of a problem on newer PCs and not at all on Macs.

> *Tip: Only burn CDs when all other applications are closed, and then walk away from the computer when the burn starts, to avoid the temptation to touch anything. This will give better results.*

Once the CD is burned, remove it from the PC and insert it into your Mac. Note that there is an Eject key on your Mac keyboard, useful for opening the CD drive on your new machine.

After a bit of whirring, an icon for your CD appears on your Mac desktop. Open the CD and start dragging your old files to their new locations, all the while cussing under your breath that using Move2Mac would have been much easier.

Now that I've given you the 30,000-foot overview, let's get started finding the right files on your PC and moving them to the proper folders to prepare for burning to CD.

Moving Your Email Address Book

Here's what Apple says to do to move your Microsoft Outlook Express Address Book from your PC to your Mac.

On the PC:

1. Launch Outlook Express on your PC, and open the Address Book by choosing Tools > Address Book.

2. Choose Edit > Select All to select all of your contacts.

3. Drag the selected contacts to the Addresses folder that you will burn onto the Switch CD.

   Outlook Express will automatically change the format of these to one that is Mac-usable as it exports them.

And here's what you do on the Mac side once you burn the disc.

On the Mac:

1. Put the Switch CD in your Mac's optical drive; it mounts on the Desktop.

2. With the Finder active, choose Go > Applications or press Command-Shift-A.

   Alternatively, you can click the Applications icon in an open Finder window or click the Address Book icon in the Dock (**Figure 4.2**).

⌐ Address Book icon

Figure 4.2 It's even easier to find the Mac OS X Address Book if you use the Dock, where the icon for the Address Book looks like an address book—that is, if you haven't removed it from the Dock.

3. Find the Address Book application icon, and open it (**Figure 4.3**).

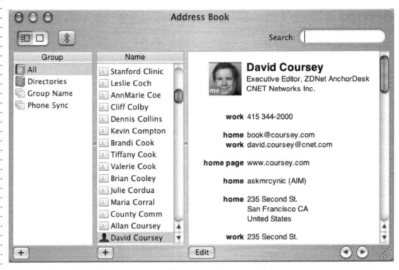

Figure 4.3 The Mac OS X Address Book is useful in part because it's a very nice, if somewhat basic, address book, but mostly because it works with the Mac OS X Mail client and iSync. It is also available to applications from other companies as they develop connections between the Address Book and their applications.

4. Open the Switch CD from its icon on your Desktop, and navigate to the Addresses folder.

5. Select your contacts by choosing Edit > Select All or pressing Command-A, and drag those contacts into the Address Book window.

You can use this technique with Microsoft Entourage and Palm Desktop. I recommend using the built-in Mac OS X Address Book for contact management, though.

Why? Because the information in the Apple Address Book is available to all applications and is what iSync uses. Sure, you can use Entourage if you like, but I find the Microsoft contact manager and email client less compelling than their Apple counterparts. But that could change with the next version of Microsoft Office for Macintosh, so decide for yourself.

One Big Caveat

What you read in this section is just fine *if* you use the Windows applications that Apple conveniently expects you to use. I say "conveniently" because if you're using other applications—most notably Outlook—migrating can be more difficult. Even the first version of Move2Mac doesn't solve this problem, although by the time you read this, a later version may take care of it.

My suggestion for a workaround: Use a Palm OS-based personal digital assistant and iSync to move your contacts, calendar, and email from the PC to the Mac. With these PDAs selling for less than $100, this is the best way to move Outlook information to your new Mac.

Your Mac already comes with Palm software, and iSync supports synchronization between your iCal and Address Book and your Palm PDA. So, synchronize the PDA on your Windows machine and then synchronize it with your new Mac. It's an easy way to move calendar and address book entries between the two platforms.

Moving Your Favorites

If you use Microsoft Internet Explorer on Windows, you'll be happy to know that it's also available on the Macintosh (Apple also offers its own fine browser, called Safari). It's easy to move your Favorites from the PC to the Mac, but it's not necessarily something I recommend.

Why? Because your Mac browser comes preloaded with a few zillion useful Mac links already (and see Appendix B for a few more). You can find a list of them at www.apple.com/switch/howto/mac/applefavorites.html, where you will also find instructions for adding specific links back into Internet Explorer on your Mac. I'd rather see you keep the existing links on the Mac and re-create the links you want from your PC, and here's why. Unless you're hyperorganized, I'll bet your PC favorites aren't really that useful, including perhaps half a dozen links you really care about. Better to add those URLs manually on your Mac than to wipe out all the helpful links Apple provides.

But if you must copy over all the useful links, here's how.

On the PC:

1. With Internet Explorer running, choose File > Import and Export.

2. In the Export dialog (**Figure 4.4**), save the file as Favorites.html in the Favorites folder you will burn onto the Switch CD.

Figure 4.4 Here's what it looks like when you begin exporting your favorites from your Windows machine.

On the Mac:

1. Put the Switch CD in your Mac's optical drive, and open it when it mounts on your Desktop.

2. Open the Favorites folder on the CD.

3. With the Finder active, choose Go > Home (or press Command-Shift-H; see **Figure 4.5**), and then navigate to Library > Preferences > Explorer.

4. Drag the Favorites.html file from the Favorites folder on the CD to the Explorer folder you just opened. If you're asked if you want to replace the file, say yes.

Just know that in the battle between the Mac and Windows, you've now committed a war crime.

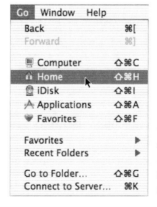

Figure 4.5 One way to get to your home folder is to choose Home from the Go menu (or use the keyboard shortcut combination, shown on the right).

Moving Your Music

If you keep your music library as a collection of MP3 files, this is an easy process, because iTunes happily plays MP3 files—no file translation necessary. Here's how to move them over.

On the PC:

1. Select the folder that contains your MP3 files—typically My Music inside the My Documents folder—and then select Edit > Copy.

2. Open the Music folder of the Switch CD folder set, and transfer your music by choosing Edit > Paste.

   If you have any other folders that contain music, use the same process to transfer those files.

On the Mac:

1. Put the Switch CD in your Mac's optical drive, and when it mounts on the Desktop, open the music folder on it.

2. Open iTunes by clicking its icon in the Dock or by navigating to Applications > iTunes and double-clicking its icon.

   Select all of the files in the CD's music folder, and drag them to the iTunes main window.

When you release the mouse button, iTunes adds every song to your music library. If you have more than one CD's worth of MP3 files, repeat this process until all of your files are moved to your Mac.

> *Note: This works only if you have been storing your music in MP3 format, which won't be the case if you've been using Windows Media Player to pull music off your music discs. My recommendation is to convert your WMA Windows media files to MP3 files before moving them over to the Mac. The newest Microsoft Plus Pack for Windows XP includes a transcoder that can do bulk conversions of WMA files to MP3 files. It sells for $19.99.*

Moving Your Office Documents

If you use Microsoft Office on Windows, I think you'll be very pleased with the Mac version. It's fully file-compatible with the Windows version, and while the two programs look significantly different, in some ways (most of which make Office a real Mac program) the actual feel of Office is very much the same across both operating systems.

Here's how to move your Office files.

On the PC:

1. Go through your My Documents folder and identify any folders that contain Office documents—such as word-processing documents, spreadsheets, or presentations.

    Some would include PDFs in this category, so if you don't have enough of these to warrant a whole folder, just include them in the Office Documents transfer procedures.

2. Select one of the folders, and then choose Edit > Copy.

3. Open the Office Documents folder in the Switch CD folder set, and choose Edit > Paste.

    This copies the documents to the folder.

Repeat these steps if you have more than one folder of documents to transfer.

 Note: Don't forget to look through every location that might contain documents you would want to transfer. You can use the Windows built-in search function to help.

On the Mac:

1. Insert the Switch CD in your Mac.

2. When the Switch CD shows up on the Desktop, open it so that you can see the Office Documents folder.

3. Choose Go > Home to go to your home folder (or press Command-Shift-H).

    There is a Documents folder in the window that appears.

4. Drag the Office Documents folder from the CD to the Documents folder in your home folder.

   You should see a progress bar showing the name of each file as it's transferred from the CD to your Mac's hard drive.

If you've installed Office, you can now double-click a Word, Excel, or PowerPoint document, and it will open, looking just as it did on your PC.

> *Tip: If you haven't installed Office (and in any case before you buy a copy), I'd recommend you first open the Office files using AppleWorks, which probably came preinstalled on your new Mac. AppleWorks is happy to read Office files (via a file translator) and, depending on what you need to do, may save you the $459 that Microsoft wants for Office v. X for Mac. Apple's Keynote presentation application can also easily import PowerPoint files.*

Palm

The great news for PDA users is that you can move the information on your Palm to your Mac as easily as syncing the device on both machines—using the same USB cradle you already own. Just synchronize your Palm on the PC, move the cradle to the Mac, and sync there. That gets your information into Palm Desktop, which is already installed on the Mac.

If you want the information to land in Address Book and iCal—highly recommended—set up iSync on your Mac and then do a synchronization. You may have to download the iSync program from the Apple Web site, but setting it up is quite simple if you follow the onscreen directions. Also, iSync uses Palm's HotSync software, which is already installed with Mac OS X.

PDF

Apple folks are frequent users of Adobe Acrobat files (or PDFs). I've never had any that I wanted to move to a Mac, but if you do, and for the sake of completeness with Apple's Switcher Guide, here's how you move them.

On the PC:

1. Go through your My Documents folder and identify any folders that contain PDFs.

2. Select one of the folders, and then choose Edit > Copy.

3. Open the PDFs folder in the Switch CD folder set, and choose Edit > Paste.

   This copies the PDF documents to the folder.

Repeat these steps if you have more than one folder of PDFs to transfer.

On the Mac:

1. Insert the Switch CD in your Mac.

2. When the Switch CD shows up on the Desktop, open it so that you can see the PDFs folder.

3. Choose Go > Home to go to your home folder (or press Command-Shift-H).

   A Documents folder appears in the window.

4. Drag the PDFs folder from the CD to the Documents folder in your home folder. Your Mac will copy all of the PDFs into the Documents folder.

 Note: Acrobat Reader is a fine program, but you don't have to have it to read PDF files on your Mac. Mac OS X includes the Preview application, which can open PDF documents.

Pictures

The Mac is a great machine for digital photography, and many people buy a Mac for that specific reason. If you already have some digital photographs on your PC, however, here's how Apple says you should move them.

On the PC:

1. Navigate to My Documents > My Pictures (or what-ever folder you use to store your digital photos), select that folder, and then choose Edit > Copy.

2. Open the Pictures folder in your Switch CD folder set, and select Edit > Paste.

Repeat these steps for any other folders that contain digital photos you'd like to transfer, and don't forget to look at your Desktop for pictures.

On the Mac:

1. Insert the Switch CD in your Mac's optical drive, and open it when it mounts on the Desktop.

2. Launch iPhoto by clicking its icon in the Dock or by navigating to your Applications folder and double-clicking its icon there.

    (Get to the Applications folder by pressing Command-Shift-A or by selecting Go > Applications in the Finder.)

3. Drag the Pictures folder from the Switch CD to the iPhoto window.

iPhoto dutifully copies your photos from the CD into its library, where you can work with them.

Email

I'm a big fan of the Mac OS X Mail application, which comes with every Macintosh. It's easy to use, does what I need done, and has the best spam filter of any mail program I've seen. You might have configured your email account when you first set up your Mac. If so, you're already sending and receiving email, perhaps through your new .Mac email address.

Mac OS X's Mail will, however, support multiple email accounts. All that matters is that your server be able to work with the POP3 or IMAP protocols. Most do, but Microsoft Exchange may be an exception. (If you need to get mail from an Exchange server, ask your mail administrator to allow POP3 access to your mail or create a remote account for you that automatically redirects mail sent to your Exchange server address, such as you@yourcompany.com to another address, such as you@mac.com.)

If you want to add an email account to Mac OS X's Mail program, here's the information you need:

- Name
- Email address

- Reply address
- Server information
- Incoming mail server (IMAP or POP)
- Incoming mail (mail server address)
- Outgoing mail (SMTP server address)
- Account name (your account name)
- Password for your email account

You also need to determine whether your email server requires you to send any authentication to send mail; if so, turn on this feature in the Mac OS X Mail client.

All the above information is available from whomever provides your email account, typically your Internet service provider (ISP), employer, or school. If you are already using the account on your PC, this information is stored in the Mail control panel or in the account settings in the mail client you're already using. You can copy it (on paper) from there and enter it into Mac OS X's Mail program.

Here's how to do it:

1. Open Mac OS X's built-in Mail application by clicking its icon in the Dock (the postage stamp) or by navigating to its icon in Applications > Mail.

2. Choose Mail > Preferences, and click the Accounts icon in the Accounts window.

3. Click the Add Account button.

4. On the Account Information tab, enter the account settings you've noted from the setup on your PC in the appropriate fields, and click the OK button (**Figure 4.6**).

Repeat the steps above if you have multiple email accounts to reestablish. It's that simple.

If you use AOL for email, just locate the AOL installer on your new Mac. After you have installed AOL, open the AOL application and it will walk you through the setup process. You just need to know your AOL ScreenName and password. It's that easy.

Figure 4.6
Here's where you enter information necessary to create an email account in the Mac OS X email program.

Note: Be sure to download the latest version of AOL: AOL updates its software occasionally, and the version that comes with your Mac may not be the most current.

You can also use Netscape software for Mac OS X to access both AOL and your POP3 email, which is what some of my friends do. The decision is really based on where you receive most of your important messages. Mine come over my personal email server at my ISP and very little over AOL, so I use the Mac OS X Mail client. Others with the opposite situation might choose Netscape, though I would recommend they just tell their AOL friends to send mail to their other mail address.

If you are using a Hotmail account, you will need to use the Entourage program included with Office v. X to access it. The instructions included with Entourage will help you set up a Hotmail account.

Although I have nothing against Entourage, I think the Apple programs are better, so I recommend accessing your Hotmail account over the Internet using your Web browser.

Email messages

This is complex, so I will quote extensively from Apple's switching guide. But before following these instructions, please refer back to the mail-migration method, using Netscape 7.0, that I outlined earlier in this chapter. I think it's easier, but here's how Apple would do it.

According to Apple, you can use Mac OS X's Mail application and a .Mac email account to move your saved mail from your PC to your Mac. You can use the PC versions of Outlook and Outlook Express to connect to your .Mac account.

Note: I have not tried this, but I don't see any obvious reason why this technique wouldn't work with Outlook as well as Outlook Express.

To use this method, you'll need a .Mac account, which you can sign up for at www.mac.com or when you set up your Mac for the first time. Be sure to note your .Mac user name and password.

Note: This presumes that you already have the Mac OS X Mail application configured on the Mac, which happens automatically when you sign up for a .Mac account.

How to Create a New .Mac Account

1. Open System Preferences from the Dock or the Apple menu, and click the Internet icon in the window that appears.
2. Select the .Mac tab in the Internet panel. Click the Sign Up button (**Figure 4.7**).
3. Your Web browser opens and takes you to the sign-up section of .Mac, where you can fill in some information to get a .Mac account—just follow the instructions.

Do note that .Mac is a fee-for-service proposition, so be prepared to spend $99.95 per year.

You're done. Be sure to note your account name and password.

Figure 4.7 Here's where you create a new .Mac account, in the Internet panel of System Preferences. Some people (like me) think having a yourname@mac.com email address is kinda cool.

On your PC:

You're going to configure Outlook Express on your PC to connect to your new .Mac email account. Why? Well, you're going to use this account to transfer your mail from your PC to your Mac over the Internet.

> *Note: If you use an email program other than Outlook Express, don't panic—you can probably easily adapt these instructions for use with that program.*

1. Open Outlook Express on your PC, and select Tools > Accounts.

2. Click the Accounts button to launch the wizard, and select Mail.

3. Enter your first and last names in the Display Name field, and click the Next button.

4. Enter your new Mac.com email account name (probably something like yourname@mac.com) in the next screen, and click the Next button.

5. In the incoming-mail pop-up menu of the E-mail Server Names screen, select IMAP—not POP3, which is the default.

6. Enter the following server addresses (**Figure 4.8**), and then click the Next button:

- "Incoming mail (POP3, IMAP or HTTP) server": mail.mac.com

- "Outgoing mail (SMTP) server": smtp.mac.com

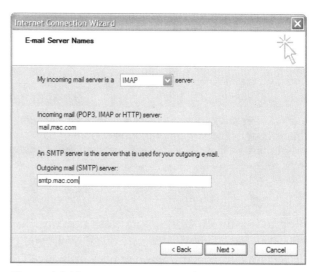

Figure 4.8 Here we are entering the .Mac account information into Outlook Express's setup wizard.

7. In the next screen, enter your .Mac account name in the Account Name field and your password in the Password field (go figure). Leave the "Remember password" checkbox selected, and click the Next button.

8. When you see the congratulations screen, click Finish.

You're done setting up Outlook Express on your PC.

(If you are prompted to download Mail folders, choose Yes, and click OK.)

Depending on where your mail is stored in Outlook Express, moving it can be very simple. If you have multiple mail folders in Outlook Express, you'll have to create folders with the same names in your .Mac email account and then transfer the mail one folder at a time. Here's how you transfer the saved mail in your Inbox.

1. With Outlook Express open, select the Inbox and choose Edit > Select All.

    This selects all of the mail messages in your Inbox.

2. Drag the selected messages from your Inbox to the Inbox mailbox folder below the mail.mac.com account icon.

    This will email all of the mail in your Inbox to the Inbox folder in your .Mac account—which is hosted on Apple's .Mac servers.

Once you've transferred your mail to your Mac using this method, you'll need to set up your .Mac email account.

Here's how to set up Mail to connect to your .Mac account.

1. Choose System Preferences from the Dock or the Apple menu, click the Internet icon, and enter your .Mac member name and password in the .Mac tab of the Internet panel.

2. Click the Email tab, and make sure the "Use .Mac Email account" checkbox is selected.

3. Choose System Preferences > Quit System Preferences.

4. Open Mail, and click the Get Mail icon in the program's toolbar.

    Make sure that the mail you transferred is available on your Mac.

If you're transferring more than 5 MB of mail using this method, you're going to get an IMAP error message. It's OK, though—no mail is lost, and everything that was sent before you got the message was copied successfully. To finish transferring the mail, you'll need to open your .Mac account and transfer the mail to your local hard drive on your Mac before transferring more.

Here's how to do that (on your Mac):

1. Open Mail by clicking its icon in the Dock or by double-clicking its icon in the Applications folder.

2. Create a new mailbox in Mail by choosing Mailbox > New Mailbox and then selecting On My Mac in the window that appears.

3. You need to give this mailbox a name, so call it something like "Mail from my PC," and then click OK.

4. Select View > See Drawer to open the Mail drawer if it's closed.

5. Select the messages you want to store on your Mac's local hard drive in Mail's In Mailbox, and then select Message > Transfer > *the name of the mailbox you just created.*

Mail moves those messages over to your hard drive.

Note: *Now's a good time to delete any unwanted messages before you transfer them to your local hard drive. Just drag them to the Trash, or select them and click the Delete button in Mail's toolbar.*

6. Remove the transferred mail from your .Mac mailbox by selecting the messages and choosing Message > Delete or pressing the Delete key.

7. Choose Mailbox > Erase Deleted Messages, and then choose Mailbox > Rebuild Mailbox.

Now you have room in your .Mac account to copy more mail using the procedure above.

You can use the procedure to move mail from additional mailboxes on your PC to your Mac.

I am sorry that got a bit windy, but if you follow Apple's instructions, it works just fine, and it may be the easiest way to migrate your mail from Outlook Express over to your Mac. If you happen to be using Outlook instead of Outlook Express, I'd probably just switch cold turkey and not move the mail over, or perhaps forward only the most important messages to a different email account, retrieving them on the Mac to transfer them. If you keep the PC around for a while you can make a gradual change, answering new mail from the Mac and old mail from the PC.

If you go into your mail settings and tell Outlook to allow your mail to remain on the server, both the PC and the Mac will receive all your mail. This can be confusing—What have I responded to?—but can also smooth the transition.

It will also highlight how well the Mac OS X Mail program's spam filter works.

The Lazy Way to Move Email

There's another way to move your mail from the Windows machine to your new Mac, and it appeals to the slacker in all of us.

At the first thought of moving your email, go to your Windows Mail control panel, click the E-Mail Accounts Button, and click the Next button to view or change existing accounts.

Next, select your email account, choose More Settings, and then select the Advanced tab.

At the bottom of the tab select "Leave a copy of messages on the server" as well as "Remove from the server after 10 days." But change the 10 to 30.

You will now leave email on your mail server for a month. When you start your Mac and set up your existing email account, it will download the accumulated messages from your mailbox, giving you as much as a month's worth of your old mail on your new Mac. Messages downloaded to your Mac will be deleted from your account.

Those are the instructions for Outlook users. The Outlook Express instructions are even easier: Select Accounts from the Tools Menu, choose your account from the Mail tab, and then make changes on the Advanced settings tab.

In Summary

I have presented two ways to migrate your files and data from your Windows machine to your Mac. I don't think it's a terribly difficult process, but it's certainly complex. Although you can do the move manually using the instructions provided here (and on Apple's Web site), I think most people are better off buying a copy of Move2Mac and letting it handle the detail work.

I'll correct any errors uncovered in this chapter on my Web site at www.coursey.com.

Switcher Diary: FABIOLA TORRES

Switcher Diary: FABIOLA TORRES

College professor Fabiola Torres says her lectures have to be exciting to keep student interest and contain current media content to be relevant. Her Mac makes it possible to achieve both those goals, but before finding the Macintosh she spent many years as a frustrated PC user.

Fabiola: I have been a PC user since 1989. Was it called Windows back then? I remember finally using the term *Windows* in 1995 (I think). I was going through college, and all I did was research, research, and more research. I didn't even use PowerPoint. With this response you can see that my "Windows" world was reduced to Office. Now as for my skills using Windows, well, all I did was save in drive A and/or the desktop. If I had to install anything, I would just call my friend who worked for IT for Cal State Northridge. I didn't even bother knowing how the system worked. I would just see the long list of directions for installation, refuse to do it—for fear of doing something wrong—and call up my IT friend. What I hated about Windows was I didn't understand it. Any time something would go wrong—like an error message, safe mode, an invalid something or another, that blinking white cursor—I would freak out and once again call my friend. Luckily, he lived upstairs: Thanks, Will.

I still use Windows when I'm at work—again just for Office and Web work. It's really frustrating because the computers available to part-time faculty are only PCs.

David: How did you become a Mac user?

Fabiola: There were many factors that made me switch. One commercial that attracted me to the Mac was that one of a kid asking his dad to download a new program on dinosaurs. Of course, the father is confused and is taking a long time to install it. Then the kid says, "I'm going next door. They have a Mac." Right then and there, I realized there was a less complicated machine. But I was still seeing computers as a high-tech word processor. Then the magic moment came. I saw an iMovie on women in sweatshops done by a high school student that blew my mind. It was informative, visually descriptive, and empowering because it delivered new and clear information. Here I was … a college professor … and my students would have received more information about global economics and the feminization of labor through an 8-minute film. I was doing something wrong. This happened two years ago.

David: Is your Mac a good value? How do you feel about Mac pricing?

Fabiola: My Mac is an investment. I realized it was more expensive than a regular PC, but when you look at it, it's actually worth it. First of all, most PCs do not have FireWire or applications like iMovie, iTunes, iPhoto, iCal, iChat, or iSync. You have to pay a lot more for such applications. These come standard.

A Mac is like buying a luxury car. You may be spending a lot of money, but once you have it, you get quality standard equipment and great customer

Switcher Diary: **FABIOLA TORRES**

service. If you get a low-cost car like a standard Toyota, you will have to pay extra to get good components like air conditioning, cruise control, power windows, nice rims, leather seats, remote access, or a better engine. Now, if you buy a standard Volvo or a BMW, you will get a great car with all the features needed to make your drive safe and comfortable.

David: What do you consider to be the most important differences between using a Mac and using a PC?

Fabiola: PCs are not creative machines. They are not geared toward creative expressions. Macs welcome creativity; they inspire creativity.

David: What do you consider to be the most important differences between Mac OS X and Windows?

Fabiola: Mac OS X is visually appealing. Your eyes flow with the click of the mouse. Also, the standard applications that come with Mac OS X are practical and inspirational—they make you want to be creative. For me, Windows hasn't changed since 1996. It's a great word processor.

David: What do you wish you had known before switching? And what were your biggest concerns?

Fabiola: I think the switching moment came at the right time. I was a graduate student required to write papers. There was no room for creativity—sad to say. When I began to teach, I realized that my teaching environment needed to be appealing. If I have to compete with MTV, quick sound bites, and entertainment that require a short attention span, I had to take my lectures beyond just lectures. They had to be exciting!!!

I use iMovie with my digital camera to make short films on a topic. Or I record commercials, TV shows, and movies into my camera and then I import them into iMovie, compress them through QuickTime, and then import them into PowerPoint. I take my presentation on a CD-ROM and then I show it in the class. I also use iPhoto the same way. I may take a picture of a billboard, a neighborhood, or a landmark, import it into PowerPoint, and then show it in class.

Sometimes I just make a slide show. I also use music lyrics in the class, so I have to use iTunes to then import them into PowerPoint. So in a way, I still use Office, but it's the Mac applications that make my PowerPoint presentations exciting. Anyone can make concepts fly across the screen. My goal is to add value to the presentations.

David: Anything else I should have asked but didn't? Anything you want to tell me?

Fabiola: I'm a college professor (going through finals right now) who teaches Chicano studies (Mexican-American studies), ethnic minorities in the U.S., and women's studies. Pop culture is very important to my curriculum. That is why I need to be able to bring the world into my classroom. I want my students to understand their surroundings and not get fooled by what is being shown on TV (regarding minorities in the U.S. and women).

In this post 9/11 era, I need to provide a well-rounded classroom that includes images and sounds to empower my students to *not* misjudge others.

Meet Your Macintosh

Much of the remainder of this book is formatted as questions and answers. My goal is to present a tremendous amount of information one morsel at a time, with the hope that it will be less overwhelming than if it were all dropped on you at once. This format will also help you skim the information so you know what's here and can come back to it later when you need it. At the same time, I've tried to make it easy to read the book straight through, if you like.

The questions are collected into broad topic areas, beginning with what happens with you open the box.

Where's the Manual for My Mac?

You haven't lost it; there isn't one. But there *is* a nice help system on your Mac, and searching it will find answers across all the help files on your machine. The help system tends to be very task-oriented, so asking it questions about things you want to do is a good way to find information.

Curiously, some things you'd expect to be in the help files aren't there, such as how to uninstall an application. I've tried searching using the words *uninstall* and *remove,* which seemed like a friendlier way of describing what I wanted to do. No luck.

So while I find the help system to be generally pretty good, it's not perfect. If you want to know more about your Mac, let me recommend some books also published by Peachpit Press: Robin Williams's *Mac OS X Book,* Maria Langer's *Mac OS X: Visual QuickStart Guide,* and Ted Landau's *Mac OS X Disaster Relief.*

Also, Apple has excellent online help resources on its Web site (www.apple.com; **Figure 5.1**), and if you buy the extended warranty (called the AppleCare Protection Plan), you get long-term access to human assistance as well. And don't forget your local (or online) Mac user group. I've found Mac users to be exceptionally helpful, and I suspect you will, too.

Figure 5.1 Apple does a very good job of providing free support online. This is your starting point, the AppleCare home page at www.info.apple.com. I have always been able to find answers to my questions here, even if sometimes the search took a little while.

The answer to my question above: Except for a few applications that have their own uninstall programs, just drag an application you no longer want to the Trash, and it's gone.

How Do I Get Started Using My Mac?

I'm betting that you have already started your Mac and have been through the setup wizard, so you don't need my help with any of that. Computer makers generally—and Apple in particular—have concentrated on improving the "out-of-box experience," as they call it.

Apple for the most part makes an excellent first impression. That's important to you because it gets your computer up and running in less time with less frustration. It is also your first experience with the Apple way of doing things.

What Are Those Connectors on the Back of My Mac?

Here's a tour of those ports—many of which are similar to PC ports—using an iMac as the example. On the back of the iMac you will find the following, from left to right (**Figure 5.2**):

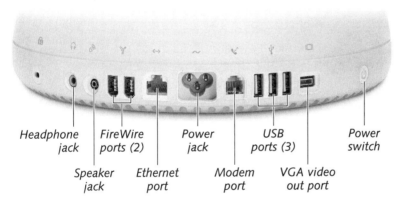

Headphone jack | FireWire ports (2) | Power jack | USB ports (3) | Power switch

Speaker jack | Ethernet port | Modem port | VGA video out port

Figure 5.2 The iMac sports several ports to let it connect to peripherals, networks, and power supplies. These are the same ports you will find—someplace—on all current Macs. From left to right: headphone jack, speaker jack, two FireWire ports, an Ethernet port, power jack, modem port, three USB ports, VGA video out port, and the power switch. There is also a port over on the far left for attaching a third-party locking mechanism for tying your Mac to something heavy, such as a desk. (Courtesy of Apple)

Headphone jack. Stereo minijack. Plug in your headphones here.

 Speaker jack. This looks like a stereo minijack, but it isn't. It's a special connector that the Apple Pro Speakers (which may have come with your machine) use. The iMac has a built-in speaker and an 18-watt amplifier to drive it all. If you don't like the way the Pro speakers sound, you can choose from a variety of aftermarket speakers.

 FireWire ports (two). Also known as IEEE 1394 or iLink, FireWire is an Apple invention that provides a high-speed peripheral connection. These ports have a rated speed of 400 Mbps and are ideal for connecting digital video cameras or external hard drives to your Mac. These are also the ports that you connect an iPod to, both for music downloads and for charging its battery. If you plug something into this jack, your Mac will probably automatically recognize and mount it. Just to make sure, however, check Apple's Web site for a list of devices.

The 17-inch PowerBook G4 (and possibly other models by the time you read this) comes with one FireWire 800 port, which runs at 800 Mbps. An adapter lets you connect a 400 Mbps device to the 800 Mbps port.

 Tip: It is possible to turn your Mac into a FireWire hard drive for another Mac. Start up your Mac while holding down the T key, and it will go into FireWire target disk mode. Connect a FireWire cable between your Mac and the other FireWire-equipped machine, and your Mac's hard drive will appear connected to the other computer. Not something I do all the time, but it's occasionally useful.

 Ethernet (RJ-45) port. This is the connector for a wired local area network (LAN). It's also how you connect your Mac to a cable or DSL broadband modem or even to another Mac using a special cord called a *crossover cable*. I hardly ever use this port, since I use a wireless network at home.

Power jack. Your Mac is Energy Star–compliant and works with a variety of voltages and frequencies; this allows one piece of hardware to be sold worldwide.

 Modem port. Apple thoughtfully includes the phone cable—and what a nice cable it is—to connect from the wall jack to the modem jack on your computer. Your Mac has is a 56K (v.90) modem that is also capable of sending and receiving faxes.

 USB 1.1 ports (3). It's important to note that these are 12 Mbps USB 1.1 jacks, not the newer and faster USB 2.0 jacks intended to compete with 400 Mbps FireWire. There are three USB jacks on the back of the machine and two on the keyboard. Since the keyboard plugs into the back, that leaves you with four, and since most people plug the mouse into the keyboard, you end up with three open USB ports, two in the back and one on the keyboard.

Some Words About USB

USB is the primary method for connecting peripherals to the Mac, except those that require the high throughput that FireWire provides. USB is how you connect a digital camera, printer, key-fob storage, or PDA cradle.

If you are buying from a dealer that isn't a Mac specialist, always check for Mac OS X compatibility in the peripherals you plan to purchase. The compatible-device list (check the Apple Web site) is surprisingly long, but please check to avoid the potential for disappointment.

A few words about USB printers: They are great values; most install automatically; and since they also have a traditional PC printer connector, you can use USB to connect to the Mac and use the old Centronics connector to link the printer to a Windows PC. This generally works pretty well.

Bluetooth warning: Apple promotes compatibility with the Bluetooth wireless protocol. You can buy a very tiny Bluetooth adapter from D-Link (www.dlink.com) that plugs into your USB port if your machine doesn't have Bluetooth built in. My recommendation: Don't, unless you are buying a Bluetooth-enabled cellular telephone. At this writing, Apple does not support printing over Bluetooth, which is sad since Bluetooth is being built into some new printers. I expect Apple to address this, as well as compatibility with future Bluetooth-enabled cameras and other devices.

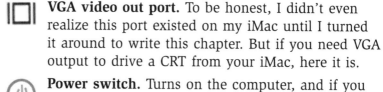

VGA video out port. To be honest, I didn't even realize this port existed on my iMac until I turned it around to write this chapter. But if you need VGA output to drive a CRT from your iMac, here it is.

Power switch. Turns on the computer, and if you hold it down long enough, it will force an emergency power down, which is almost always a last-resort thing to do.

Help! I Need More USB/FireWire Ports!

It's fairly easy to run out of these, especially if you're using a third-party keyboard that causes you to lose the USB port available off the stock Apple keyboard. You can buy external hubs to add more USB or FireWire ports to your Mac, and as long as they're USB- or FireWire-compliant, they should work. But I try to avoid hubs for aesthetic reasons.

If you buy a hub, there's no reason to select a more expensive USB 2.0 model, as your Mac can't increase its speed to match the hub. Stick with plain USB 1.x, and you'll be fine.

Can I Install More Memory in My Mac?

Yes. Although some Macs come with memory that requires a service technician to upgrade, some you can upgrade yourself. For example, getting to the iMac's full 1 GB of RAM capacity requires a trip to the service center, although you can get to 512 MB of RAM without a service technician's assistance. Desktop Macs are easier to upgrade, and unlike those from the olden days, Macs now use standard PC memory, so adding more RAM isn't nearly as expensive as it used to be.

The precise type of memory your Mac uses may be different from the model before or even an earlier release of the same model, so always check to make sure you are buying the right memory for your specific model. Fortunately, there are many online sources of Mac memory, so finding the right type shouldn't be too difficult.

I could give you more information about memory upgrades, but this changes frequently enough that I don't want to risk misleading you and having you end up with the wrong memory, so use the online resources from the memory vendors and you shouldn't have any problems.

Can I Install More Hard-Drive Space in My iMac?

I'm not one to tempt fate, so I recommend using external FireWire drives to add additional storage, which have the added bonus that you can easily use them on any machine with a FireWire port. Here's some more information on how to add storage.

How do I add an external hard drive to my Mac?

Just plug it in. Seriously, if it's a FireWire or Iomega drive, your Mac probably has the proper drivers installed, and the drive will just work. I don't recommend USB hard drives to use with Macs as they will be too slow, so always buy FireWire.

Iomega Zip drives plug into the USB port on the Mac, but the drive speeds are slow enough that USB works fine for them.

Always try a new USB or FireWire device with your machine before installing any drivers that come with the hardware. If the device works without adding drivers, the software on your Mac is likely to be more current than the software that came with the drive, so why tempt fate by installing software you don't need?

How Do I Get Sound in to or out of My Mac?

I would like to meet the genius at Apple who removed audio input and anything other than speaker output from a generation of Macs—one of which you probably own. The good news is there's a microphone hidden in the iMac's screen and below the screen in the PowerBooks and iBooks.

That may or may not solve your audio problems. But an inexpensive device called the Griffin iMic ($35; www.griffintechnology.com) *will*. Not to be confused with an actual microphone, the iMic is really a line-level-audio-to-USB converter that also has an audio output (**Figure 5.3**). I use one of these—it plugs into the Mac's USB port—to connect my semipro mixing board to my iMac. If you need something more sophisticated, several higher quality interfaces are available.

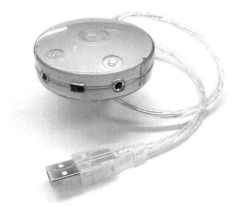

Figure 5.3
The iMic is a must-have accessory for people who want to get quality audio in to and out of an iMac. I use one to produce content for my CNET Radio programs.

And there is hope for the future: Some of the new desktop and PowerBook machines now include analog audio-input jacks, just like a good computer should. This is one case where Apple made things too simple for its users' good. (Although a point can be made that most users will go through their lives never needing to plug anything besides a pair of speakers into their Macs.)

Can I Install a FireWire Port in My PC?

Yes, and probably for less than $50. This allows you to connect your iPod to a Windows machine (but why?), but mostly it's used so you can move a hard drive or digital video camera between the two platforms. FireWire/1394 adapters are available that fit either inside your desktop PC (in a PCI card slot) or in the PC Card slot of your portable.

Are There Any Hardware Upgrades You Recommend?

Yes. Although your iMac (or whatever you bought) will work just fine out of the box, there are a few things you may find are worth adding.

- **RAM.** If your Mac didn't come with at least 256 MB of RAM, increase it—Mac OS X likes lots of RAM, and memory prices are relatively low. I'm thinking about adding another 256 MB to my iMac, but it's not a necessity.

- **Multibutton mouse.** Many people will replace the one-button mouse that comes with their Macs with a more "button-rich" mouse from a company such as Macally or Microsoft (yes, Microsoft makes Mac-compatible mice). I've played with third-party keyboards, including a Microsoft unit designed specifically to work with Office. It worked fine, and what you use is a matter of personal preference. Right now, I am using the standard Apple keyboard and a Macally trackball. If you like trackballs (as I do), you might also look at the models Kensington sells. Pricey but sweet.

- **Audio and video accessories.** Apple's standard speakers are fine, but I have added a USB volume control (Griffin Technology's PowerMate, $45, a cool looking silver knob that sits next to the iMac; see **Figure 5.4**) and an iMic audio connector to my setup. I also bought a Web cam that I am not entirely happy with. There is not (yet) a Mac OS X driver for my beloved Logitech 3000 camera. The only thing I use the camera for is Yahoo instant messaging, but it's a nice accessory.

Figure 5.4 Griffin Technology's PowerMate is an add-on control for your Mac that connects to a USB port. Besides controlling volume and muting your speakers, the device can be used with applications and is especially useful for video editing.

- **iPod.** Is an iPod a hardware upgrade? Sure—any reason to buy an iPod works for me.

- **Backup device.** Backing up your data is always a smart idea. You should check the section on backups in Chapter 9 to see if you want to invest in some sort of backup device.

How Do I Install an AirPort Card in My Mac?

If it is not already built in, every current Mac includes a socket for an AirPort wireless network card as well as built-in antennas. On the iMac, you'll be asked to remove the bottom plate of your computer, a process made easier because the retaining screws are captive and won't fall out, even when loose. This is yet another nice touch that Apple builds in to your Mac. There are specific instructions for installing an AirPort card in each Mac model. You should follow them, as the cards can be somewhat challenging to install. The instructions often are in your Mac near the AirPort socket itself. For example, the 15-inch PowerBook features the instructions inside the space where the battery lives.

Be very careful with the antenna cable that you must connect to the AirPort card. The cable and coaxial fitting are tougher than they look, but you still need to avoid damaging the connector or the AirPort card. Also, make sure the card is right side up before trying to insert it into the connector on the Mac. It will only go one way, and trying to force it will only result in a broken card, Mac, or both. And although it looks a lot like a PC Card, don't plug it into the PC Card slot on your PowerBook. It won't work there.

Note: *You will find much more on networking your Mac in Chapter 8.*

Switcher Diary: SARA WHITE

"Who wants to click Start to shut down their computer? It just doesn't make sense!"

Sara White, a student, told me it took a major virus outbreak to persuade her father to buy her (and himself) a Mac. Though she had been using Windows for five years and was comfortable using the Windows Registry Editor (I'm not), Sara said the basic design of Windows never really made sense, especially when compared with Macintosh.

David: What did/do you like least about Windows?

Sara: I hated having to constantly worry about my PC crashing. I soon learned from experience to save my work about every minute, as I never knew when I would be interrupted with a freeze, crash, or the blue screen of death.

And there was the ugliness factor. Some people may not care about the way their computer looks, but I sure do! The fact that every single computer in the Windows world seemed to be some sickly shade of beige really bothered me, and I found the Windows interface to be counterintuitive, counterproductive, and just plain hideous.

Let's put it this way: Who wants to click Start to shut down their computer? It just doesn't make sense!

David: Please tell me the story of how/why you switched.

Sara: I used to absolutely hate Macs. Although I had not really used Macs much (except for some ancient ones at school), my friends and family had told me that there were no programs available for the Mac OS and that Apple was going to go bankrupt in a few years.

Not knowing any better (I was only in fifth grade at this point), I was glad when my family announced that they were buying our first computer—a PC with Windows 95 installed. The troubles soon began.

Besides being hard to use and ugly, it would crash very often. My dad, having heard that defragmenting the disk could reduce crashes, tried to run the defragmenter program. Unfortunately, he accidentally formatted the disk instead, erasing everything—including my large school project. I was not impressed.

My dad decided that something must have been wrong with the computer and bought another one, this time with Windows 98. Of course, the problems persisted, along with the added threat of viruses from the Internet. After several years of unpleasant, highly unproductive computing, I was beginning to think that computers were a big pain.

Then everything changed.

Switcher Diary: SARA WHITE

By this point, I was in high school and was sitting in the school library during lunch break surfing the Web on a school PC. Somehow, I ended up at the Apple site, staring right at a photograph of a newly released iBook. Wow. I knew I *had* to have that computer—it was the most cool-looking laptop on earth! But this was a Mac and I hated Macs. Didn't I?

It was sure hard to dislike something that looked so good, so I decided to explore the rest of the Apple Web site. After reading about the soon-to-be released Mac OS X, my opinions of computing were changed forever. I was determined to save up enough money to buy this incredible computer.

Convincing my dad that a Mac was the best choice for a computer was a hard task. However, I am a very persuasive person, and after a few months not only the new iBook but also a Power Mac G4 Dual 800 (for my photo-enthusiast father) arrived on my family's doorstep.

Amazing! Everything about my iBook was so simple. In all of 10 minutes I had it out of the box, turned on, set up, and connected to the network. I had never seen an operating system as nice as Mac OS X. Everything just worked, no matter what!

The story didn't end there, however. Although my dad and I were now total Mac fans, my mom and sister were still stuck using the always-crashing family PC. Several months later was the turning point in their computing lives. At this point, the PC now contained at least five different viruses, all of which refused to go away.

When a particularly nasty, pornographic virus invaded it, the family was faced with a decision: Format the hard disk or buy a new computer. We settled on the second option, because as expensive as buying a new computer would be, it would be a better option than reinstalling every single program that had gathered up on the PC over the years, only to get another virus. So, a while later, a brand new G4 iMac joined the family. To this day, none of the Macs has crashed once, and I am far more productive now than I was with Windows.

David: What do you consider to be the most important differences between using a Mac and using a PC?

Sara: To me, the most important difference is the user experience. A Mac does everything a PC does and more (with the exception of crashing and freezing), but it will do everything in a far more intuitive manner. Things just work the way you want them to, and a Mac actually feels "friendly," if that's possible in a machine.

But one of the nicest aspects of using a Mac is the integration between the software, the OS, and the hardware. There is absolutely *no* comparison between iTunes, iMovie, iPhoto, and iDVD and similar software for the Windows world. Apple's "digital-hub" concept is incredible, and there's nothing else like it!

Taming
Your Jaguar

At 10:20 p.m. on Friday, August 23, 2002, Mac OS X became a real operating system. Previously, it had been a nice attempt that still lacked some essential features, such as the ability to easily connect to Microsoft Windows networks.

I know the exact time for this because it's when Apple Stores began selling the new 10.2 version to hundreds, perhaps thousands, of the faithful who gathered for the in-store launch parties. Those attending in Palo Alto, not far from Apple's Cupertino campus, actually got a glimpse of Steve Jobs, who has rock-star status among the really hard-core Mac users.

Mac OS X 10.2 is an excellent operating system with a silly nickname: Jaguar. The tropical cat had provided the code name used during development, and somehow it stuck with the final release.

Even if you are only barely able to use Windows, you shouldn't have any trouble making the transition to Mac OS X. Give it a week, and you will feel very comfortable with your new computer, especially if you can avoid going back to a Windows machine until you feel competent on the Mac. That will give you time to internalize how the Mac works without being constantly confused by moving from one platform to another.

Not everyone has this option, especially if your job requires a Windows machine, so I don't want to make to big a deal out of this. If you spend a weekend working on your Mac, by Monday morning I bet you'll be OK.

The first thing most people notice about the Mac OS X user interface is how pretty it is. Almost as quickly they think back to their busy-looking Windows desktop and wonder what's missing.

Nothing, really, is missing. And to prove that, I'd like to take you on a tour of Mac OS X 10.2 Jaguar, explaining the basics of how you interact with the operating system. Later, I'll introduce some applications as well, including Microsoft Office and all of the Apple "i" applications that come free with your Mac.

In my writer fantasies, you are holding off on doing anything with a Mac—including buying one—until you finish reading this book. And I'm sure that describes some of you. But a bunch of you have already either purchased a Mac or spent enough time hanging around the Apple Store lusting after the hardware that what I'm about to tell you won't be entirely new.

Feel free to skim this section or just look at the pretty screen shots or do whatever makes sense. I will try to make this tour of the operating system useful to newcomers and interesting to people who already have a little Mac experience.

Or you can do what I generally do when I get a new toy: Rip open the box and have at it, perhaps reading the instructions later. Women tell me that's a guy thing, and it's gotten me into trouble more than once, so perhaps you might want to look at this chapter before embarking on an unguided tour of Mac OS X. You'd hate to miss any of the sights, right? And you've already paid for the book.

A Brief History of Jaguar

It took Apple a mere seven years and several tries from the time it first started talking about a "next-generation" operating system to the time Mac OS X was released. Even then, the new operating system was out for a year before it was safe enough to take home for dinner with your parents.

But what an operating system it turned out to be—clearly the best OS ever built for a desktop computer, combining most of what people like about Unix with everything people like about Macintosh.

This is the story of that operating system, or rather the stories of the operating systems that were in development basically between the time Steve Jobs left Apple and when he (and a flock of engineers from his startup, NeXT) returned and began development of Mac OS X.

During the long wait while Steve was in exile at Pixar, his animation studio, and NeXT, his computer company, Apple executives made promises using code names such as Gershwin and Copland and talking of technologies called Pink and Blue (after the colors of the Post-it notes used in meetings where the technologies were first described— one set of features was written on one color and another set of features on the other).

It's not surprising that nothing came of these development efforts, aimed at taking Mac OS forward without losing compatibility with old applications. Making real progress sometimes requires starting over—something Apple should have remembered from the end of the Apple II and the arrival of the Macintosh in 1984.

When Steve Jobs returned from his years of exile at NeXT, he essentially scrapped the old projects, brought in the NeXT engineers, and let them have a go at a next-generation Mac operating system. That led to people describing Apple's purchase of NeXT as a reverse acquisition— it was really NeXT that took over Apple, and from an engineering sense it was true.

These engineering geniuses—and I mean that seriously—decided to replace the guts of the Mac OS with Unix technology. This was to prove a very wise move, as it linked the Mac OS to an operating system known for great maturity and stability.

The hard part of this equation, technically, would be to make the old Mac OS run atop the new Unix one, which was necessary for compatibility, especially during the time it would take the new OS to gather momentum. Software developers, used to years of unfulfilled promises, were naturally leery of investing development dollars in an operating system Apple had yet to ship.

The idea of a desktop Unix, which is what Apple's new OS would be, is an attractive one, though it has eluded a large part of the computer industry. Unix, an operating system developed at AT&T Bell Laboratories, remains a darling of academics, scientists, students, and some large corporations. It is stable, scalable, and quite mature; and its "open" nature—meaning that most of the code is available for anyone to use—appeals to many users.

continues on next page

A Brief History of Jaguar *continued*

Despite 20 years of attempts, Unix had never gained popularity on desktop computers, except workstations used by scientists and programmers. One reason for this was the lack of a capable graphical user interface to compete with Windows. Nor was there—or was there ever likely to be—a Unix version of Microsoft Office, which had become the standard applications package for corporate customers.

Unix also has a deserved reputation as an operating system designed by engineers for engineers. To be widely popular, any Unix-based operating system would have to hide the native Unix controls with something much simpler and accessible to the mere mortals who would be using it.

While Mac OS X would offer "Classic-mode" compatibility with older Mac applications, it would eventually force developers to rewrite their applications to take advantage of new features and the benefits of Unix.

As right as it might be for Steve Jobs to make Apple a Unix company, the decision was a risky one. Computer companies are loath, with good reason, to do anything that forces customers to reconsider their decision to buy in the first place.

While Jobs was away at NeXT—never itself a success—Apple had seen its share of the education market, which it once enjoyed almost exclusively, drop by half. Corporate America, whose embrace of the Macintosh was always tentative at best, had been bailing out of Macs for several years. A mass defection to Windows by the company's remaining customers would take a large, even fatal, bite out of Apple.

Something had to be done, and based on what Jobs's engineers learned at NeXT, building the next Mac OS atop a Unix kernel (called "Mach") seemed like the best option.

On Apple's side, however, was the almost cultlike allegiance of many of its customers, who consider anything with a Cupertino, CA, postmark to be handed down from the gods.

Nevertheless, the first betas of Mac OS X drew gasps of shock from many in the Apple user community who saw it. The Apple name appeared to have gone on the OS well before any features familiar to longtime Macheads had gone in.

Over time, Mac OS X gained a certain Macishness, but it would still prove to have a learning curve for the faithful. In that way, someone switching to Mac OS X from Windows may actually have an easier time than someone switching from Mac OS 9. At least the Windows users have no expectations, which the Mac users had in bushel baskets.

The first official release of Mac OS X, in 2001, was premature (Apple released a "public beta" in 2000). Though not crashy, the operating system was slow and, of course, had few applications. It did, however, prove that Apple was serious and really had a next-generation OS this time. That was reinforced by Jobs's decision to ship the new OS on all Apple hardware, with Mac OS 9.2.2 available to run the older apps everyone was still using.

Not many Mac OS 9 users actually upgraded, at least not until Microsoft released Office for Mac OS X, and then other developers began following suit. By late 2001, it was clear that Mac OS X would succeed as Apple's future direction, but Apple had to make it faster and more compatible with the Windows networks on which many Apple machines would have to make their homes.

The introduction of the flat-panel iMacs, in January 2002, got Apple a controversial *Time* magazine cover and helped put Mac OS X solidly on the map, with Apple promising significant improvements later in the year.

Those improvements, released in August 2002 as Mac OS 10.2 Jaguar, finally gave Apple an OS that lived up to the claims (and goals) of its "Switcher" campaign, an in-Microsoft's-face attempt to lure Windows users to the Mac and the jumping off point for this book.

Many people who never before considered Macintosh are now switching because the new operating system offers the ability to develop and run Unix applications, as well as the added benefits of a real desktop user interface supported by many applications.

Meet the Desktop

Let me start by introducing you to the basic Mac OS X 10.2 Jaguar Desktop—the first thing you see when starting to work on your Mac, especially if you never power it down. Yes, Mac OS X is stable enough to leave running all the time. Whether or not you do that is between you and the Global Warming folks, though the new Macs are remarkably energy efficient.

Our tour begins on the Desktop of the wide-screen iMac that I'm using to write this book. I am imagining you at the keyboard and me looking over your shoulder. This is a book version of the tour I've given many times to friends interested in Mac OS X.

When you start up a new Mac, it will probably look something like this, except that hopefully your machine won't have either my picture or the icon for my ABS backup drive sitting on the desktop (**Figure 6.1**). But if you do happen to have a desktop that looks exactly like this, please contact me immediately (coursey@mac.com) so I can get my machine and backup drive back.

Figure 6.1 The Mac OS X 10.2 Desktop, at its most basic, consists of a menu bar at the top, an icon on the right for the hard drive, and the Dock at the bottom. Your Mac won't have my FireWire-connected backup drive or my photo, I hope.

I will explain all the screen elements in more detail later, but let's start with a high-level view to get our bearings.

At the top of the screen is the menu bar. Windows has two of these, one top and one bottom, but Mac OS X has only one. The menu choices change depending upon what application you're running (**Figure 6.2**).

Figure 6.2 This is the menu bar, which is always at the top of your screen. It changes slightly when you change applications—here it's showing the Finder application—but the major elements are always the same.

At the far left is an Apple icon, and clicking it opens the Apple menu, which is as close as Mac OS X gets to the Windows Start menu (**Figure 6.3**).

Figure 6.3 The Apple menu, always available from the Apple icon on the left end of the menu bar, provides access to a handful of useful features.

To the right of the Apple menu icon is the name of the current application—in this case the Finder, which is your tool for navigating disks and folders on the Mac. The menu choices to the right of the application name are specific to the Finder yet typical of what you will see across many applications.

At the far end of the menu bar are some pretty useful icons (**Figure 6.4**). The first appears if you have Bluetooth networking installed, and the second appears if you are using AirPort wireless networking, which I strongly encourage you do to. This icon shows signal strength (excellent in this case), and clicking it opens a menu of AirPort options.

Next to the AirPort icon is the icon for iChat, Apple's version of America Online's instant-messaging client. When it's dark (as it is here) the icon signifies that you are logged on to the AOL Instant Messaging (AIM) network. The speaker icon provides access to a volume-control slider.

Figure 6.4 At the right end of the menu bar are icons for Bluetooth, AirPort, iChat, and your speaker. Clicking any of them opens a menu related to that function.

The Apple Menu

When you click the Apple icon, you open a menu that gives you access to a few features that roughly compare to some of those in the Windows Start menu, including turning off the machine and changing users. Here are the menu choices:

About This Mac. Gives you simple information about your Mac—such as processor speed and memory. Clicking the More Info button in the dialog opens the Apple System Profiler, mostly of interest to geeks and to someone who's helping you solve a serious problem with your machine.

Get Mac OS X Software. Opens your default browser and takes you to a downloads page on Apple's Web site. You will find a variety of freeware, shareware, and demo versions of commercial applications there. Worth an occasional visit.

System Preferences. Opens the Mac equivalent of Windows's control panels, discussed below.

Dock. Provides basic control over the Dock as well as the ability to open the Dock's System Preferences, explained below.

Location. This useful feature allows you to easily select a set of specific settings for the location where you are using your computer. (I'll explain more fully later in this chapter.)

Recent Items. Gives you instant access to your recently used applications and documents. To be honest, this isn't a feature I have used often, as I am not the world's most efficient computer user. If a keystroke can be wasted, I probably have. But having to write about this feature got me thinking about using it, and I recommend it to you as an easy way to open apps and docs.

Force Quit. Opens a list of applications and allows you to use brute force to quit an app that has started misbehaving. You can also access this function by simultaneously pressing Command-Option-Escape. Mac OS X hardly ever crashes, but applications sometimes do freeze up, and this is where you handle that problem. Windows uses Ctrl-Alt-Delete to get you to essentially the same place in its operating system.

Sleep, Restart, and **Shut Down.** Operate as expected.

Log Out. Allows you to easily change users.

The Dock

The most noticeable feature of the Mac OS X user interface is the Dock, a bar found at the bottom of the screen (by default but it can be moved) that holds application aliases, making it easy to find, start, and switch between your favorite applications (**Figure 6.5**).

The Dock does the same things the Windows taskbar does but looks better doing it and is more flexible.

Figure 6.5 The Dock is the first thing most Windows users notice about the Mac desktop. It provides fast access to applications and important places like your home and Applications folders.

Looking at the Dock, the first icon on the left is always a link to the Finder, and the home folder and Trash are at the other end. Somewhere in between are System Preferences and Sherlock, the Apple Web-services search utility.

In order, this Dock contains: the Finder, Mac OS X's Mail, iChat, Address Book, Microsoft Internet Explorer, iTunes, Microsoft Word, iPhoto, iMovie, Sherlock, iCal, a link to my home folder, a link to the Applications folder, and the Trash.

> **Hint:** *Dragging a removable disc to the Trash causes it to eject. This will also unmount a network disk.*

To add a program to the Dock, simply drag its icon over from the Finder and drop it into the Dock. Removing an item is even easier: Drag it onto the Desktop and watch it disappear in a puff of smoke.

To start an application from the Dock, simply click (once, although double-clicking doesn't hurt) and watch the icon bounce, indicating that the application is starting. You will also see a black triangle, indicating that the application is running. (Notice that the Finder and Word are running in Figure 6.6).

While an application is running, if you click an icon and keep the mouse button pressed, a pop-up menu opens that allows you to close the application or locate it in the Finder. (I use the Quit command frequently and the Show In Finder option not at all.)

Some applications give you other options from a click-hold on the icon as well. iTunes, for example, offers some player controls. Word presents a list of open documents and allows you to select between them (**Figure 6.6**).

Figure 6.6 Clicking and holding an icon in the Dock often provides access to application-specific functions. In Word, this means a list of open documents.

After using Windows's encyclopedic Start menu, Apple's Dock may seem too small. Although it's certainly true that the Dock won't organize 100 or more applications as well as the Start menu, it does a better job of making your most-used apps immediately accessible. My bet is that Macintosh users generally have fewer applications than Windows users, making the simplicity even more of a win.

You will probably want to customize the Dock, perhaps changing its size, playing with the magnification feature, or moving it to either the left or right side of the screen.

To change Dock preferences, from the Apple menu choose Dock > Dock Preferences (**Figure 6.7**).

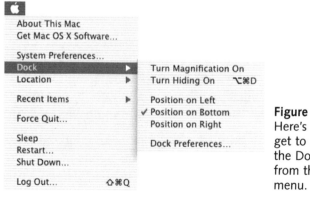

Figure 6.7 Here's how you get to some of the Dock settings from the Apple menu.

The Dock's System Preferences panel gives you several options to change its appearance and functionality (**Figure 6.8**).

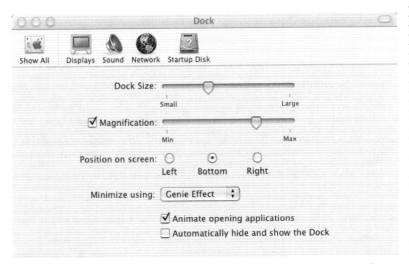

Figure 6.8 In the Dock's System Preferences panel you can control its behavior and screen placement.

The Dock Size slider allows you to change the size of the Dock. I like mine on the small side.

Magnification, selected with a check box and controlled by a slider, is a fun feature to play with—the sort of thing Apple does that makes its computers more playful than the competition's. Turning Magnification on causes the docked icons to grow as your pointer rolls over them. The slider controls the amount of magnification. Have fun with this feature, which might actually be useful if you forget your reading glasses or load the Dock with a zillion teensy icons (**Figure 6.9**).

Figure 6.9 The Dock's magnification feature, besides looking cool, allows you to make your Dock really small, knowing that you'll still be able to find the icon you need even if you can't see it until you slide your pointer across the Dock and watch the icons grow.

"Position on screen" gives you three choices for where the Dock will appear—left, bottom, or right. For no reason in particular I keep mine on the right. You might think you should be able to drag the Dock and just leave it where you want it, but you can't.

The "Minimize using" menu offers two options, which control the visual effect used when you minimize an application (by clicking the yellow button at the top left of the application window) or maximize it by clicking the application in the Dock. The difference between Genie Effect (default) and Scale Effect is minor, except that scaling is faster. The important thing here is that minimizing uses an animated effect to remind you where your window has gone.

"Animate opening applications" controls whether or not the icon bounces in the Dock while the app is opening. Kinda cute but not necessary, and unselecting this check box will remove some whimsy from your Mac if you so choose. But isn't whimsy part of why you bought a Mac?

"Automatically hide and show the Dock" mimics a similar feature in Windows. It makes the Dock disappear when you aren't using it. I leave this feature turned off, but you may want your Mac to have a really empty screen.

> **It's Not Just Windows Users Who Are Confused by Mac OS X**
>
> If it makes you feel any better, users of previous Macintosh operating systems feel pretty much the same way as you might feel when they see Mac OS X for the first time. Mac OS X is so different from Mac OS 9 that having previous Mac experience may actually slow the transition. That's because Windows users expect Mac OS X to be really different. However, Mac users look for similarities and are more likely, perhaps, to be confused.
>
> My experience is that it takes a few days to a week for a new user—from either Windows or Mac OS 9—to feel fully comfortable with Mac OS X. The goal of this chapter is to help you make it through that week.

Bring Back Happy Mac!

As a new Mac user, you have already missed the departure of a bit of Mac history. Gone with the release of Mac OS X 10.2 Jaguar is the friendly "Happy Mac" face that had previously greeted Mac users when they powered up their machines (**Figure 6.10**).

Figure 6.10 In one form or another (an earlier version on the left; a more recent on the right), a happy Mac face has always smiled on folks starting up their Macs—until Jaguar.

Or at least Mac users hoped for Happy Mac when booting, because the alternative was another face, the aptly named Sad Mac. He didn't appear often, but when he showed up, it was always the beginning of a pretty bad day, as Sad Mac meant a hardware problem, and your computer was unlikely to start at all.

In Jaguar, the Mac faces are replaced by a gray Apple icon and an animated gray wheel that appear while the machine is starting up. Many of us are counting on Apple's realizing the error of its ways and bringing back Happy Mac. Sad Mac we're happy to see go away—as long as the hardware always works.

The Finder

If you click the Apple "face" icon at the far left of your Dock or any empty spot on the Desktop, you will enter the Finder, analogous to My Computer in Windows. This is where you navigate to find files and folders. From every Finder window you can enter a search phrase and find anything that eludes you (**Figure 6.11**).

The Finder is your graphical file manager. It offers you three views to choose from—icon, list, and column—and each has its purpose. Icon view is what many people use as a default, switching into the other views as needed. The most useful view, however, is the column view. It allows you to explore your Mac via a series of columns that open as you dive down into the machine. You can choose a view by either opening the Finder's View menu or clicking one of the View buttons in the toolbar of a Finder window.

Figure 6.11 The Finder window is how you navigate your computer. Here are the top-level folders on the hard drive of the Mac used to write this book. Notice the toolbar at the top of the window, which offers several Finder controls and a search function.

Icon view. Displays the contents of a directory as file, application, or folder icons (**Figure 6.12**). If you double-click an icon, it will open the file, launch the application, or display the contents of the selected folder.

Figure 6.12
With the icon view, you can arrange icons several ways, including by name, by date modified or created, by kind, and by size. Here I've organized them by name.

List view. Displays the contents of a folder as a list of files, applications, and directories (**Figure 6.13**). Clicking the black triangles next to folders displays their contents as part of the list.

Column view. This is a variant of the list view, with the difference that when you click a folder, a new column opens to the right of the column you are working in (**Figure 6.14**).

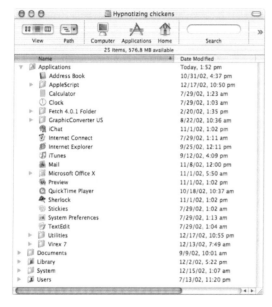

Figure 6.13
In the list view, you can quickly see the contents of a folder by clicking its black disclosure triangle.

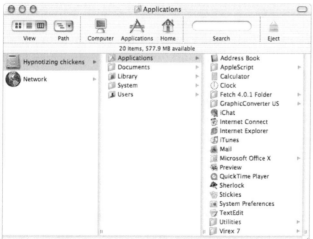

Figure 6.14 The Column view provides a handy method of navigating through folders: click a folder, and its contents show up in a column to the right.

The Finder toolbar

Every Finder window has a Finder toolbar located near the top (see Figure 6.11). It provides a Back button to retrace your steps, three View buttons, and a place to drag and drop icons for files, folders, and applications. Single-clicking these icons causes them to open, just like they do in the Dock. You will also find a clear button in the upper right-hand corner that hides (or unhides) the Finder toolbar.

The Finder menu bar

When you are using the Finder, the menu bar at the top of the screen contains some useful functions and navigational tools. Most of these will immediately make sense to a Windows user—except one.

The Go menu allows you to navigate around your Mac, but it also allows you to get to network servers via the Connect to Server command. Selecting this option displays other computers (both Macs and Windows machines) visible on your network. Double-clicking the computer allows you to connect to the shared folders on the other machines. You may need a user name and password, depending on how the other machine is configured.

The traffic lights

I'll bet you've already noticed these, but every window you open in Mac OS X has three "traffic lights" in the upper left-hand corner. Roll your pointer over any of these red, yellow, and green buttons and you'll notice that X, –, and + symbols, respectively, appear inside all of them. Here's what's up:

Red. On the far left and dressed with a X in the center is the red, or stop, light. It closes the window. If you haven't saved changes you've made to a document, you'll see a dot here instead. Save the document and the dot will go away.

Yellow. In the center, wearing a minus sign, is the minimize button. Click this and your window takes an animated trip into the Dock, where you can click it to reopen it.

Green. On the right and wearing a plus sign is the maximize button, which doesn't so much make a window full-screen as it makes the window the size the application wants it to be.

You will often find other, application-specific functions across the top edge of a window. None them should ever do anything that can't be easily undone, so feel free to play when you come across them.

What Are System Preferences, and How Do They Compare with Windows Control Panels?

They are pretty much the same thing, except the System Preferences panels in Mac OS X are less likely to ruin your day than the control panels in Windows.

The names of the individual Mac OS X System Preferences panels should give you a good idea of what they do, but to avoid confusion I've created a chart that compares the functionality of the control panels in Windows 98 with their Mac OS X equivalents.

Table 6.1 Windows Control Panels versus Mac OS X 10.2 System Preferences

Windows 98	Mac OS X 10.2	Comments
Accessibility Options	Universal Access	On the Mac, provides controls for seeing, hearing, keyboard, and mouse to assist persons with special needs.
Add New Hardware		No Mac OS X equivalent (which is good—there isn't a need).
Add/Remove Programs		No Mac OS X equivalent (also good, because there's little need).
	Bluetooth	This preferences panel appears when you connect a Bluetooth wireless adapter to your Mac.
Date/Time	Date & Time	
Desktop Themes	Desktop, Screen Effects, General	Among these three preferences panels are the controls that govern the look and feel of your Mac OS X Desktop.
Display	Display	
Fonts		
Game Controllers		

Table continues on next page

Table 6.1 Windows Control Panels versus Mac OS X 10.2
System Preferences *(continued)*

Windows 98	Mac OS X 10.2	Comments
	Ink	This preferences panel provides handwriting-recognition features when you connect a tablet to your Mac.
Internet Options	Internet	.Mac and iDisk settings. Default email client and account settings. Default Web browser and home-page settings.
Keyboard	Keyboard	
Mail	Internet (and email client settings)	
Modems	Network	The modem settings are on a tab in this Mac OS X preferences panel.
Mouse	Mouse	
Multimedia		In Windows, this control panel changes settings for multimedia devices. No similar control panel on the Mac, which is good since Windows manages to make this way too complex.
Network	Network	Apple allows you to define locations and create a separate connection profile for each. For most people the default settings work fine and need not be changed.
Passwords	Keychain Access (Not a preference panel; rather, a program found in Applications > Utilities.)	Mac OS X offers a very understandable system to manage all your passwords.
PC Card (PCMCIA)		Mac Support is built in.
Power Management	Energy Saver	
Printers	Print Center (Not a preferences panel; rather, a program found in Applications > Utilities.)	Controlled by the Print Center utility.
Regional Settings	International	Apple is very proud of its support for international languages. This panel is worth a sightseeing tour.
Sounds	Sound	Controls sound effects, input, and output.

Windows 98	Mac OS X 10.2	Comments
Speech	Speech	This is a fun preferences panel that allows you to control both voice recognition and the Mac's ability to read text and system alerts to you. Have fun selecting from the 22 default voices ranging from serious to hilarious. Your Mac is happy to read you alert messages or help if you cannot read the screen.
System		Thankfully, Mac OS X doesn't have anything that really compares to Windows's system settings.
Telephony		On Windows, configures telephony drivers and dialing properties. Not needed for Mac. See Modems and a program called Internet Connect in the Applications folder.
Text Services	International	
Users	Accounts	Who can use your Mac and what they can do are determined by this panel. Remember that each Mac OS X user gets a private (and secure) home folder allowing that user to store his or her own programs and documents away from prying eyes.
	Dock	Controls how the Dock behaves.
	Login Items	Determines the programs that start immediately when you log in.
	My Account	Change your user name, password, personal startup icon, and default address card here. You can use a small photo of yourself as your icon.
	CDs & DVDs	Tell your Mac what to do when you insert a blank CD or DVD; a music CD or picture CD; or a video DVD.

Table continues on next page

Table 6.1 Windows Control Panels versus Mac OS X 10.2
System Preferences *(continued)*

Windows 98	Mac OS X 10.2	Comments
	ColorSync	Controls how your Mac works with color. Unless you have a specific reason to change these settings, it's best to leave them alone.
	QuickTime	Controls Apple's multimedia player of the same name.
	Sharing	Controls file sharing over both your local network and the Internet—also remote access, printer sharing, and the built-in firewall.
	Classic	If your Mac is set up to also run Mac OS 9.2.2 for compatibility with pre-Mac OS X applications, this is where you will find the controls.
	Software Update	Controls the automatic down-loading of software updates from Apple.
	Startup Disk	Determines which disk (or operating system) your computer uses at startup.

Mac System Preferences are easier to use than Windows control panels because they don't have to do as much. Many settings that Microsoft must include to be compatible with absolutely everything in its universe aren't needed by a company that builds both its own hardware and its operating systems. This is not to say that Apple has done this perfectly and that sometimes I don't wish for a few more features, such as a more functional firewall, better support for virtual private networks, and the ability to decide how often my computer connects to a time server and resets its clock. But overall, Mac OS X's System Preferences are much less intimidating, and a wrong setting is much less likely to mess things up (and then be impossible to fix) than Windows's control panels.

How Do I Change System Preferences?

To open the Mac OS X System Preferences, simply click the light-switch icon in the Dock (provided you haven't removed it; **Figure 6.15**) or choose System Preferences from the Apple menu. Either way, a window much like the one in **Figure 6.16** will appear.

Figure 6.15 You can open System Preferences by clicking its icon in your Dock.

Figure 6.16 Here's a view of the System Preferences window, with a few of my third-party software panels in there too.

The System Preferences are divided into four sections: Personal, Hardware, Internet & Network, and System. At the top of the window is a customizable toolbar, much like those in a Finder window, which allows quick access to certain preferences panels. You might want to drag the icons for your most used System Preferences to this toolbar. And if you don't like an icon that's already in the toolbar, just drag it off. If you'd rather see the panels organized alphabetically, choose View > Show All Alphabetically (**Figure 6.17**).

Figure 6.17 You can choose which way you want to view System Preferences as well as select a particular preferences panel from the View menu when you have the System Preferences folder open.

Clicking one of the Preferences icons causes that particular panel to open, although the rest of the window remains the same—it may change shape to accommodate more or fewer controls. (You can also choose preferences panels from the View menu.)

Note: *You can make the toolbar disappear by clicking the transparent capsule-looking hide-toolbar button at the top right of the window. I'm not sure how useful this function is, but it's there if you want to use it.*

When you're done with a particular item, clicking the Show All icon in the toolbar (or pressing Command-L) again displays all the preferences icons. When finished with System Preferences, you can choose System Preferences > Quit System Preferences or press Command-Q.

> **Important:** *Some settings are for administrators only. If you are asked for a password, enter the one you used to log in to the Mac. If that works, you're in business. If not, you need to find someone who knows the admin password to help you. And if you ask very nicely, maybe that person will go to the Users preferences panel and add administrator privileges to your account so you won't have to ask again.*

What Do the Individual Preferences Panels Do?

I'll now take you through the four System Preferences categories and give you an idea of what each panel is used for. I'll also provide a cross-reference between Windows 98 control panels and the equivalent System Preferences panels in Mac OS X.

Personal preferences

These panels control the Mac OS X look and feel, which is called "Aqua." And these settings really are personal—each user with an account on the Mac can set these however he or she chooses, and the settings will only be in effect when that person is logged in and using the machine (**Figure 6.18**).

Figure 6.18 The Personal Preferences panels include Desktop, Dock, General, International, Login Items, My Account, and Screen Effects.

Desktop. This panel is an excellent example of what it means to be a Macintosh. On its face, this panel allows you to choose a background image for your computer's Desktop. But look at the Desktop-picture choices and note that there are people at Apple with the good taste to offer this many Desktop choices to you.

Play with the various collections to find something you like, including the option of using an image from your Pictures folder. If you are easily bored, you can set the Desktop image to automatically change at a variety of intervals, ranging from daily to every 5 seconds.

Dock. These settings control the placement and behavior of the Dock, which I explained in detail earlier in this chapter.

General. The General panel determines the colors used for items you select and buttons, scroll-arrow locations, and whether clicking in the scroll bar advances you a page or to that location in the document. You may also specify how many recent applications and documents are displayed in Apple menu > Recent Items.

Finally, you should set the font-smoothing style to match the type of display you are using. I leave that last setting, "Turn off font smoothing," alone, since smooth fonts have always seemed preferable to me, although you're welcome to have jaggy fonts if that pleases you.

International. If you selected the proper language when you set up your Mac, then you don't need to open this panel at all. I won't go into detail, but you should take a look at the various settings that could make your Mac just perfect for a Turk, a Thai, or an Icelander just by selecting a few check boxes—which could also make it perfect for a Czech.

Login Items. This panel allows you to select applications that will start every time you log in. It also shows background-only applications, such as the Microsoft Database Daemon (a helper for Microsoft Entourage).

My Account. This is where you change your password and the image associated with your user name, as well as the details of your personal address card (doing so launches Address Book, covered in Chapter 7). If you want to use your own picture (or some other image) as your icon, drag it in here.

Screen Effects. This is Apple's name for what Microsoft calls a Screen Saver (and Apple used to). Apple offers several very attractive screen savers, enhanced by what some call the "Ken Burns effect." Named after the documentary filmmaker of public television fame, some Apple screen effects use still photographs but zoom and pan to create a very pleasant visual experience. Burns uses this same effect to give the appearance of movement to the historical still photos.

Hardware preferences

These settings affect all users of a single Mac, and they govern, not surprisingly, your Mac's hardware (**Figure 6.19**).

Figure 6.19 The Hardware System Preferences panels include Bluetooth (if your machine has it running at the time), CDs & DVDs, ColorSync, Displays, Energy Saver, Keyboard, Mouse, and Sound.

CDs & DVDs. This panel allows you to decide what happens when you load a blank CD, blank DVD, music CD, picture CD, or video DVD. For prerecorded media you will probably choose to open the appropriate Apple application: iTunes for a music CD, iPhoto for a picture CD, and DVD Player for a prerecorded DVD. Those are excellent default choices for recorded media. For blank media, the default is "Ask what to do," giving you the choice of opening one of several applications appropriate for disc burning.

Color Sync. Color management is very important to Mac users in the graphic arts. Normal mortals won't use this panel very often, if at all (although we are big beneficiaries of Apple's attention to graphic quality in its operating systems and hardware). Don't make changes in this panel unless you have a reason.

Displays. This is where you adjust the screen resolution and number of colors your Mac will display. You can also calibrate your display so that it displays accurate color. This is another panel I wouldn't mess with unless I had a specific reason. If your Mac has an LCD flat-panel display, you are probably best off with the default resolution setting, as LCDs generally display one resolution beautifully and all the others not so well.

Tip: *If you need to change your display resolution or color depth frequently, you can check the "Show displays in menu bar" check box to put a display system menu in your menu bar.*

Energy Saver. This is where you do your part for or against global warming by setting how long your hard drive and display are inactive before going to sleep, among other energy-consumption–related settings. The automatic setting is a good choice, though you can make changes if you feel like it. If you leave your Mac on most of the time, you can set it to restart automatically after a power failure.

Keyboard. Two settings here determine the key-repeat rate: how long you must hold down the key before it starts repeating the character, and how quickly the characters are repeated. A second screen turns Full Keyboard Access on and off. With it on, you get access to six keyboard functions and can select the key sequences that invoke the functions. I don't use these. If you use a third-party keyboard, it may install its own keyboard software, as either a preferences panel or a separate application.

Mouse. Controls the mouse or trackpad settings. If you use a third-party mouse, it may install its own application or preferences panel.

Sound. From this panel you can select the alert sounds your Mac uses and the speaker volume, as well as input and output devices your Mac will use. If you change sound settings often, you can use this panel to put a volume system menu (one that's always present) in the menu bar.

Internet & Network preferences

There settings are shared by all users, and they control how your Mac interacts with networks, including the Internet (**Figure 6.20**).

Figure 6.20 The Internet & Network System Preferences panels include Internet, Network, QuickTime, and Sharing.

It's important to note that the Internet System Preferences panel controls what programs you use when you are connected to the Internet, and the Network System Preferences panel controls how you make the connection. In general, don't mess with the Network panel unless you have a specific reason and know exactly what needs to be done.

Internet. This panel includes settings for your .Mac online services account, the iDisk online storage associated with your .Mac account, your default email program, your default Web browser, your home page, and the location where you store downloads.

Network. Although this is the most complex System Preferences panel, you shouldn't need to open it very frequently. For most people the default settings should work just fine. Let's walk through this panel one element at a time.

At the top is the Location pop-up menu, which defaults to automatic. This is a neat feature that allows you to create settings for all the places where you use your computer as well as the ways you connect from any given place. For example, if you have a PowerBook and you use an AirPort network at home and an Ethernet network at work, the Network System Preferences panel lets you create a location (a set of settings) for each place.

This is mostly of interest to iBook and PowerBook users but could also help a college student who perhaps takes an iMac home on the weekends but generally uses it in a dorm room.

By creating a location, you can control how your Mac tries to access the Internet, whether over the built-in Ethernet port, a wireless AirPort card you've installed, the built-in 56K (v.90) modem, the infrared port, or some other means. You will find these connection choices in the Show menu.

Depending on the connection method you've chosen, the tabs present various options for setting up the connection. Enter these settings on the appropriate tab in the Network preferences window.

Again, if you don't understand any of these settings, I strongly recommend not touching them.

QuickTime. This panel contains settings for Apple's QuickTime media technology—not something you are likely to interact with soon, unless you buy the Pro version and need to register it or you want to check for an update. This panel has a built-in software updater for QuickTime.

Sharing. This is a very important panel that controls how your computer does or doesn't interact with other computers over the Internet. This is also where you can change the Internet and Rendezvous name of your computer, which is what people will see when they connect to your machine.

The tabs are labeled Services, Firewall, and Internet. Here's what each does in detail:

- **Services.** This is where you control the services your computer offers other computers over the Internet. These are:

  Personal File Sharing. Allows other Macs on your network to see your shared files.

  Windows File Sharing. Allows Windows machines on your network to see your shared files and you to see theirs.

  Personal Web Sharing. Allows other computers to see the personal Web site on your computer. The files for this site live in your home folder in the Sites folder. Go there and click the Index.html page to learn more. Although this lets you use your Mac as a Web server, it's more likely that your public Web site—open to everyone on the Internet—lives on .Mac, on AOL, or on a server at your Internet service provider (ISP).

  Remote Login. Not for beginners—lets you log in to your Mac from another computer. Leave it turned off.

  FTP Access. Not for beginners—lets you turn your Mac into an FTP server for file transfers. Leave it turned off.

  Remote Apple Events. Not for beginners—lets your Mac respond to Apple Events sent over a network. Leave it turned off.

  Printer Sharing. If you have more than one Mac on your network, turn Printer Sharing on and the other Macs will see printers connected to this Mac as if the printers were connected to the networked Macs. This allows expensive printers to be share by several machines or a portable-Mac user to connect wirelessly to a printer via AirPort.

- **Firewall.** Your Mac includes a built-in basic firewall, intended to keep hackers from accessing your computer. If you are using a static IP address (provided by your ISP) and your Mac is directly visible on the Internet, this is probably not enough protection. Consider buying a copy of Symantec's Norton Personal Firewall for your Mac.

   If your Mac is directly connected to your ISP over a cable or DSL modem that's directly attached to the machine, you would probably be safer with this firewall turned on—although the Norton software does a better job.

   If you're connected to the Internet via a home gateway or router of some sort, which itself is connected to a cable or DSL modem, you're probably already protected by a firewall inside that device.

   If your Mac is always connected to the Internet, some sort of firewall protection is necessary. If you always turn off your Mac when you are not using it and stay on the Internet only a few hours each day, your chances of being victimized are much lower. If you're only on AOL or some other dial-up connection just long enough to send and receive email, don't worry about being hacked.

   Tip: If you have just added or changed a firewall setting and some communications, mail, conferencing, chat, file-transfer, browser, or other application stops talking to the Internet, try changing back to the previous firewall setting and see if the problem isn't solved.

   Warning: A firewall is in no way a replacement for effective antivirus software and doesn't provide the same kind of protection. If I could have only one or the other—firewall or antivirus—I'd choose antivirus protection every time.

- **Internet.** If your computer is connected to the Internet, you can use this tab to share its connection with other computers on your local network. Let's say your Mac is connected to the Internet using a DSL or cable modem, but you also have an AirPort card. With Internet sharing turned on, all the other computers on your network would be able to connect to the Internet via AirPort to your machine and then your DSL or cable modem to the Internet.

But here's a warning, straight from the Apple help files:

"If your Internet connection and your local network use the same port (built-in Ethernet, for example), investigate possible side effects before you turn on Internet sharing. In some cases (if you use a cable modem, for example), you might unintentionally affect the network settings of other ISP customers, and your ISP might terminate your service to prevent you from disrupting their network."

In other words, this is serious power-user stuff—proceed with caution.

System preferences

These settings affect all users of a given Mac, and they govern general system settings (**Figure 6.21**).

Figure 6.21 The System preferences panels include Accounts, Classic, Date & Time, Software Update, Speech, Startup Disk, and Universal Access.

Accounts. In Mac OS X you can create different user accounts, each password-protected (or not) and each having a home folder of its own. Information in the home folder is protected from viewing by other users if you have password-protected the account—except the Public folder, which is called that for a reason.

The Accounts preferences panel is where you create and manage these user accounts, both for people who will actually touch the machine and for Windows users who will log in over the network to share files with you (**Figure 6.22**).

If you wish to see another user's folder on your machine, look in the Users folder (at the root level of the hard drive) and select the folder named after the user whose files you want to access. There will be small "do not enter" symbols on the folders you don't have permission to access (**Figure 6.23**).

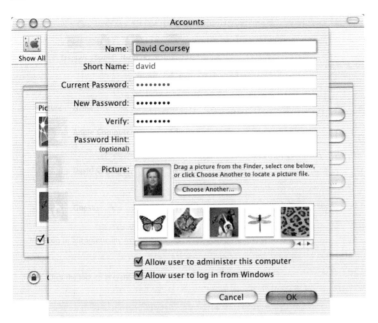

Figure 6.22 The Accounts preferences panel gives you control over the various user accounts on your Mac. Each user on a Mac has his or her own personal (and secure) file-storage area.

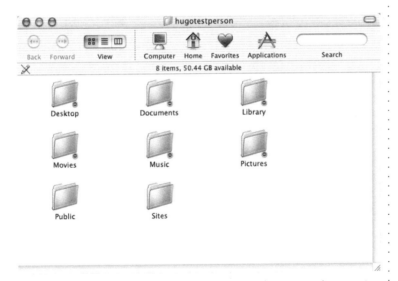

Figure 6.23 This is what you see if you go exploring another user's home folder and don't have access to some of the folders stored inside.

If you want to access your home folder from a Windows machine, be sure to select the box next to "Allow user to log in from Windows" in your Accounts preferences panel. And make yourself an administrator so you can install programs and make other changes to the system. This is done by selecting "Allow user to administrate this computer."

Tip: *You may not be able to select either of those boxes until after you have entered your password in the Current Password field and clicked OK. It took me about half a hour to figure this out one day. Sure, you are already logged in and can make changes, but before you make those changes, Mac OS X wants to be sure it's really you making them.*

Classic. This preferences panel controls how Mac OS X runs Mac OS 9 applications. (It some day may not be on your Mac once Apple stops shipping Mac OS 9 with every copy of Mac OS X, but for now it's here.) I have never needed to open this panel, so I won't explain it. Classic works just fine without tweaking any of these settings, but if you need to do some troubleshooting or tweaking of the Classic environment, this is the place to do it.

Date & Time. This is a fun panel to play with, if you're into such things, although you may never open it if you're not. From here you set the clock and calendar inside your Mac and select your time zone on a cool graphical map of the world. Be sure to also pick the closest city to you from the list provided. This panel controls the setting for daylight saving time and is occasionally used by other Mac applications.

The Network Time tab allows you to use a network time server and select which server to use. Turning this on causes your Mac to periodically set its clock based on information from the server, which is connected to some sort of atomic time source calibrated to the National Institute of Standards and Technology. That's about as accurate as time can be.

You can force your clock to set itself immediately by clicking the Set Time Now button.

When the "Use a network time server" box is selected, you can't manually set the time using the clock and settings on the Date & Time tab. Also, it isn't clear how often the computer will automatically check the time when you've turned the feature on. I am betting there's a setting down in the Unix guts of Mac OS X that controls this, but I have yet to find it.

The final tab contains settings for the Menu Bar Clock, the useful little timepiece located in the top right-hand corner of your screen.

Software Update. This is one of the more important System Preferences panels, as it controls how often your Mac checks back with the Mother Ship at Apple to see what new system software is available. I don't even know why it's possible to unselect this feature, though I suppose if you're traveling and using a portable it might be useful.

I have my Macs set to check for new software daily. Most of the updates are worth accepting, but occasionally you may want to skip one (for example, I refused some new Italian-language software) by choosing Make Inactive from the Update menu when an update arrives (**Figure 6.24**). If you later decide to install the updates you have taken a pass on, you can find them by choosing Show Inactive Updates from the Update menu. Apple also keeps a list of available updates on its Web site.

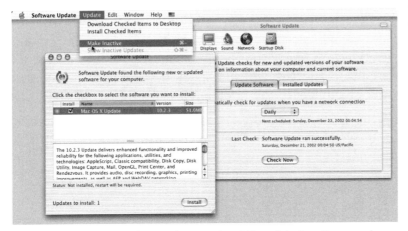

Figure 6.24 If I wanted to make a major OS update inactive—and never load it to my Mac—this is what it would look like when I made the update inactive. Not to worry—once I did this, I would be able to display the inactive updates, activate this one, and download the update without a problem.

The Installed Updates tab shows you what updates you have installed on your machine. And yes, I felt really stupid writing that sentence. But I warned you that most of these preferences panels were pretty easy to figure out.

Note: *Although Software Update will download new versions of system software and even some iApps, as well as the occasional (much more occasional than Windows users are used to) security patch, this is not how antivirus updates will appear on your machine. Software Update should be the all-purpose software updater for applications—security and everything—but it isn't.*

Tip: *If you're looking for a way of updating all the software on your Mac, you might consider VersionTracker Pro ($49.95/year; www.versiontracker.com), which is a Web-page/software combination that checks the software on your Mac and finds updates for it. VersionTracker is also an excellent source of freeware and shareware applications for your Mac. Highly recommended.*

Speech. Another fun panel that controls your Mac's voice-recognition and screen-reading functions. Very few people use the voice-recognition features, which allow you to control certain aspects of the Finder and some applications with spoken commands. I have not tried this but have seen it done.

Your Mac will also speak to you, reading alerts, prompts, and even the word under your pointer. You also get to choose from more than 20 voices, which range from fairly normal-sounding (for a computer) to the intentionally bizarre or hilarious.

Startup Disk. Selects the system you wish to use when starting up your computer. The name Startup Disk is a bit of a misnomer; you can start up from Mac OS 9 or Mac OS X on the same disk.

Universal Access. This section contains special settings that make Mac OS X easier to use for people who have difficulty seeing, hearing, using the keyboard, or using the mouse. You don't have to think of yourself as being disabled to benefit from these features. I encourage everyone to spend a few minutes looking at these settings so that you will be able to recommend them to people who might benefit.

The Other Category

If you've installed third-party software, the preferences panels for those programs may show up in a new category at the bottom of the main window called Other. Likewise, some preferences panels, such as Ink and Bluetooth, only appear when you have the appropriate hardware, in my case a tablet and a Bluetooth adapter, installed.

Switcher Diary: PATRICK GANT

Patrick Gant is a public relations professional who decided he didn't want to base the communications business he was starting up in his home on Windows. He had used PCs for more than a decade and tried all the versions, but when it came to his own business, he realized he would need a computer more reliable than a Windows machine.

Patrick: I used Windows- and MS-DOS–based machines for over a decade. Started with MS-DOS 4, then 5.0, then Win 3.1, Win 3.11, Win 95, Win 98, Win Me—and that last edition was the proverbial straw that broke the camel's back for me. Heck, I even gave Linux Mandrake a whirl, just to see what all the fuss was about.

David: What do you like most about Windows?

Patrick: In general, Windows loaded quickly, it permitted considerable customization, and compatible software was always easy to find. Prior to the release of Windows XP, I would have also said that the product was priced fairly and was fairly nonintrusive about registration.

David: What do you like least about Windows?

Patrick: Stability was an ongoing concern for me. I had reformatted and reinstalled Windows at least three times in as many years. This was not as a result of any careless tampering on my part: It was as if the OS simply degraded over time. I later found out that this was a "known issue" for people who are daily users.

Another issue for me was value for price. Every time I would buy an upgrade, Microsoft would sell the new OS as if its main function was to fix the bugs that were in the previous release. I got tired of feeling that my consumer dollar was being taken for granted. Worse still, there was an implicit expectation by Microsoft that if I wanted my computer to always run properly, I would need to remain part of an endless cycle of updates, service releases, and patches.

Value was also a growing concern. When XP was released, I was annoyed to discover that MS crippled some key features in the Home Edition, nudging users to buy the Professional Edition, adding another $100 to the price tag!

One more thing … aesthetically, I always thought that the Windows interface was ugly—plenty of drab, gray square boxes. The design always made me think that they put the needs of Microsoft ahead of their users. Related to this was the annoying habit of Windows apps to clutter up the desktop upon installation. That always drove me nuts.

David: How did you become a Mac user?

Patrick: My switch was borne out of frustration. Two years ago, I was in the process of setting up my business and everything was going according to plan, except for one thing. My three-year-old PC had a disturbing habit of crashing—in some cases requiring a reboot in safe mode. I even had occasion to reformat my hard drive once and reinstall everything. Fun. An astute friend pointed out to me that when you're self-employed, you have to fix these things on your own (there is no IT department to call). Worse still, a broken PC would essentially cripple my ability to make money.

Another friend of mine (of the self-employed variety) mentioned to me that he had been using Macs for years and swore by them. He convinced me that a Mac would be a reliable machine, but I was still unconvinced that I could get used to all the changes (or at least that's what I thought at the time). To be frank, I was never a fan of Mac OS 9, and it sure wasn't the factor that tipped the scale for me. The OS did have merit but also an annoying habit of seizing up at times. It was my trip to the Apple Store where I had my epiphany of sorts. There, I saw Mac OS X for the first time. I was hooked right away. I liked how it borrowed some ideas from Unix and Linux and then added some of Apple's remarkable common sense to the interface.

It wasn't until I bought my Mac that I began to appreciate the finer points of its design. The cleverly organized keyboard. The headphone jacks, located in the front of the machine, right where I needed them. The ability to put the machine to sleep reliably and repeatedly. The location of USB ports on the keyboard and at the side of the machine.

So the OS was the thing that sold me on my first iMac, yet it was hardware and design that convinced me to buy my second Mac, an iBook 600. To be fair, I did give PCs the benefit of the doubt. I went to my local big-box retailer and lined up the iBook side by side with a host of PC laptops. Sure, some PC models were faster, but none were as compact, light, and simple to use as the iBook. And all the PCs had this cheapness to them, as if a $2,000 machine had been slapped together by the manufacturer in haste. Another selling factor for me was the simplicity of AirPort (and later on, the equal ease with which Rendezvous helped me customize my office network).

David: Is your Mac a good value? How do you feel about Mac pricing?

Patrick: Just having a reliable computer has made my purchase worth the money I spent. Growing up, my dad often reminded me that when it comes to tools, always buy the best you can afford. In my work as a PR consultant and writer, my computer is my main tool and my lifeblood, so buying the best just made sense. No point in saving a few bucks on a cheap PC if the thing breaks down regularly.

David: What do you consider to be the most important differences between using a Mac and using a PC?

Patrick: In a nutshell, I think the biggest difference is that the folks at Apple go out of their way to let you know they appreciate your business. Much of my company's success is tied to service excellence, so I really appreciate it when I work with a company that puts users' needs first, ahead of all other things.

David: What do you wish you had known before switching? And what were your biggest concerns?

Patrick: In order of concern (ranked from highest): reliability, compatibility, versatility, and value.

Switcher Diary: PATRICK GANT

David: Is there something someone could have told you that would have made it easier for you to make the Switcher decision?

Patrick: The assurance I received from a fellow writer made a big difference for me. It demonstrated that I could invest in my Mac with confidence, knowing that my stuff would be compatible and that my machine would be far less prone to crashes … and easier to recover data if that should ever come to pass.

David: What do you do with your Mac and where do you do it?

Patrick: I run a small public relations/communication company from my home-based office. It's a business tool: I write everything on it, from speeches to press releases, from fact sheets to articles. I also keep track of expenses on it as well as invoicing. And I do all of this with the software that come with the machine. It's also a creative tool. My daughter uses it to draw pictures for her dad. I also use it heavily to edit family movies and to manage, fix, and print family photos. It's also a great jukebox. I like to have music playing when I'm hammering out a speech, and I think that iTunes and iPod are just about the finest music players ever built.

David: What Mac applications do you use?

Patrick: iMovie, iPhoto, NetNewsWire Lite, Mail, AppleWorks, Address Book, iSync, iTunes, Chimera, ViaVoice, iCal, Sherlock, WeatherPop, Guitar Tuner, Halime, LimeWire, PodWorks, Palm Desktop.

David: Is there anything you want to do on your Mac that you cannot do because the software is Windows-only?

Patrick: Just one. I use a cheap MP3 recorder to record interviews for stories (I write a lot of features and annual reports). I have to depend on my PC to upload it (via serial cable), and convert the voice files from the player's proprietary format to MP3. Then I fire it over the network to the Mac. Of course, if Apple should ever release an iPod with a built-in mike, I would be on it like a hungry dog on a bone!

Software Questions

The big question everyone asks when they consider switching from Windows to the Mac is, "Are the applications I need available?"

We're too good of friends for me to lie to you—or merely shade the truth—by telling you this isn't a legitimate concern. So let's have a talk about that and some other software-related issues.

Should I be concerned because there aren't as many applications for Mac OS as there are for Windows?

I think most people will do fine with the number and variety of applications they will find for the Macintosh. That's as long as you don't need highly specialized business or leisure software.

Most Macs come with free software (including the widely lauded iApps such as iTunes and iPhoto) that may turn out to be all the software you need. There is also a version of Microsoft Office for the Mac. For those not wanting to spend the money on Office, AppleWorks (an Office-like application suite built by Apple) is also able to read and write Office documents through MacLinkPlus (a file translator from DataViz included with AppleWorks). This gives your Mac all the basic functionality most people will ever need—and the freely available iApps are, as a group, better programs than what you'd be likely to buy for your Windows machine.

Having said that, Windows is the default platform for software developers, and many applications will never be developed for Macintosh. I am thinking particularly of games, a category where Apple lags way behind Microsoft. Of course, if you want games, I recommend a game console over a PC, anyway.

When new devices are released, such as the Sprint PCS Vision wireless data modem card I'm using in my Windows XP laptop, they rarely include Mac drivers. The same goes for my ham radio and search-and-rescue software.

There also isn't a really great low-end Web-page–building package for Mac OS X, nor is there any really good mapping software.

My solution to this dilemma is to use a copy of Connectix's Virtual PC ($219 to $249; www.connectix.com) to run Microsoft Windows 2000 and Windows applications right on my Mac. You might also use your old Windows machine or perhaps one at a friend's home or the office when you absolutely, positively have to use a Windows app and Virtual PC won't do.

In my discussions with Switchers, this issue rarely comes up.

How does the Mac version of Microsoft Office compare with the Windows version?

Quite favorably. Some Windows users actually believe that Office v. X for Mac is a better product (**Figure 7.1**). The important thing to know is that Microsoft claims 100 percent file compatibility, and so far I haven't been able to prove it wrong. That means you can start a document on one platform, move it to the other for editing, and send it back without breaking anything.

You should not confuse file compatibility with feature-set compatibility. There are many features in Windows Office that are not in Mac Office, and a few in Mac Office that aren't in the Windows version (**Figure 7.2**). I have been trying to assemble a list of these things, but Microsoft says it doesn't have one. That sounds odd to me, but considering that the programs are built in different states (Washington for Windows and California for Mac) by different groups of developers who only sorta seem to talk to one another, perhaps it isn't surprising.

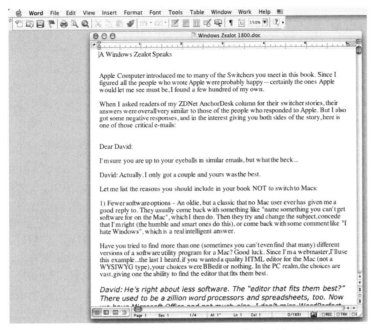

Figure 7.1 This is what Word v. X for Mac looks like. It should seem pretty familiar to most Windows users. The only exception is the Formatting Palette, which can be used with or instead of the Formatting Toolbar.

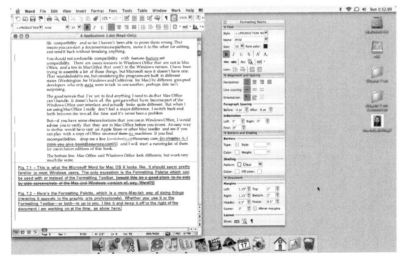

Figure 7.2 Here's the Formatting Palette, which is a more Mac-ish way of doing things (meaning it appeals to graphic arts professionals). Whether you use it or the Formatting Toolbar—or both—is up to you. I like it, and I keep it off to the right of the document I'm working on, as shown here.

The good news is that I've yet to find anything I need to do that Mac Office can't handle. It doesn't have all the gewgaws that have become part of the Windows Office user interface and it looks quite different. But when I am using Mac Office I really don't feel a major difference. I switch back and forth between the two all the time, and it's never been a problem (**Figure 7.3**).

But there are some obscure features that you use in Windows Office, I would advise you to verify that they are in Mac Office before you invest. An easy way to do this would be to visit an Apple Store or other Mac reseller and see if you can play with a copy of Office on one of its machines. You can also download a "test drive" of Mac Office from Microsoft's Mactopia site (www.microsoft.com/mac), but be aware that Microsoft has hobbled the text drive by stripped out some of the features. If you find incompatibilities, drop me a line (book@coursey.com), and I will start a running list of them for use in future editions of this book.

The bottom line: Mac Office and Windows Office look different but work very much the same.

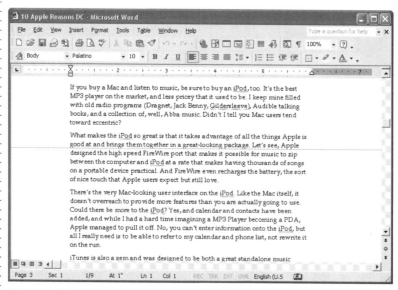

Figure 7.3 For comparison, this is what Word XP looks like on my Windows machine. I don't think moving from this to the Mac version will be a problem for you.

There is something only in Windows Office that I must use. What do I do?

In my case, it isn't a missing feature that I need but a whole missing application. My personal Web site uses FrontPage extensions, and there appears to be no Mac Web building application that supports these. (The extensions give me access to some cool features and allow the site to build its own navigational buttons).

My solution has been to run Windows Office in Virtual PC, a program that makes it possible for me to run Windows 2000 on my Mac (**Figure 7.4**). The effect is that of turning a window on my Mac's screen into a slow but serviceable Windows desktop. And that is where I run FrontPage, as well as some other Windows programs I need. I describe Virtual PC in greater detail elsewhere in this chapter.

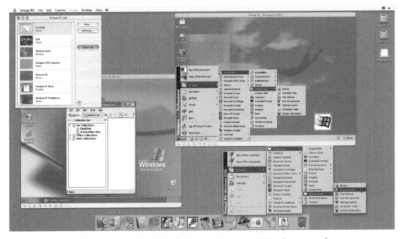

Figure 7.4 When you absolutely have to run Windows software, turn to Virtual PC from Connectix. This software turns your Mac into, well, a virtual PC capable of running several versions of Windows, as shown here. The 6.0 version, new as this book goes to press, offers performance enhancements and the ability to place Windows applications and a new Windows Start menu right in the Dock!

So there are Office programs that aren't available for the Mac?

Yes. Mac Office includes Word, Excel, PowerPoint, and a program you've never heard of called Entourage (it handles email, calendaring, and task management, and it synchronizes with Palm PDAs;

Figures 7.5 to **7.7**). It does not include FrontPage or Access. There is no Outlook for Mac OS X, nor are there programs such as Visio, which I have often heard requested by Mac users.

Figure 7.5 The biggest difference between Windows Office and Mac Office is that there is no Outlook (or Outlook Express) for Mac OS X. Instead, Microsoft ships a close-but-no-cigar application called Entourage. It works pretty well but won't connect to a Microsoft Exchange server. Here's a look at the Entourage Address Book.

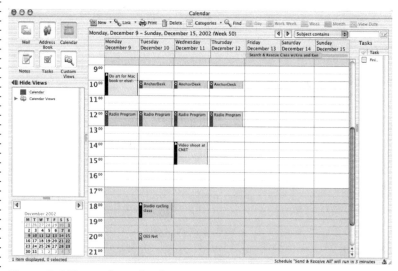

Figure 7.6 This is the Calendar view in Entourage.

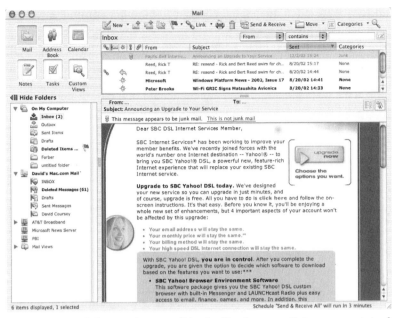

Figure 7.7 And this is what email looks like from an Entourage point of view. Over all, this is a nice application, but because it won't connect to the Exchange server at the office and the Apple applications work as well or better, I use them instead. (I introduce you to iCal, iSync, the Mac OS X Mail client, and the Mac OS X Address Book later in this chapter.)

There are charting programs for Mac OS X that the Visio user can adapt to, such as Chartsmith and ConceptDraw. Office v. X includes Microsoft Graph and Organization Chart X, which allow users to create basic charts and graphs. Or Visio can be run in Virtual PC. I haven't tried this myself, but I hear it's fairly slow because Visio is so graphics-intensive.

What do I use to replace Access?

If you are already a big Access user, I am not sure anything can replace it. But if you're asking what databases are available for the Mac, there are a couple—but everyone I know uses FileMaker Pro.

FileMaker Pro is an excellent product, and as it's grown and changed, it hasn't disappointed me. There are currently five products in the FileMaker line, including desktop, server, developer, and mobile versions.

Rather than do a not-very-good job of explaining FileMaker here, I'd rather you visit its Web site (www.filemaker.com), take a look around, and download the trial software. This will give you a great deal of insight into a very useful and usable database.

So I will leave it at this: FileMaker has my highest recommendation (**Figure 7.8**). Access never will.

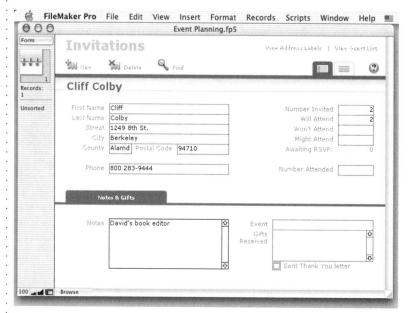

Figure 7.8 FileMaker Pro, sold by an Apple subsidiary, is my favorite database on both the Mac and Windows. FileMaker has relational capabilities and is a very handy development and publishing tool (though this figure just shows that you can make a nice-looking data-entry screen). If you hate Access (or were never willing to try), you will find FileMaker much simpler to learn and use.

Why no Outlook for Mac?

Actually, there used to be one, just as there was—a long time ago—a FrontPage for Mac. My belief is that Microsoft is doing this in an attempt to keep Macintosh out of corporate accounts. Microsoft currently provides no method for accessing the full features of an Exchange server from a piece of Mac OS X client software.

How do I access my company's Exchange server from my Mac?

There are several options, most of which require a little cooperation from your company's mail administrator.

Ask your Exchange server admin if Outlook Web Access is available. This is the best option and allows access to your email, contacts, and calendar from any Web browser. The caveat is that you have to be able to get to your server in the first place, and that may require a VPN (virtual private network) connection between your Mac and your company's firewall. Mac OS X 10.2 added a VPN client as a standard feature, but it doesn't work with all firewalls. Some firewall companies, however, have built their own Mac OS X clients, and Apple is working on fixes to its own client to make it more compatible and robust.

You can also ask your administrator to allow POP3 or IMAP access to your mail. This won't help with your Exchange calendar or contacts, but you will be able to download your messages. Technically, IMAP is the better choice, since it allows you to see messages without actually downloading them, but I have found it troublesome in practice. POP3 email is more commonly used and works better.

Or you can ask your admin to divorce you from the Exchange server—useful if you are not using the calendar or contact manager—by having the server automatically redirect (not forward) your email to another email address. Redirecting has the benefit of keeping the original sender in the "from:" address. Forwarding replaces the original sender with the email address the message is being forwarded from. This is what I do with my CNET email.

You can use a Palm OS personal digital assistant as a bridge between your Mac and a Windows machine. The only concern here is the possibility of accidentally creating duplicate contacts and calendar entries.

Virtual PC can also come to the rescue here, allowing you to run Outlook on your Mac and connect to your company's Exchange server using a Windows VPN client. This isn't a preferred solution, but I have seen it work. Alternatively, you can keep a Windows machine around for when you need Outlook and nothing else will do.

Finally, Microsoft still sells the older Mac OS 9 version of Outlook, and you can run the application in Mac OS X's Classic environment.

Microsoft estimates that a large majority of its Mac Office customers still have a PC they also use.

Windows on Your Mac

I am writing this column while running Windows 2000 Professional—but I am doing it on my iMac. How is this possible? My iMac is running Virtual PC 6.0, a program that allows Windows to run in a virtual Intel-based computer that is itself running as a Mac OS X application on the Mac.

Virtual PC is the application for people who absolutely, positively must run a Windows application and want to do it on their Macs. It is especially useful on a portable Mac, since carrying two notebook machines on a trip doesn't make very much sense (although I've done it for reasons I have thankfully forgotten and that never seem to have presented themselves again).

I grabbed a screen shot of my Mac while writing this (**Figure 7.9**). Connectix just released the new 6.0 version of Virtual PC, and only moments ago I installed it on this machine. If you look at the top-left side of the screen, you will see the Windows 2000 "machine" in its own window, with this sidebar, which I'm writing in WordPad. Now, look at the Dock where a Start menu icon has been added—a Windows Start menu. Here, I'll open the Start menu so you can see it, and then I'll grab the screen shot. Hold on a sec …

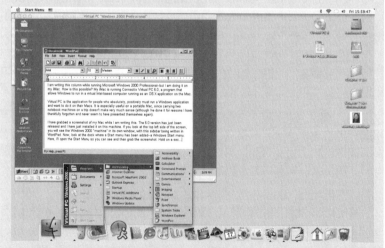

Figure 7.9 Here I am writing this sidebar in Windows 2000, which is running in Virtual PC running on my iMac.

When I did that, I realized it pretty much covered the Start menu, but it's there. Also, look over at the right end of the Dock, right next to my home folder. See the pen-and-notebook icon? That shows that WordPad is running on my Virtual PC. This is about as tight as Mac/Windows integration can get.

But since behind every silver lining lies a big dark cloud, what's the downside of Virtual PC? Well, it's slow. This new version is a good bit faster than the 5.0 release I was using previously, but it's still slow. For this word-processing application it works just fine, and the slowness isn't noticeable after the application starts. But the more graphics the application requires, the slower it becomes. Many games you simply cannot play on Virtual PC.

Virtual PC comes in several versions; each includes a fully licensed version of a Microsoft operating system. I am running Virtual PC with Windows 2000 Professional ($249 list) for a reason: It works really well on my iMac. I have not been able to get Windows XP to run with decent performance on my Mac, so I am most hesitant to recommend it to you. And Windows 98 isn't more stable on Virtual PC than on a regular PC, so I am not using it, since the more stable Windows 2000 is available.

I would not recommend Virtual PC for hours-a-day use. And since you can buy a PC that will perform at least as well for $600 or less, that would be a better option for some. Or just hold on to an old PC for those occasions when you need one.

But I must admit that I like having Virtual PC around, especially on my portable Mac where I've installed most of the Windows applications I use frequently. I have a copy of Windows Office, Streets & Trips, and some ham radio software I use occasionally. They all run fine, albeit more slowly than I am used to on a PC.

So I recommend Virtual PC to you with reservations. It works just fine and does what it promises, although the Windows XP edition seems to take more horsepower than my iMac has (I hear the dual-processor Power Macs run Windows XP pretty well). I would not want to run an application I had to use all day on Virtual PC, but for the occasional app you just can't live without, it's fine. If do you know, however, that you want to run Virtual PC all the time, I'd recommend buying the most powerful Mac you can afford.

Suppose I don't want to use Microsoft Office?

Most Macs come with AppleWorks already installed (**Figure 7.10**). This is a simple but quite good suite of applications that have the ability to read and write Office documents. They include most of the functionality most users need most of the time (**Figures 7.11** and **7.12**).

Figure 7.10 Before you automatically drop $$$ for Microsoft Office, consider AppleWorks, which probably comes free with your Mac ($79 if purchased separately). However, do this in the store so that if you decide you want Office after all, you don't miss out on promotional pricing that often gets you a copy of Office for less than half price when purchased with a new Mac. Here are what AppleWorks calls it's "Starting Points" for projects.

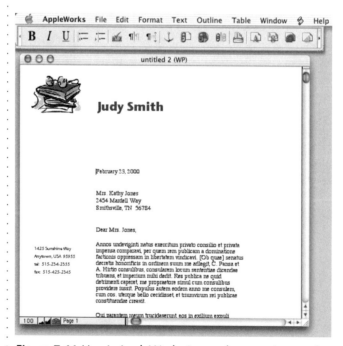

Figure 7.11 Here's AppleWorks in word-processing mode.

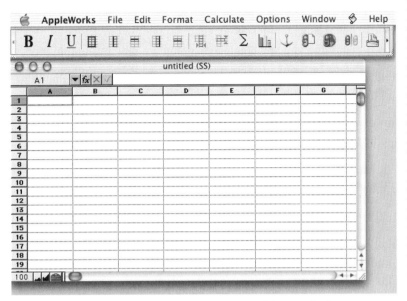

Figure 7.12 And this is the AppleWorks spreadsheet, which you aren't likely to confuse with Excel.

I won't lie to you: AppleWorks isn't Office, but it's very useful on its own terms and may be all you need. Read about it later in this chapter in the iApps section—which also talks about the other software that comes bundled with your Mac.

Another Alternative

As I write this, OpenOffice.org has begun the beta test of a version of its Office-compatible suite running on Mac OS X. The problem is that the program still needs to be turned into a Mac OS X–native application using the standard user interface. When this is completed, OpenOffice for Mac OS X could be very interesting.

If you are not familiar with OpenOffice, this is the open-source version of a program called StarOffice, which Sun Microsystems purchased in 1998 from the German company Star Division. StarOffice is intended to be fully compatible with Microsoft Office and able to run on a variety of operating systems, including Windows and various Unix variants.

Sun gave StarOffice away until Mac OS X was released, when it began charging $79.95 for a single copy. At the same time, Sun gave the StarOffice source code to OpenOffice, which was created to promote a version of the program that would be developed by volunteers and continue to be given away for free.

continues on next page

Another Alternative *continued*

The completion of a real Mac OS X version of OpenOffice, with the look and feel that Mac users expect, could be a major development in the future of Mac OS X and the Switcher movement. It may not be too long before a copy of OpenOffice ships with every Macintosh, giving all Mac users immediate and high-level compatibility with Microsoft Office.

Of course, no Office knock-off will ever really be Office, especially if Microsoft wants to do something that would damage file compatibility. But since such a move would be likely to do more damage to Microsoft than to Mac users, it doesn't seem likely. So, as the Microsoft/Apple relationship seems to sour, OpenOffice gives me hope that the potential loss of Microsoft Office as a Mac OS X application might not really matter after all.

Mac Office seems awfully expensive!

A new copy of Mac Office sells for $459, although there are occasional promotions that reduce the cost to $199 if the program is purchased with a new Mac. You'd think Microsoft would do something about this, rather than just whine that sales haven't been to its liking.

Office is priced for corporate buyers, most of whom don't pay nearly full price and are generally upgrading old copies. Most individuals have never purchased a copy of Office, but even if we had, there's no inexpensive way to upgrade from the Windows version to Mac Office.

Tell me about the software that comes free with my Mac.

Everyone knows that software sells hardware. The best way to kill an operating system or a hardware platform is to starve it to death. Cut off the flow of new software, and sooner or later the platform goes away.

But the software business has been pretty rough for the past decade or so as Microsoft has wiped out competitor after competitor. Many of these companies used to publish Mac applications, but the combination of Microsoft predation and Apple's declining market share led to a situation where Apple had to take matters into its own hands.

We should all face such misfortune, as Apple has countered this adversity with a bravura set of applications of its own creation. This is software that literally sells hardware—stand around an Apple Store for an hour or two and you'll see it happen (if it hasn't already happened to you, that is).

Collectively dubbed the iApps (after the original iMac), these programs include iTunes, iPhoto, iDVD, iMovie, iChat, iCal, and iSync. These applications are good, simple, and approachable enough that people are willing to buy Mac hardware because it's the only place you can find them.

But not all of Apple's software is an iApp. Also worth talking about are Mail, Address Book, AppleWorks, Safari, and Sherlock (which are essentially iApps without the cute moniker).

The iApps are excellent applications, the sort of things Windows users pay money for but Mac users get for free. Whole books have been written about some of them, so I won't explain them in detail. But I do want to give you a taste of what each iApp looks like, what it does, and why they may—all by themselves—be a good enough reason to switch.

iApps for Creativity

The first set of iApps are designed to help you organize, edit, and distribute your digital photos and movies.

iPhoto

Here's a program that I think has been a tad overrated, mostly because of confusion over what it does.

If you always take perfect digital photographs—or are just too lazy to make them better—then iPhoto may be all the digital photography software you need. It will download photos from your camera to your Mac, do some repairs, help you print the images, and allow you to create Web pages and assemble your images into very cool books that Apple will have professionally printed for you.

None of those things are really what iPhoto is about, however; the heart and soul of iPhoto are its organizational capabilities (**Figure 7.13**). iPhoto is the only tool I know of that makes it easy to organize all those thousands—maybe tens of thousands—of images that quickly move from digital camera to hard drive (often never to be seen again).

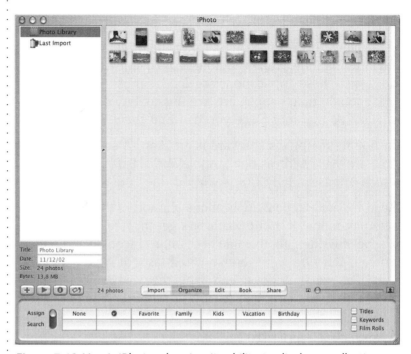

Figure 7.13 Here's iPhoto, showing its ability to display a collection (albeit a small one) of pictures as small thumbnails. In a larger photo library, this mode allows you to scroll through thousands of photos pretty quickly. The slider at the lower right controls the size of the thumbnails.

With iPhoto, your entire photo collection, or whatever portion of it you want to see, is immediately available for viewing, using one of the sharpest visual interfaces I've ever seen.

Most digital photography programs make use of scaled-down *thumbnail* images so you can see a number of pictures on the screen at once. iPhoto, however, is the only program I've seen that makes it easy to zoom in and out, so you can quickly go from many images on your screen to just one, if that's all you want.

You use a slider to easily control the zooming and scroll bars to control your movement through your photo collection

(**Figures 7.14** and **7.15**). This is about as easy as wading through a zillion digital images can be.

Figure 7.14 Moving the slider makes the photos larger (and makes it easier to find the one you're looking for).

Figure 7.15 With the slider at the far right you are now focused on a single image and can use iPhoto's editing capabilities which include enhance and retouch tools.

Where iPhoto falls short is in assigning keywords and managing the collections of photos, called Albums, that you can create. For most people, what Apple provides is probably adequate, but when I look at the program I see this as an opportunity for improvement in a future upgrade.

As I said, iPhoto is not the best choice for fixing problem photographs, although many will be perfectly happy with what the program is able to do with retouching and enhancing photographs. This is especially the case when buying a better piece of software—I recommend Adobe Photoshop Elements—could set them back $89 (less if rebates are being offered).

Maybe I'm vain, but I'd never show anyone a digital photo that hadn't been through Photoshop, and Photoshop Elements makes a large part of this powerful (and otherwise expensive) program available at a very decent price.

iMovie and iDVD

Having neither children nor an exhibitionistic streak, I am not in the target audience for iMovie and iDVD. As you've guessed, one is for editing movies downloaded from your digital video camera and the other is for creating DVDs, complete with menus and graphics.

Both programs are entry-level versions of larger programs—Final Cut Pro and DVD Studio Pro—that Apple sells to people who earn their living doing this sort of thing. Both are excellent programs, and Mac users get them for free when they buy a Mac.

iMovie and iDVD also make up half of iLife, a suite of applications that come bundled on all new Macs. The other members of the suite are iTunes and iPhoto. Except for iDVD, all are also available as a free download, and users can buy the group of four integrated applications for $49.

The first time I used iMovie, I shot some video at the going-away party for a coworker as a demonstration; it took me about 30 minutes to feel comfortable with the program (**Figure 7.16**). There is no big manual for iMovie—just help files—because the program doesn't need one. It was only later that I discovered the tutorials on the iMovie Web site.

You may at some point want to invest in a book about iMovie, when you want to improve your skills—not when you are just getting started.

Figure 7.16 iMovie has a simple interface yet provides the novice videographer with much of the functionality of a professional software package. iMovie 3 comes with a handful of new effects, including the Ken Burns Effect (up there in the top-right corner), which lets you add a sense of motion to still images. (Courtesy of Apple)

With a compatible FireWire digital video camera (there is a list on Apple's Web site at http://guide.apple.com/), getting video off the camera is plug-and-play simple—with iMovie able to fully control the camera. Editing is easy to learn, but making the proper artistic edits takes some skill and learning. Fortunately, television has made most of us fairly video-literate, so it's easy to imitate something we've seen before. And iMovie 3 includes a basket full of new special effects, including the "Ken Burns" effect, which lets you zoom into and out of as well as pan across still photographs.

iDVD, included with Macs that have a built-in DVD recorder (which Apple calls a SuperDrive), makes it pretty simple to put one or more movies, as well as slide shows, on a single DVD. iDVD creates the menu structure that's necessary for using the disc with a consumer DVD player. It's lots of fun to use (**Figure 7.17**).

Figure 7.17 iDVD allows you to easily create a disc that can play in almost all consumer DVD players and provides a set of templates to help you build professional-looking user interfaces like this one. (Courtesy of Apple)

In Appendix D is a column I wrote singing the praises of these two products as well as explaining my plans for a new career if this book fails to make the *New York Times* best-seller list.

iApp for Entertainment

Next are Apple's Mac music player, iTunes, and its iPod companion.

iTunes

When the first MP3 players came on the market, I sorta wondered what the fuss was about. Sure, you could carry music with you, if you call carrying an hour or two of tunes actually "carrying music." Hope that bike ride won't be a very long one, or else you'd better like those tunes a whole lot.

And yes, you could download the music you'd stolen over the Internet onto an MP3 player—in only slightly less time than it would take to play it. OK, I exaggerate, but moving music to an MP3 player via USB cable is pretty slow.

Then along came Apple's iPod. The iPod—basically a multi-gigabyte hard drive with an operating system, a little processor, a headphone jack, a cute little spinning dial for cursor control, and a FireWire port—is one of the coolest inventions I've seen.

Coupled with a Mac and iTunes, the iPod can—through the miracle of FireWire—download a CD from the Mac in about 10 seconds. With its large hard drive, you can literally carry a thousand songs in your pocket.

The first versions of iTunes left a lot to be desired in ease of managing those 1,000 songs. But now we have iTunes 3 (**Figure 7.18**), along with less expensive and higher capacity iPods that take advantage of features such as Smart Playlists.

Figure 7.18 This is what iTunes looks like. Decide for yourself whether this is really part of my personal music collection.

The new iTunes software lets you store more information about your music, including a personal rating and how often you play a particular song. Smart Playlists uses this information to create collections of, say, your 50 highest rated songs, or the tunes you listen to most often, or music by a specific composer or from a specific year.

Dragging and dropping songs is no longer the only way to create a playlist. Smart Playlists significantly automates the process, even down to noticing new music that's added or statistics that change after the playlist is created. And the new version is part of iLife and has hooks into the other members of the suite.

iTunes also has a feature that automatically adjusts the volume on your entire music collection, preventing one song from playing dramatically louder or softer than the others.

Audible.com's collection of downloadable books and other spoken content—such as public radio programs—is now supported by iTunes and iPod as well. I used to carry books around on my Pocket PC, but the iPod's much larger capacity means that I can both carry more books and download higher fidelity versions of the files.

The one thing I don't like about iTunes is that it's only an MP3 player. That means iTunes will only "tune in to" Internet radio stations that broadcast an MP3 stream. Although streaming MP3 tends to be very high quality (high bandwidth, too), very few stations broadcast in the format.

For that reason, I find the iTunes's Internet radio tuner to be essentially useless, although in the scheme of things it's not all that important. RealNetworks's RealOne media player will tune in to all the Internet radio I care to listen to.

If you buy a Mac, you should dig a little deeper and get an iPod. But until you do, there are many enjoyable hours to be had using iTunes alone to rip songs from your CD collection, manage them on your Mac, and then burn them onto CDs you can use in the car or on a portable player.

Windows users will point out that Windows Media Player, MusicMatch (which ships with the Windows iPod), and RealOne will all do these same things. If you like those applications, knock yourself out. But I hope you enjoy all the advertising and other attempts to separate you from your money that get built right into these applications and are completely absent from the Mac versions.

Remember: Apple is so happy you bought its hardware that it gives you really great applications for free and doesn't try to turn them into ongoing revenue streams, except by offering you things you might really need, such as Kodak prints of your digital photos or one of the cool iPhoto books.

Windows apps are, to my taste, way too far into "stoking the star-maker machinery behind the popular songs," as Joni Mitchell might say.

iApps for Organization

And then there are iApps for keeping your life and Mac in order.

iCal

iCal is a personal calendar application that does a very nice job of helping you manage your time. Apple's description of it as "elegant" is appropriate, and comparing iCal to Microsoft Outlook is an excellent example of the differences between Apple's way of thinking and Microsoft's.

iCal lets you create separate color-coded calendars for your work, home, school, or other activities (**Figure 7.19**). You can view all these calendars at once in a single day-at-a-glance, week-at-a-glance, or month-at-a-glance window.

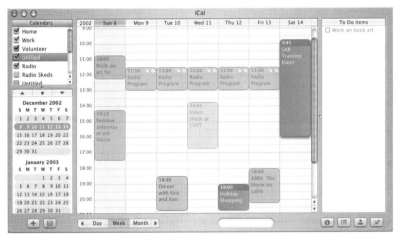

Figure 7.19 iCal, as I write this, is a first-generation product and shows some rough edges, but it's a nice, functional application that allows me to manage multiple calendars, share them (via .Mac) with other iCal users, and easily sync with the PDA and phone using iSync.

You can use iCal to remind you of appointments, watch approaching deadlines, send and receive email and text-based notifications, set alarms, and create and prioritize to-do lists associated with each calendar.

With iCal, you can easily view or hide your various calendars, making it easy to view and print calendars for specific parts of your life. By turning off home events while in the office, you can focus on just those events that matter at the time.

Turn on all the events, and you can easily spot conflicts and empty spaces in your schedule.

You can share iCal calendars online, using Publish from iCal's Calendar menu. You must be a .Mac member to do this unless you have a Web server configured to serve the calendar, which seems much more difficult than being a .Mac member.

Should You Buy .Mac?

One question you as a new Mac owner will doubtless be confronted with is whether to spend $100 a year for a .Mac subscription. Apple offers a 60-day trial membership in the hopes that you'll become a paying member when the free trial ends. The question? Is .Mac a good deal?

If you're only considering price, you can probably make better purchases than .Mac, as all the .Mac services are available from other vendors, who generally do a better job than Apple has in its first .Mac release.

But none of the services from these competitors are as tightly integrated into Mac OS X as .Mac is. And I feel confident in predicting Apple will keep it that way. So whatever you may save in dollars you may lose in convenience. And if you've already bought a Mac, you have accepted the idea that style and convenience can be worth some extra money, so .Mac is merely Apple's attempt to extend that value equation to online services while extracting another $100 from your wallet.

Here's what the subscription buys, in my perceived order of value.

iDisk

Your account includes 100 MB of space on Apple's servers—and you can purchase more. You can access files you store on your iDisk from almost any Windows or Mac machine with an Internet connection. And you can store on your iDisk your iCal calendar and contact information as well as backups of your most important files.

While writing this book, I always kept a copy of the book's files on my iDisk, just in case something bad happened to my computer or even to my whole house. I also occasionally use iDisk to send large files to friends, either because my ISP or theirs won't accept large multi-megabyte files. (.Mac has a 3 MB limit, for example.) With iDisk, I can set up a user account for my friend if I want to protect the files from unauthorized eyes or I can merely drop the file into my Public folder if I don't care who sees it. Either way, my friend uses a browser to download the files.

With iCal, I can store public copies of my calendar on iDisk, and iSync uses iDisk to maintain a backup of all my contact and calendar information, which it synchronizes with my PDA, iPod, and cellular phone.

Of course, iDisk is typically too slow to use as though it were a local hard disk. For example, I accidentally started saving my book document files directly to iDisk. It was so slow that I thought at first my computer had gotten sick before I realized my error. After that, I was careful to only save final copies or to drag and drop files over to my iDisk.

Backup

A .Mac membership gets you access to Backup, a program that allows you to automatically copy specific types of files over to your iDisk. I have mine set to run every day at 2 a.m.

Now it's my duty to inform you that you shouldn't rely solely on .Mac Backup to keep a full backup of your machine. I am also supposed to tell you that you should also use something else—such as a CMS Peripherals Automatic Backup System—and that you need multiple backups to be really safe.

Having informed you of this, I am also aware of the reality that most people *never* make a backup, so something that backs up your most important files every day puts you way ahead of the vast majority of computer users, Mac or PC.

Still, Backup isn't a highly capable application. For example, you cannot back up more than one Mac to your .Mac account, as someone with a desktop and a portable might want to do. You also can't back up to a hard disk or a tape drive, although you can make CDs and DVDs to your heart's content.

Overall, Backup, in its current (albeit first) incarnation, is worth having only because it's better than nothing. Why do I use it? Should my other backups fail or my house burn down, I'll still have something stored on my iDisk.

Virex

This antivirus program is well respected as a standalone product but needs some serious help as part of .Mac. The big complaint is that .Mac makes it pretty hard to download virus updates, something you end up doing yourself by going to either the .Mac or the McAfee Web site and downloading the latest virus update, which you then install on your Mac.

Although virus protection is much less critical on a Mac than on Windows—as there are many fewer threats to a Mac—Apple has let us down with this one. I suspect that Apple will fix this and offer automatic updates some time in the future.

My recommendation is to buy a copy of Symantec's Norton AntiVirus—or better, Norton SystemWorks, which has an automatic update feature. SystemWorks also includes other utilities to help keep your Mac working properly.

continues on next page

Should You Buy .Mac? *continued*

Mac.com Email

Yes, you probably already have an email account, but if you don't, .Mac offers a nice mail service, which gets you a mail address in the form of *username@mac.com*. Some people think that's pretty cool, and it is nice to have an email address you don't have to change if you move to a different job or school. You can also check your .Mac email through a Web browser, and for $10 more a year, you can purchase additional mailboxes for others in your family.

HomePage Web Publishing

If you would like to publish a simple Web site, perhaps to share photos and files, .Mac's HomePage makes this pretty easy. Because .Mac throttles heavy usage, this isn't a good place to keep all those music files your friends want to download by the zillions. But it integrates nicely with iPhoto for building pages from your photographs and is generally easy to use.

What's the Answer?

So what should you do? Having read what I've just written, I've painted a pretty sad picture of .Mac, which is odd because I actually like it and use it. (Of course, I get a free account from Apple, so I am doubtlessly biased.)

If you are pretty sure (perhaps from your PC experience) that you won't make regular backups or install antivirus software, then .Mac is easy insurance against some forms of catastrophe. If you don't have an email account and think having a .Mac address is cool, there's another reason. I am fond of having a copy of my Address Book saved to my iDisk every time I use iSync (having lost an address book some years ago). And HomePage and iPhoto do work nicely together.

Is .Mac a great online service? No. It may become one as Apple expands and updates it, but that's tomorrow, not today. Is it worth $100? I think for many people, yes, if only because it's integrated and convenient. If you find yourself giggling after reading this, then you're not a good candidate for .Mac. But you already knew that, right?

Publishing a calendar gives others access to your events or to public calendars (sporting events, club meetings, and so on) that you create. Mac users subscribe to published calendars via .Mac. Windows users can view (but not subscribe to) calendars by viewing a page on the creator's .Mac Web site. When you upload an iCal calendar to your .Mac account, you're provided a URL on your .Mac Web site where the calendar can been seen, and you can also create an email message so you can tell friends.

One warning: The calendars you publish to the Web can be seen by anyone who knows or can guess the name of the calendar itself. There are ways to password-protect your calendars, but not with the .Mac service. This is odd because you can password-protect your .Mac Public folder. This lack of security makes a valuable feature much less useful. Put another way: I'll publish my calendar when Steve Jobs publishes his. In the meantime, I expect Apple to address this obvious problem.

Apple offers several of its own iCal calendars that you can subscribe to. While exploring the Apple Web site, I subscribed to public calendars for U.S. holidays, Swedish holidays, and events at my local Apple Store.

iCal makes it easy to remind yourself of important events. Besides screen pop-ups and sounds, iCal can send an email message at a specified interval before the event. These can go to any device with an email address, such as a pager or cell phone.

Here are the major elements of the iCal user interface:

Calendars window. This is where you select a calendar to work with.

To Do lists. At the bottom-right corner of the iCal window is a pushpin icon. Clicking it opens the to-do window, where you can enter to-do items with due dates and priorities. These items won't generate the email reminders that calendar items do, but this element is still useful. To-do items are attached to a specific calendar, allowing you to categorize them.

Event Info window. This is where you enter specific information about an event on a calendar and set associated alarms. You can set how often the event repeats. You can also use the Address Book application (which we'll discuss later) to invite others to your event. To do this, click the People button and then drag people's names from your Mac OS X Address Book and drop them onto the event in the calendar. This gives a new meaning to having to drag in a crowd.

Minicalendars. Like every other calendar, iCal offers month-at-a-glance minicalendars. You can click a specific date in the calendar to go there. The up and down arrows in the bar above the minimonth calendar allow you to move forward and backward a month at a time.

Transparent layers. iCal uses transparent layers to let you see more than one calendar at a time. You can see all your calendars at once and choose the ones you want to see.

Day/Week/Month buttons. Sometimes it's boring writing about how Mac software works, because it usually works pretty much the way you'd imagine. Guess what these buttons do to the way calendars are displayed?

Searching. Type what you are looking for, and iCal will find it, quickly.

The best part about iCal is that it uses iSync to keep all my devices—Handspring PDA, iPod, my other Macs—synchronized with one another. Didn't know an iPod can store your calendar? Well, it can store your contacts, too.

Address Book

Here's something Microsoft has had years to get around to but never quite managed: a single address book that all the applications on a computer can share (**Figure 7.20**). You will find this systemwide address book in Mac OS X 10.2, and although many Mac applications don't yet use it—and some may never, considering that there are companies selling Mac contact-manager software, including guess who—Apple is committed to the concept. Already, it's starting to pay off.

I am not generally in favor of operating-system vendors telling application developers what they can't do, but I'd sure support Apple's turning the lights off on all the other Mac OS X address books out there. Although Apple's needs some additional fields and more user configurability, the world of one computer = one address book is a great place.

Address Book is another example of Mac OS X's doing the right thing. The Address Book itself is functional and not nearly as overwhelming as the contact manager in Outlook can be.

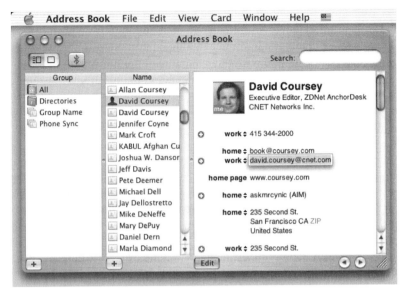

Figure 7.20 The Mac OS X Address Book does not include all the information you can save in Microsoft Office. But it does include all the information most people are likely to use, as well as some user-definable fields you can customize.

Clicking and holding an address will take you to a map showing its location, and clicking the phone number gives you the option of making it display very large across the middle of the screen—just the thing for when you have to walk over to the fax machine.

Address Book also works with iSync as well as Bluetooth-enabled (meaning expensive) cellular telephones.

Like Mail, Address Book searching is fast and full-text by default.

iSync

This is another of those things Apple is doing that Microsoft should have done first. iSync keeps your contact and calendar information synchronized across multiple devices, including Palm OS–based personal digital assistants (PDAs), the address book and calendar on the iPod, a handful of Bluetooth-enabled cell phones, and other Macs via your .Mac account (**Figure 7.21**).

Figure 7.21 This is what iSync looks like. Here you see my .Mac account, my PDA, and my cell phone, all of which can be synchronized by clicking the Sync Now button. The phone uses Bluetooth wireless to sync, and the PDA uses a copy of Palm's HotSync as a conduit between the Mac and the PDA. The Palm software comes preinstalled on the machine.

Synchronizing a PDA, iPod, and my .Mac account using iSync is a one-button process. Setup is straightforward, as iSync looks for devices connected to your system and helpfully offers to connect them as well as your .Mac account. This was accomplished in 15 minutes for .Mac, a PDA, and an iPod. I don't have a Bluetooth phone, but you aren't likely to, either— it's a brand-new technology. It appears, and I am told, the setup for the phone works the same way as for other devices. Remember that Macs prior to 2003 don't come with Bluetooth support built-in, so you have to buy one of those tiny D-Link USB adapters.

Since I'm using a Handspring PDA, I start the synchronization process by pressing the HotSync button on the PDA's charging stand. There is also a Sync Now button on the iSync panel I can use if I don't want to synchronize the PDA.

You might want to consider using your PDA to help move information from your Windows machine to your Mac and vice versa. The benefits and potential problems of this are discussed in Chapter 4.

One limitation is that iSync works only with the Mac OS X Address Book and iCal. It would be nice if other personal information managers (such as Entourage) were also supported, although there are Palm synchronization tools for them already.

Something I am not sure I like about iSync is how it handles synchronization conflicts caused by changes having been made on more than one device at a time. Although iSync appears to make intelligent choices when solving problems and presents the solutions to me for approval, I'm still not always absolutely certain that I'm picking the most current data. It's not a huge problem, but Apple could do more to help me make the right choice.

One more thing: How about Pocket PC support, please?

Sherlock 3

Here's an application that I'd like to get excited about but probably won't. Why? Because Sherlock has been a heartbreaker, and I am not putting myself through that again.

The pitch goes like this: "Sherlock 3 displays custom information in a context-specific window so you can grasp the information you want quickly." That's what Apple says about Sherlock, which you might also think of as a particularly nifty Web-search utility (**Figure 7.22**).

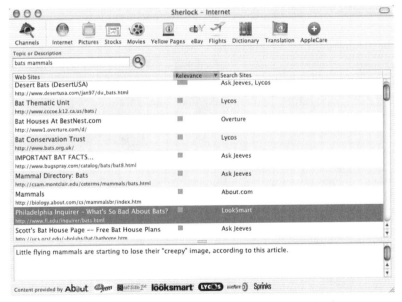

Figure 7.22 This is what a Sherlock Web search returned when I went out looking for bats (the warm-blooded kind).

Included with Sherlock are "channels" dedicated to finding pictures; tracking stocks; getting movie listings; tracking flights; looking up words in a dictionary; letting your fingers do the walking in an online Yellow Pages; translating text to and from a variety of languages; getting support from Apple; and buying trash, trinkets, and treasures on eBay.

Type the name of a person in the Pictures channel, and you'll get a bunch of thumbnails, hopefully of the person you are looking for. (Google works better, by the way.)

The movie finder is very cool, if you like sitting in dark rooms with a few hundred other folks. It lists movies: where they are playing and what's playing at which theater. And it also shows movie trailers, a chance for Apple to show off QuickTime (**Figure 7.23**).

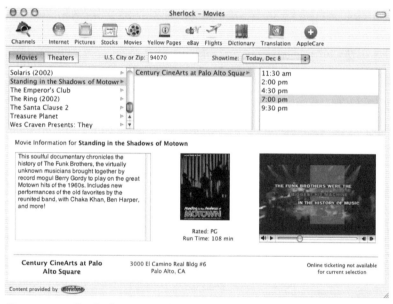

Figure 7.23 Sherlock goes to the movies! Movie buffs really like Sherlock's ability to find what's playing at the local cineplex. And here's a movie I actually want to see!

Yellow Pages finds businesses and offers helpful directions to their locations (**Figure 7.24**), and the stock tracker does a good job of watching your portfolio.

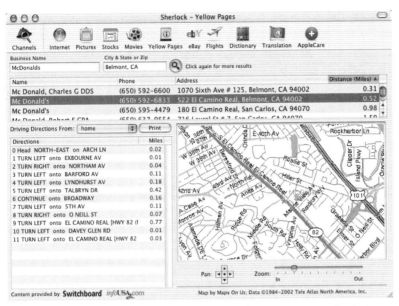

Figure 7.24 In Yellow Pages, tell Sherlock where you are and what you want to find, and it will even give you a map and directions, such as to a McDonald's in my old neighborhood.

Because Sherlock is just a nice front end to other people's information, you're stuck if you don't like the services Apple has partnered with. One useful setting will store addresses you can use with the Yellow Pages to tell it where you are so it will find nearby stores.

So why am I reserving a measure of affection? Well, there are the earlier versions, which never lived up to their promise. Here's another quote from Apple's description of Sherlock 3: "And you can look forward to asking Sherlock to perform more and more services for you as time goes by."

Did I hear someone say, "Play it again"? Apple has made that promise before—that Sherlock would gain support from other developers and offer new services. That never happened, although a guy did create a more useful Sherlock clone named Watson (www.karelia.com/watson/).

The problem with being Apple is the company has little ability to persuade other companies to create a bunch of Sherlock channels that you and I can use. The only good news is that Sherlock uses a technology called XML to get data from Web servers that it then displays. XML is likely to become more and more common, meaning that creating a Sherlock channel might not be as big a deal as it has been in the past, and we'll see more channels.

I have cried too many tears over Sherlock's failed promise. But this is the nicest and most useful version yet, and the XML stars may be lining up in Sherlock's favor.

iApps for Communication

Next are the applications that help you stay in touch with others.

iChat

Jaguar's built-in iChat instant-messaging (IM) program marks the beginning of what could become a close relationship between Apple and America Online. iChat is the first outside client software that AOL has licensed to use its instant-messaging network. That gives iChat users immediate access to 150 million AOL Instant Messaging users as well as .Mac users (**Figure 7.25**). You can also use iChat to join any AOL chat room just by entering its name, but since iChat can't give you a list of names, this feature looks better on paper than it works on your screen. My recommendation: Use real AOL software if you want AOL chat rooms.

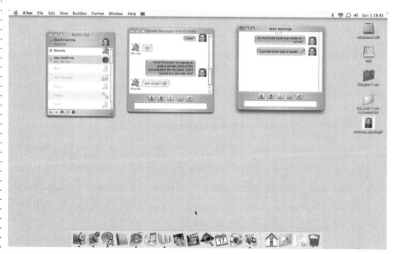

Figure 7.25 Here is iChat, where I am talking to two friends, both AOL members. And yes, the personalized icons are optional, as are the cartoon bubbles. I thought they were silly right up to the moment when I decided they were fun and turned them back on.

Using a new Mac OS X 10.2 technology called Rendezvous, you can see which people are available on your local network without even knowing their screen names. Although you may not want to type-talk to someone that close to you, it's an excellent drag-and-drop way to send or receive files.

The first thing most people notice about iChat is that the chats look different. First, it's easy to use a picture—yourself, perhaps—as an icon, and the dialog itself appears in "thought bubbles" that look like cartoons. If this bothers you, just turn the bubbles off by selecting View > Show As Text. You also get to select how people are identified; the best way is to display names and maybe pictures, if you like.

> *Tip: Don't use pictures alone, because people without pictures get generic icons, and you won't be able to tell who they are.*

The program provides the usual font, color, and smiley options that allow you to make your messages either more personal or merely annoying, depending on the mood of the recipient. And there is also a chat-log feature, which may prove useful or incriminating, depending on your online habits.

iChat is integrated with the Mac OS X Address Book and Mail applications, so you don't have to endlessly retype contact information. The .Mac and AOL Instant Messaging (AIM) account names for your contacts are stored along with their email addresses and other contact information. Adding someone to your Buddy List is as simple as dragging his or her Address Book entry to the Buddy List. Mac OS X Mail is also "buddy-aware" and gives you the opportunity to IM rather than reply to an email if the sender is online when you are.

There are lots of instant-messaging clients in the world—including several for the Mac, such as Yahoo, MSN Messenger, and AOL Instant Messaging. iChat happens to be one of the nicer ones. The Mac versions as a group tend to be a little behind their Windows counterparts, most noticeably in the lack of audio and video chat features on the Mac. Yahoo Messenger rates tops with the largest feature set, but iChat is the most fun to use.

Mail

I have always liked the Mac OS X Mail client, but since Jaguar I've started loving it (**Figure 7.26**). Why? Because of something called "latent semantic analysis" that allows this mail program to do a better job of stopping spam than any email program I've used. The result is that only two or three of the dozens of junk messages I get each day ever make it to my desktop—without my having to worry too much that real messages are being trashed with the spam.

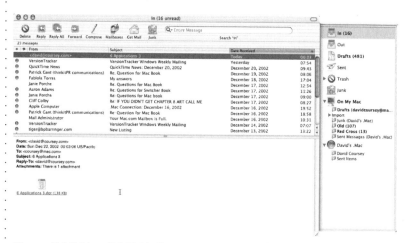

Figure 7.26 Mac OS X Mail is a very nice email client with an even nicer junk-mail filter. If I could have only one email client, this would be it. It can be used with POP mail, IMAP mail, and your .Mac mail account. And it works with multiple accounts.

When you first use Mail, its junk-mail filter is in training mode, identifying junk mail, turning it an appropriate brown color, but still delivering it to your mailbox (**Figure 7.27**). Then, if you agree with the program's junk-mail determination, do nothing.

Figure 7.27
Here's how you select the modes for Mac OS X Mail's junk filter, which does a good job of clearing spam from your mailbox.

You will, however, find some messages that are junk that were missed and some messages that aren't junk but were labeled that way. In each case, you simply click a button that toggles between Junk and Not Junk, enabling you to change the status of a message.

When you're satisfied that the junk filter understands what you think is and isn't junk, turn on automatic mode and the spam is automatically sent to the Junk folder, which is automatically emptied weekly.

At least that's how I set my Mail program to work. Every few days I take a look at the Junk folder to make sure nothing important got put there by mistake (very rarely), and about twice a day I need to click the Junk button to handle a piece of spam that snuck through.

Considering the amount of spam I get each day, I consider the ease of use and spam-fighting features of the Jaguar Mail program to be remarkable.

Mail is capable of managing several POP, IMAP, and .Mac email accounts, enabling you to view them individually or in a single combined view. You can also create folders to store messages you need to hold on to. Any message from any mailbox can be dragged to any folder for storage. The program handles drag-and-drop attachments, displays photos in the message body, and uses the common Address Book available to all Mac OS X 10.2 applications.

Mail is also great for people who lose things: The built-in search is quick, even when searching the entire contents of all your messages.

Safari

Back in 1996, Apple released a Web browser called Cyberdog. Although those who used it loved it, Cyberdog never caught on, and Apple quietly put it on the shelf. The company, however, apparently never stopped dreaming of having its own browser, because Apple kicked off 2003 by releasing another Web browser. Called Safari, it employs a handful of clever features that makes browsing the Internet a snap. For example, the application included a Google search field right up in its address bar. Clicking the SnapBack button takes you back to the point where you last typed a Web address or selected a bookmark. The software lets you easily block pop-up windows. Safari's method of displaying and organizing bookmarks is handy. And Apple claims the free browser is up to three times faster than the Mac version of Internet Explorer. In its initial release, the application lacks several popular features—including a tabbed interface and a scrapbook—that other Mac browsers include, but that didn't stop 1 million Jaguar users from downloading Safari in its first two weeks (**Figure 7.28**).

Figure 7.28 Apple's zippy Safari Web browser offers many handy ways to navigate the Internet, including putting a Google search field in its address bar.

iApps for Productivity

Although they don't start with an *i*, AppleWorks and Keynote share a common bond with the other iApps: They are smartly designed, easy-to-use applications.

AppleWorks

Many Macs include a free copy of AppleWorks, a six-function basic productivity suite that includes word-processing, spreadsheet, painting, drawing, presentation, and database functionality. It also knows how to read and write Word and Excel documents.

I will not try to convince you that AppleWorks does everything Office does—it doesn't. But I would challenge you to spend a week or two with your new Mac and see if the combination of AppleWorks, iCal, Address Book, iSync, Safari, and Mac OS X Mail doesn't meet most of your software needs.

Sure, if you then decide you need full-bore Office v. X for Mac and have $459 burning a hole in your pocket, go right ahead. But before you do: That money will buy you a very nice iPod and a few CDs to put on it.

Or just save the money for an older-model iMac or a new eMac for the kids—$459 makes a good down payment.

Most people buy way more software than they need because the software companies keep telling them that they need to buy more and more features. Sure, there are new bells and whistles in new software, and I love many of them, but before you spend money for features you don't need, give AppleWorks a chance.

However, in the interest of full disclosure, every word of this book was written in Word.

Keynote

Whether it means to or not, Apple looks to be assembling its own set of software alternatives to Office for the Mac. Apple's $99 Keynote application fills in another piece. The slick presentation program comes with 100 images and 12 themes to help you quickly assemble slides. The application offers a useful way of managing and navigating through your slides, uses handy alignment guides for squaring up one slide with the next, and can import from and export to PowerPoint.

Switcher Diary: BEN DINGER

"I work for an ISP and go to college. My Mac seems to have been made for both jobs."

Here's a Switcher who left Windows after 15 years, having reached a level where he's comfortable calling himself a "Windows god," even if having such knowledge embarrasses him a little. Ben Dinger is also a college student and works for a local Internet company.

Like many people, Ben developed an interest in the Macintosh after being introduced to Apple by a friend who already owned a Mac. When we traded email, Ben was just four days away from getting rid of his last Windows machine.

Ben: I have a Windows XP PC that I just didn't get rid of because, well, I paid a lot of money for it and now find just over a year later that it is worthless. Well, I hate it enough that I'm selling it for nothing on Friday. And thank you, Jesus, I won't have to use that thing anymore.

What am I going to do with that money? Well, I think I may just buy another Mac!

David: Tell me about your first Mac.

Ben: I bought the CD-ROM version of the iBook. I purchased it at the University of Nebraska Computer Shop new for $1099, thanks to the education discount.

Since then, I have acquired a bunch of Macs at surplus auctions—everything from a Classic Mac II to a Quadra 800 with 136 MB of RAM, to a Power Computing PowerPC 603e clone. Yes, I'm an addict.

In the future I plan on purchasing a blue-and-white G3 or a dual 867 Power Mac G4. Just depends on the cash situation. :)

David: Is your Mac a good value? How do you feel about Mac pricing?

Ben: I feel that mine was an amazing value. It fits my needs perfectly. For other Macs, I think the pricing is good. Why? Because they use quality components and come with a vast array of software from the factory. Really, the only thing I have purchased for my Mac is Microsoft Office for Mac OS X (for $8 at school).

Everything else is, well, already there. Oh, I guess I did buy Mac OS X 10.2 for $79.

David: As a self-described "Windows god," what do you think are the differences between using a Mac and using a PC?

Ben: The Mac is just completely user friendly and completely flexible. I can do anything with my Mac. In fact, it fits my needs so perfectly, it's uncanny.

Switcher Diary: BEN DINGER

Mac OS X is light years beyond Windows. It's stable as a rock—the only time my iBook gets rebooted is for a software update—it's fast and just great looking. Windows XP looks like Fisher-Price made it.

David: What do you wish you had known before switching?

Ben: My biggest concern was that Mac OS X would be everything I thought it would be. Also, that it would be able to connect up to my various Windows and Unix boxes. It does. Finally I was concerned that I wouldn't be able to play games or whether my Word documents would be readable.

None of these concerns turned out to be valid.

David: What do you do with your Mac, and where do you do it?

Ben: What don't I do with my Mac? I mean, it goes with me just about everywhere, and I have found it to be an unlimited platform. It's amazing what I can do with this machine.

I work for an ISP and go to college. My Mac seems to have been made for both jobs.

At school, it fits under my arm perfectly and has enough battery life for several lecture sessions. It also seamlessly connects to either the wired or wireless network at school.

At work, we are almost exclusively a Sun shop, which means that to do my job I need to have at least one Unix session going, and often two or three. Now, if I was using a PC I really don't know if I could use a laptop to do this. My Mac has all the software I need already built in. For Windows, I'd have to buy third-party software.

The Dock makes my life infinitely simpler as well. I can have all of my Unix sessions in the Dock and just click through them. With Jaguar, you can name your terminal windows, so that makes it even better. With Windows you can do this, but it isn't easy and would take valuable time away from our customers.

With Mac OS X, I have all the power of Unix and a wonderful user interface. I can do everything I would do on a Sun workstation but faster. And wirelessly.

David: Is there anything you want to do on your Mac that you cannot do because the software is Windows-only?

Ben: The only thing I could think of would be games. But I don't play enough games (or have enough time for them) for this to be an issue.

David: Anything else I should have asked but didn't? Anything you want to tell me?

Ben: Yeah, about how many of my friends have switched to Macs. The answer? All either have already or want to.

Getting Connected

Macintoshes (and their owners) tend to be social creatures, longing to communicate. To this end, each Mac comes equipped with a 56 Kbps modem and an Ethernet port. For an additional $79 to $99, you can purchase an AirPort wireless networking card, which opens up some exciting new possibilities, including sitting in a Starbucks (or other Internet *hot spot*) and using the Internet there on your Mac portable. Or perhaps someday you'll come to my house—bring steaks—and you can sit out on the porch and check your email while I'm checking the barbecue.

So here's how, in a series of questions and answers, to get connected. Some readers will find this chapter too technical, while others will find it not technical enough. For the latter, I have included things I've learned the hard way. The former get the following paragraphs, which together could be called "All You Really Need to Know About Connecting Your Mac to the Internet." Before you get too far into this chapter, take a look at the Internet and Network panels in System Preferences (**Figures 8.1** and **8.2**).

Figure 8.1 If you open your System Preferences, you will find icons for both the Internet and Network preferences panels. The Internet panel uses the .Mac logo for a reason— it's mostly used to set up your .Mac account. We will be using the Network panel in this chapter.

Figure 8.2 Should you make the mistake of thinking the Internet panel is where you set up your Internet connection, you're in for a surprise. This is where you set up your .Mac account, set up your iDisk (part of .Mac), and select the email client and browser you will use, on the Email and Web tabs, respectively. On the Web tab you can also select your default browser home page.

Connecting via Dial-Up

During setup, you were given the opportunity to sign up for an account with EarthLink, a national Internet service provider (ISP) (**Figure 8.3**). EarthLink has a good reputation, and I have used it on a couple of occasions and had good experiences with it. If you selected the EarthLink option, you are already set.

If you don't sign up with EarthLink now but want to later, the setup application is in the EarthLink folder in the Utilities folder, which is in your Applications folder.

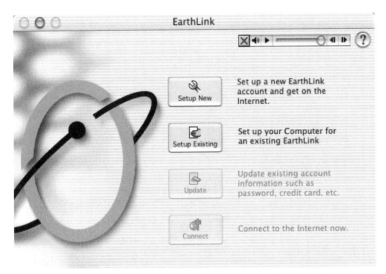

Figure 8.3 If you missed setting up EarthLink when you first turned on your new Mac, you can do so later by running the EarthLink app, located inside Utilities > EarthLink Applications.

If you are an America Online user, you will be pleased that AOL software comes preinstalled on iMacs and iBooks. (You may be interested to know that AOL was founded by Steve Case as a service for Mac users.) Although some of the most current Windows features haven't been included with AOL for Mac OS X, most users see this as a plus because it avoids the overcrowding of the user interface and blatant commercialism that hit the service after the merger with Time Warner.

If you already have your own ISP, drop over to the Network preferences panel. From the Show pop-up menu select Internal Modem and then select the PPP tab (**Figure 8.4**). Fill in your account name, your password, and the ISP's phone number, and you should be able to connect without problems.

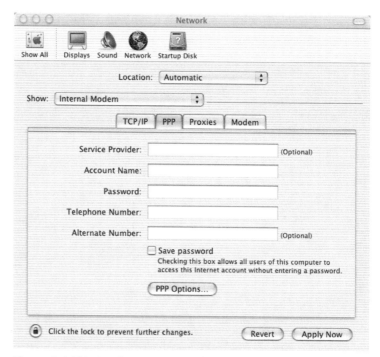

Figure 8.4 This is where you provide the information necessary for your dial-up modem to connect to an ISP. We're inside the Network preferences panel, showing the Internal Modem and its PPP (for point-to-point protocol) settings. PPP is how your computer talks to your ISP.

Connecting via Broadband

Some people think broadband Internet connections, over DSL or a cable modem, are only for people with several computers. Not so. And most broadband ISPs know all about hooking up their modems to Macs, but it is important to make sure before you pay any money.

The actual connection process is pretty simple: After the service is installed, connect the Ethernet port on your Mac to the Ethernet port on your broadband modem. Then go to the Network preferences panel; from the Show pop-up menu select Built-in Ethernet, and in either the TCP/IP tab or the PPPoE tab (whichever your ISP instructs you to use), enter your account information (**Figure 8.5**). This should get you connected without any problems.

Figure 8.5 The Network preferences panel provides a place where DSL and cable-modem users enter their account name and password to connect to the broadband network. PPPoE is one way to connect the Mac to the network.

If you already have a home network, you may find that simply connecting the Ethernet cable is enough to get you going. I've found that most networks accept the default Mac settings just fine.

The same is typically true if you have an AirPort card and want to connect to an existing wireless network. Use the AirPort Setup Assistant, located in the Utilities folder inside the Applications folder, and you'll be on the Internet very quickly.

The point I'm trying to make here is that if you use the software that Apple provides and follow Apple's and your ISP's instructions, you will probably be up and running before you actually find (and read) this chapter.

Home Networks

I love home networks and think everyone who has more than one computer should have one. The "killer application" for a home network is sharing a single broadband connection between several computers. Sharing anything else, such as files or printers, is a distant second for me. In this chapter I'll give you the basics of setting up a network that can connect both Macs and PCs to a single Internet connection. I'll focus on a wireless network, since AirPort makes setting one up so easy. I'll also tell you (again) how to connect a single Mac to a cable or DSL broadband modem.

Note: AirPort is Apple's brand name for what the PC world calls 802.11b. They're the same thing. Apple's AirPort cards are functionally equivalent to other companies' 802.11b cards. Apple's AirPort Base Station is functionally equivalent to the 802.11b access points or gateways sold by other companies. AirPort/802.11b networks run as fast as 11 Mbps.

Now here is where it gets interesting. Apple kicked off 2003 by introducing AirPort Extreme, based on the emerging 802.11g networking standard. AirPort Extreme/802.11g networks run as fast as 54 Mbps.

AirPort and AirPort Extreme devices can talk with each other, so you can mix and match (connecting, for example, an 11-Mbps AirPort-equipped PowerBook to a 54-Mbps AirPort Extreme Base Station). However, an AirPort Extreme device communicates with an AirPort device at 11 Mbps. To achieve the higher rate of 54 Mbps, all devices (Macs and base stations) must use AirPort Extreme connections. Another thing to keep in mind when joining an AirPort Extreme network: The transmission range is shorter. Two 11-Mbps AirPort devices can be as far apart as 150 feet and still talk to each other (in a perfect setting); two AirPort Extreme devices must be within 50 feet of each other to talk.

Unless I explicitly say so, when I write about AirPort in this chapter, I am using that as shorthand for both the 11-Mbps and the 54-Mbps versions. I also use here, and you will see it elsewhere, the term Wi-Fi, which is shorthand for wireless networking based on the 802.11 standard.

Just to confuse us, there is another 54-Mbps wireless LAN standard, called 802.11a. Although 802.11b (AirPort) and 802.11g (AirPort Extreme) devices can talk to each other, neither can't talk with 802.11a devices. The 802.11a adoption rate is slow, so you may never run into one these devices.

Your AirPort-equipped Mac should communicate seamlessly with any 802.11b hardware, regardless of manufacturer. Likewise, your 802.11b-equipped PCs should talk to your AirPort Base Station without any problems.

Although all 802.11b devices should work fine together, 802.11g devices are just starting to appear—and all the 802.11g kinks may not have been worked out yet—so you may come across problems trying to mix and match AirPort and AirPort Extreme devices with 802.11b and 802.11g devices from other companies. Ask the companies about compatibility before buying.

Warning: *I have never run into this, but it is possible that an ISP may not be compatible with AirPort. Ask what wireless gateway the ISP does support, and if it's 802.11b-compatible, it should work just fine with your AirPort-equipped Macs.*

What is a broadband Internet connection, and why do I want one?

Most people consider a broadband Internet connection to be anything you get from a cable or satellite company, or a DSL connection from a telephone company or other provider—something that doesn't involve dialing an ISP with a conventional modem. The precise speeds vary, but a broadband connection typically runs from 384 Kbps to as much as 6 Mbps. Compare that with your dial-up modem, which tops out at 56 Kbps.

A broadband connection is (or should be) much faster than a dial-up Internet connection, useful for moving large files; downloading music and video comes immediately to mind. A fast connection is also useful for watching video or listening to music over the Internet or for sending digital photos.

A broadband connection makes it easier to use the Backup feature of your .Mac account (if you have one) as well as to download automatic updates from Apple. With a broadband connection, your instant messaging can be left on all the time and you can listen to Internet radio as much as you like. These features alone may be worth the price.

You can easily share a broadband connection with the other computers in your home—and even with your neighbors if you use a wireless network to connect your computers to one another.

> **Caution:** *When sharing an Internet connection, you may be in violation of your agreement with your broadband provider—some don't allow sharing a connection. Use caution and find out if sharing your connection will get you into trouble. Many follow the old adage "It's easier to apologize than to ask permission."*

A broadband connection may be always on, which creates a potential security issue that firewalls are intended to handle—after all, a computer that's always connected to the Internet is more likely to be noticed by hackers than one that's only on when you dial up your ISP. Because the connection is always there, you don't have to wait to use it when you sit down at the computer. There's no waiting for your modem to dial and no busy signals. Broadband does not require a special telephone line, so if you have a separate line for your computer, you can have it disconnected and apply the money toward your broadband connection.

Typical broadband service costs about $60 or less a month as I write this. I consider it an excellent investment.

How do I connect a single Mac to a broadband (cable or DSL) modem?

This is easy: Your Mac has a built-in Ethernet jack, and all you need to do is connect the broadband modem to the jack, using the cable that probably came with your modem. You will recognize the Ethernet port on your Mac by the < ••• > symbol, and it looks like the regular modem jack, only wider. (A telephone cord will fit into an Ethernet jack with room to spare on either side, but an Ethernet cable is too large for a telephone jack.)

When ordering your broadband service, it's best if the provider (DSL or cable company) actually knows something about setting up its modems for Mac OS X. Some do, and some don't. There is generally a workaround if it can't help you.

When "Always On" Really Isn't

Broadband Internet providers like to tout the high speed of their connections and that you will never get a busy signal. Some like to talk about how the Internet is "always there" on a broadband connection.

And if you use what is called a *static IP address,* your connection always will be there, allowing your Mac be visible to other computers on the Internet at all times. If you are running a server or need to receive instant messages regardless of whether you are actually sitting in front of the computer, this is a good thing. It's what I generally use for my computers, giving each a unique address on the whole Internet.

But: Using a static IP address makes your Mac more vulnerable to hackers, and static IP addresses are generally more of a hassle than many people find they are worth.

Most ISPs, broadband or not, use *dynamic IP addresses* that are assigned to each computer as it logs on. In fact, your AirPort will assign these addresses to your own computers just as it is assigned an address by your ISP.

Likewise, most broadband ISPs require users to log on using a user name and password. This is done by the computer on a single Mac network and by the network gateway (AirPort Base Station) on a larger network.

When your computer/network is idle, the connection will time-out and disconnect. That usually isn't a problem since it will automatically reconnect when you or someone on your network starts using a computer once again. This is what I call "instant on," but it's different from "always on," and to some the difference is significant.

If you have never set up a network before, there are some voodoo terms I need to introduce you to. The first is *DHCP,* which stands for Dynamic Host Configuration Protocol. If you memorize what the initials mean, you may be able to impress your friends or even win a game show, but everyone just calls this DHCP and forgets what it stands for.

What DHCP *does,* on the other hand, is very important and a real time-saver. DHCP automatically configures your computer (or an Internet gateway or AirPort Base Station) to connect to the Internet. By default, your Mac expects to connect to a DHCP server capable of providing it with an Internet address (a series of numbers in the format of 192.168.1.1, for example) as well as an address for a DNS server. OK, this is getting way too deep, but—in general—a DHCP server is your friend and will make it easier for your Mac to connect to the Internet. Your ISP will probably tell you to use DHCP to connect.

It is possible, however, that you will be given what's called a *static* (meaning stable) IP address and some other numbers that you need to fill in your Network preferences panel. You may also run into something called *PPPoE,* short for Point-to-Point Protocol over Ethernet, that requires you to enter a user name and password to connect to the Internet.

Rather than confuse you totally, I will refer you to your ISP for specific information on connecting your computer to its Internet service. At worst, it involves filling in the Network preferences panel with some numbers your ISP provides. It's not that difficult if you follow instructions, but if I try to explain it to you, I think I am more likely to do you harm than good.

How do I connect multiple computers to the same Internet connection?

There are several ways to do this, but here's the Mac way:

1. Buy an AirPort Base Station, and buy an AirPort card for each of your Macs.

    Buy 802.11b/802.11g cards or USB devices for any PCs you want to join the party (first ensuring they are compatible with Apple's devices).

2. Install the cards in your Macs and PCs (minor disassembly required, but it's not too difficult), and connect the AirPort Base Station to your DSL or cable modem.

3. Follow the directions provided with your base station and from your ISP for connecting the base station to the Internet.

    To do this, you'll probably need information provided by your ISP (usually your telephone or cable company) to set up the base station.

Using this method, you can have a wireless network up and running in an hour or two. And besides having your computers share an Internet connection, you'll also be able to share files between Macs and Windows machines, and your Macs will be able to share printers (as will your Windows machines, just not with the Macs).

This is not the least expensive way to set up a home network, but it is the easiest—especially if you are just using Macs on it—and AirPort works very well.

If you have only one Mac and several PCs, you might want to use a more PC-centric approach, which is fine. This would involve using a wireless gateway and access cards from NetGear, Linksys, or D-Link for the gateway and an AirPort card for the Mac.

Setting up a home network has become pretty easy, especially if you stick to Macs and AirPort hardware. The benefits— making full use of a broadband connection, being able to put your computers pretty much anyplace, being able to use your portable at the kitchen table or out on the patio—can change the way you think about computing.

Here's some additional information for people who already understand networks: I have had very good luck connecting AirPort cards to non-Apple gateways and non-Apple wireless devices to Apple's AirPort Base Station. The Apple hardware is based on the Lucent/Agere Orinoco technology.

I remain concerned, however, about possible incompatibilities among Wi-Fi equipment—and between 802.11b and 802.11g devices—so I recommend buying as few brands of hardware as possible. And once you find something that works, stick with it.

At this moment, I am using AirPort cards to connect to 3Com and Linksys hardware (I have two wireless networks). I have also tested Agere, D-Link, and NetGear hardware with excellent results. You many find it easier to do initial setup on some of these non-Apple devices from a PC rather than a Mac, if only because the instructions are invariably written for PC users.

About AirPort

Apple fundamentally changed what it means to be on a network when it introduced its AirPort devices in the summer of 1999.

How does wireless Internet access work?

An AirPort network consists of an AirPort Base Station, an AirPort card for each Mac you want to connect, and an account with an ISP. The AirPort Base Station has a built-in modem for dial-up Internet connections, but you may also connect the base station to a broadband cable or DSL modem using an Ethernet cable for faster connections.

Your AirPort cards do not talk directly to the Internet but rather to the base station—otherwise known as an *access point*. The base station manages the connection to the Internet through your ISP.

How does AirPort work?

Until a few years ago, if computers needed to talk to one another they had to do it over wires. More recently, wireless networks have become popular as equipment prices have come down. As in many things, Apple was a leader in making this technology public by introducing AirPort about two years before wireless networks went mainstream.

There are three ways to create an AirPort network:

1. You can create an ad-hoc computer-to-computer network that other AirPort (or 802.11b or 802.11g) computers can connect to, provided they are within range. This method doesn't require an AirPort Base Station (or other 802.11b or 802.11g access point).

2. Using an AirPort Base Station, you can create a permanent network in which the wireless-equipped computers talk to one another, or to the Internet, through the base station. This is my recommended installation.

3. You can also connect an AirPort Base Station to an existing network, perhaps at your office or school, so computers can connect to that network wirelessly.

You may also use your wireless-equipped Mac to connect to any 802.11b/802.11g network, including those at Internet *hot spots* being set up in cafés and airports.

> **Tip:** *You can find lists of public wireless hot spots at www.80211hotspots.com, www.nodedb.com, and www.wifinder.com.*

What is the range of an AirPort network?

The maximum claimed distance is 168 feet for AirPort devices and 50 feet for AirPort Extreme devices. There are, however, many variables, so some experimentation may be necessary. In open air on a good day, with nothing between the Mac and the access point, ranges can be several times this. On the other hand, inside buildings with radio-blocking materials, ranges may be much less. This is especially true for users of the titanium-clad PowerBooks, as the metal casing restricts the radio signal the computer is able to transmit (**Figure 8.6**).

Figure 8.6 The icon on the menu bar that looks like radio waves is the signal-strength indicator for your AirPort card. This machine is close to the base station and has an excellent connection. Fewer bars mean a weaker signal.

> **Tip:** *If your Titanium PowerBook has almost no connection range, try removing the battery and firmly running your fingers along the sides of the hole where the battery used to be. This may improve your range, but no guarantees.*

Finding the best location for your AirPort Base Station (or other wireless access point) may take some work. At my house—which has three levels—I had to move the base station a few times to find a place where all the computers could talk to it. The computers must be able to talk to the base station, but they don't have to be able to talk to each other. This means that if the AirPort Base Station is in the center of the physical network, it should cover 150 feet in all directions, allowing the farthest computers to be up to 300 feet apart. The distance would be much less in an AirPort Extreme setup.

You will probably never need one, but there are antennas and special network equipment available that allow Wi-Fi to operate point-to-point across distances of 10 miles or more. This is useful for linking buildings in a campus environment but also can be used to connect someone who has a broadband modem to someone who is unable to get one for technical reasons.

At my new house, a DSL connection won't be available until 2005, and cable modems have always been, for me, less reliable than DSL. So I may be looking for someone with a DSL connection where I can install a wireless network and then use one of these special antennas to connect his or her house to mine over Wi-Fi.

Configuring your AirPort Base Station

Both your computer and the base station must be configured to talk to each other and the Internet. If your Mac is already set up to connect to the Internet, you should use the AirPort Setup Assistant software to transfer the settings from your Mac to the AirPort Base Station.

The AirPort Setup Assistant is located in the Utilities folder inside the Applications folder. If your computer isn't already set up to connect to the Internet, use the information provided by your ISP to answer the AirPort Setup Assistant's questions. You can also give your network a name and a password, which I recommend that you do.

After starting the AirPort Setup Assistant, you should select "Set up your computer to join an existing AirPort network" or "Set up an AirPort Base Station," depending on the task at hand. Follow the onscreen instructions.

Another program, the AirPort Admin Utility (also in Applications > Utilities; **Figure 8.7**), makes it easy to quickly change your settings (**Figures 8.8** to **8.12**). If you have experience with networks, especially wireless networks, you will find this much easier to use than the AirPort Setup Assistant, which is designed for newbie networkers.

Figure 8.7 This is the Utilities folder, which is "hidden" inside the Applications folder for a reason. I think of this as the Folder of Doom because most of the things that could really mess up your Mac, if used improperly, live here. Some, such as the AirPort Admin Utility and the AirPort Setup Assistant, are quite useful and relatively benign. Others—Terminal, for example, which takes you to the Unix heart of Mac OS X—can be positively deadly in the wrong hands. In generally, only open this folder when someone or the help system gives you a concrete reason to do so.

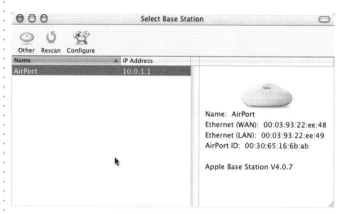

Figure 8.8 This is the AirPort Admin Utility, connected to my AirPort Base Station. Clicking the Configure icon allows me to set up the base station after I enter the base station's password (the default is *public*).

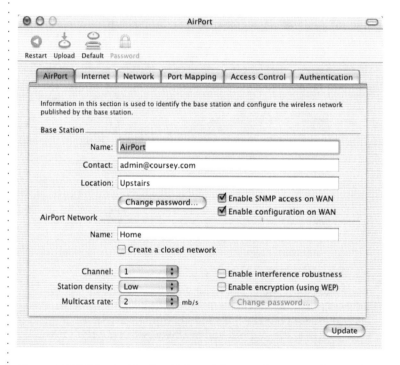

Figure 8.9 We're inside the AirPort Admin Utility now. This is where you name both the base station and your network. Note that "Enable encryption (using WEP)" and "Create a closed network" are not selected on this network. They probably should be on yours.

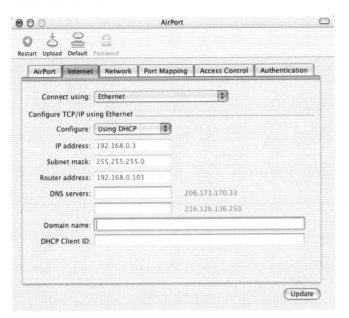

Figure 8.10 This is where you configure the IP address on your base station. Most users will select Using DHCP from the Configure pop-up menu as I have, and no further settings need be entered. If you have a static IP address, you would select Manual and enter the IP address, Subnet mask, Router address, and DNS server addresses yourself.

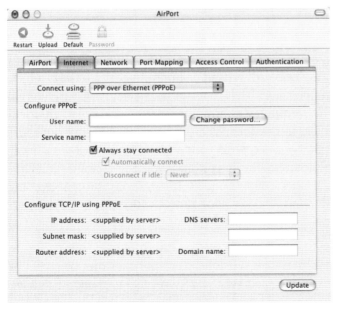

Figure 8.11 If you are using PPPoP, this is where you enter the user name and password provided by your broadband ISP into the Air-Port configuration. With this information, AirPort can automatically establish your broadband connection as necessary.

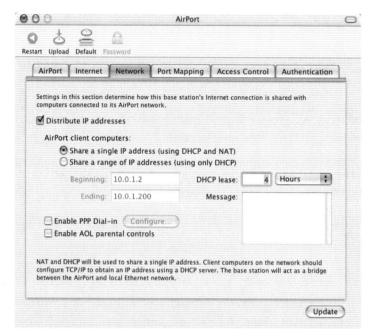

Figure 8.12 You will probably want your AirPort—or whatever broadband gateway hardware you use—to provide IP addresses to the computers on your network. In most cases your setup on the AirPort Base Station's Network tab should look just like this one.

The AirPort Admin Utility also provides access to advanced features. The most useful of these may be the ability to set the channel your network operates on. Normally this isn't necessary, but if you are near other networks or even some cordless telephones (the ones advertised as operating on 2.4 GHz, which is the frequency that 802.11b and 802.11g use), you may wish to change the frequency channel your network uses—this will help with flaky connections. Microwave ovens also put out radio frequencies at 2.4 GHz, so if your wireless network gets fuzzy when using the microwave, you may want to change the channel to see if this helps. Check http://docs.info.apple.com/article.html?artnum = 58543 for more information on interference sources.

If you are concerned about people snooping or connecting to your wireless network without your permission, you should turn on something called WEP, for Wireless Encryption Protocol.

With WEP, each computer on your network, as well as your AirPort Base Station or wireless gateway, must be set to use the same pass phrase. Most people don't use WEP, although they probably should.

To use WEP on an AirPort Base Station, select the "Enable encryption (using WEP)" checkbox on the AirPort tab of the AirPort Admin Utility. Then create a password that all users will need to enter to use your network. Note that there is a setting for using either 40-bit or 128-bit encryption. More bits mean more security but also the possibility of incompatibility with older, 40-bit networking hardware. An all-Mac network can use 128-bit without problems.

> *Hint: Only three channels don't overlap the other channels— 1, 6, and whatever the highest channel is on your base station, typically 11. Also, I'm told the highest channel is least likely to suffer interference from cordless telephones. The only reason to know this is if you need to move because you and a neighbor are both operating on the same channel. Not likely to pose a problem, but now you know what to do about it. There should always be three channels between physically adjacent networks. If your neighbor is on channel 1, put your network on channel 4.*

What do I need to buy for a wireless network?

You will need the following:

- A wireless gateway/router (an AirPort Base Station or other 802.11b/802.11g-compatible device). If money is an issue, the AirPort Base Station is relatively expensive but easy to set up from a Mac. It also allows you to share an AOL dial-up connection among multiple users, although each must have his or her own account. (Only one screen name per account can be signed on at a time.)

- AirPort cards for your Macs. They are easily installed.

- An 802.11b/802.11g PC Card for each notebook PC.

- A USB wireless adapter for each desktop PC. Yes, you might also buy an add-in PCI card for each PC, but they are more trouble to install and won't work any better.

Remember: Buy as few different brands as possible. And if you run into trouble, many wireless hardware companies provide free technical support 24 hours a day.

Are AirPort networks secure?

They're not as secure as a network that is connected only using wires. But if you use the WEP encryption provided by the AirPort Base Station and then only send confidential data (such as payment information) to secure Web sites (identifiable by Web addresses beginning with "https:") you are protecting yourself to a very reasonable degree. But all this can be cracked if somebody really, really wants to know what you are up to. My own network is secured this way, and I don't worry about it.

Will other people be able to use my wireless Internet connection?

Not if you choose a good network password. Or tell your AirPort Base Station to connect only to devices with specific 12-digit AirPort IDs. You will find these numbers on the labels of your AirPort cards, and you can enter them into your AirPort Base Station configuration utility.

You can also select "Create a closed network" on the AirPort tab of the Admin Utility (see Figure 8.9). This gives you an exttra level of security by hiding the name of the network. A user then must also know the exact name of your AirPort network to join it.

Alternatively, you can do nothing and share your bandwidth with the neighbors but only if they know your network password. If you have chosen good passwords for your user accounts, this shouldn't pose too much of a problem.

As mentioned before, there is the potential for legal problems if you share your connection. Your agreement with your ISP may include a clause intended to prevent this sort of sharing. In my mind, such sharing, done over the long term, is unethical. It costs a lot of money to install and support a broadband network, and the carriers are entitled to a fair return.

Is my DSL or cable-modem connection secure?

This is related to a question about whether you should use a firewall (the answer is yes). In the Finder, go to the Go menu, and select Connect to Server. You can then look around on the network and see if there's anything you don't recognize as your own. Some cable-modem networks are notoriously open, allowing everyone in a neighborhood to see one another's computers. This is why we use firewalls and strong passwords.

In general: If you don't need file sharing (or any of the other features of the Sharing preferences panel), turn it off for greater protection. (See Chapter 6 for information on the Sharing preferences panel.)

How do I connect to a different network at work (or someplace else)?

In many cases, you will simply take your portable Mac to the new location, turn it on, and connect to the corporate wireless network either by using either AirPort or by plugging a cable into your Mac's Ethernet port.

If all goes well, you will be connected to your network, thanks to the wonders of DHCP. That's how both my home and office networks function, and how yours probably does as well.

But, sometimes you may need specific settings—provided by your ISP or corporate system administrator—to connect. For those times, Apple conveniently allows you to save the settings and associate them with specifically named locations.

Go to the Apple menu > Location to select your location ("Automatic" is the default and works just fine for me), or open Network preferences and set up and save (via the Location pop-up menu) the name and associated settings for a specific place. You may set specific settings for each of your network ports, such as Ethernet, AirPort, or the built-in modem. Apple Help refers to these as "Network Locations."

Where do I go for more help?

Point your browser at www.apple.com, select the Support tab, and then search the Knowledge Base for *AirPort*. You will find the answers to most common questions (**Figure 8.13**). You may also search a document titled "Designing AirPort Networks 2." It runs 57 pages and should answer any questions you have on design and implementation of an AirPort network.

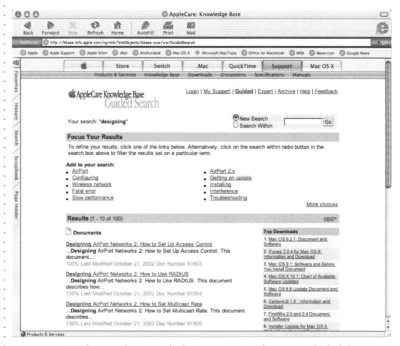

Figure 8.13 The Apple Knowledge Base provides many helpful documents for people setting up Macintosh networks, including "Designing AirPort Networks 2," which has helped me on several occasions.

Will I need this help?

If you managed to get your Mac set up, then setting up an AirPort network shouldn't be a problem. Just make sure you have the welcome kit that your ISP sent. It should contain the necessary technical details to get your Internet connection up and running, whether you use an AirPort or not.

Letting Another Computer Connect to Yours

If you want to share files with another computer, you will need to connect to it over your network. But before you can do that, there are some preliminaries. First, you must be sharing the file, folder, or disk so that someone can connect to it.

Sharing must be turned on, or the computer, whether Mac or PC, will not appear on the network. To turn sharing on, go to your Mac's System Preferences and select the Sharing panel. On the Services Tab select Personal File Sharing to share with other Macs and Windows File Sharing to share with guess what (**Figure 8.14**).

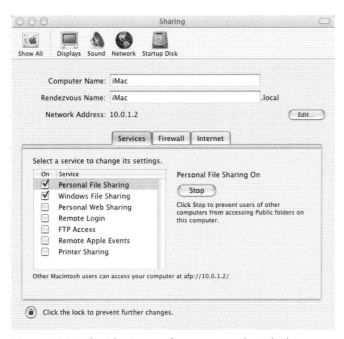

Figures 8.14 The Sharing preferences panel, with the proper boxes checked to allow both Mac and Windows file sharing.

You also need to go to the Firewall tab and turn on the firewall. Now would be an excellent time to start it (**Figure 8.15**).

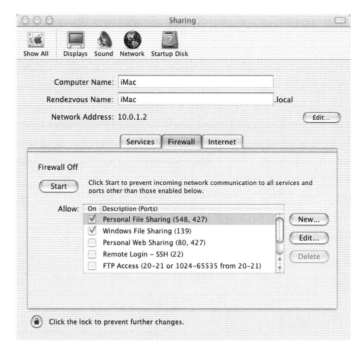

Figure 8.15 Now, what is wrong with this picture? The firewall is turned off! If you want firewall protection, remember to click the Start button.

Your Windows computer or computers must also be set up to allow sharing, which many of you already know how to do. For those who don't, and considering that you may be using any of four or five different versions of Windows, I will refer you to either a Windows book or the Windows help system.

Your goal is to set up your Windows machine on a network, select a workgroup for your network, and then share the files and folders you wish to share.

If everything has gone well, your Mac is now all set to see what's shared on your PC and vice versa. To connect to the PC, go to the Finder, and from the Go menu choose Connect to Server (**Figure 8.16**). In the Connect to Server dialog, select the server you wish to connect to (**Figure 8.17**) and follow the instructions (**Figures 8.18** to **8.21**).

Workgroup Names

Windows recognizes computers on a network by assembling them into workgroups. The easiest way to share files between Windows machines and Macs is to have them all be part of the same workgroup.

This is a problem because your Windows machine probably has a workgroup name like MSHOME or HOME or whatever someone has changed it to. Your new Mac has the very creative default workgroup name of Workgroup.

You can either change your Windows machines to be part of a workgroup called Workgroup or change the Mac to be a member of whatever workgroup already exists (similarly to adding a Mac to a Windows network you have already set up).

Here, from the Apple Knowledge Base, is how to change the workgroup setting on your Mac:

The default workgroup is WORKGROUP. To learn what a workgroup is, look on Apple's site for technical document 107138, "Windows File Sharing: What is a 'Workgroup'?"

To change the workgroup, follow these steps:

1. Open the Directory Access application (found in the Utilities folder in the Applications folder).

2. Click the padlock at the bottom of the window to authenticate to give you Admin user access.

3. Select SMB from the Services list.

4. Click the Configure button.

5. Select the name of the workgroup from the list, or type the name of the workgroup you wish to create.

6. Click OK.

7. Then click Apply.

8. Quit the Directory Access application.

Note: Changes in the Directory Access settings may take up to 5 minutes to be recognized by other computers on the network. To force a quicker update, stop and restart Windows File Sharing.

Figure 8.16 From the Finder, choose Go > Connect to Server as the first step in connecting to another computer across your home network.

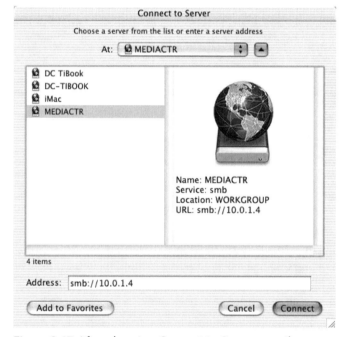

Figure 8.17 After choosing Connect to Server, you then choose the server to connect to. This is a view of my home network, showing two Macs (the way this network is configured, TiBook shows up twice), the iMac I am currently using, and a Windows machine called MEDIACTR. Note that Windows machines always have a URL that begins "smb:"

Figure 8.18 After choosing the Windows machine, you are asked to provide a user name and password.

Figure 8.19 After successfully entering a user name and password, you are asked to select from the "shares" the Windows machine makes available to you.

Figure 8.20 This is what my Mac looks like with the SHAREDDOCS folder from my Windows machine sitting on the desktop.

Figure 8.21 Here's what my Mac looks like from the Network Connections screens of my Windows XP machine. Note that the actual name of the Mac is in parentheses.

If you find all this about as clear as mud, you're not alone. What I really need to be doing is sitting there next to you and letting you watch me connect your Mac to another computer and start exchanging files. If my explanation in this book has confused you, please accept my apologies and check out the help system already on your Mac. It has step-by-step instructions for all this and what it doesn't have the Apple support Web site does (www.apple.com/support).

Switcher Diary: HOWARD YERMISH

"The key here is your brain and your productivity. I'm simply more productive and more creative with the Mac. It lets me do my job, which has nothing to do with configuring my computers."

Howard Yermish grew up in a very computer-savvy home and ended up using Windows almost by default: It was just what people, including his father the Ph.D., bought. When he started a Web design business, he naturally started with Windows and ended up on Macintosh, as he says it, "by accident."

Howard: My father has a Ph.D. in computer science, and I've been around computers since I was four years old. We always had some form of PC at the house, and I've always known how to build them from scratch. I guess what I liked was that I could tinker with and build them from scratch.

David: What do you like least about Windows?

Howard: Windows has become like voodoo computing. What used to be fairly simple to configure has turned into something that I just have no patience for. The interface manages to change in every incarnation into something different.

I think that while Windows XP is finally taking steps in the right direction, it is a far cry from friendly. I know tons of people who are scared to install software or change things on their computer because they are afraid that they may break something.

David: Do you still use Windows?

Howard: I still use Windows daily. As a Web developer, I constantly have to test Web sites on the Windows platform. I also have servers that I manage that are Windows-based. There are also a few programs that I've been using for years that are not available for the Mac, and it would be too cost/time prohibitive to change at this point.

David: How did you become a Mac user?

Howard: It was a complete accident.

I've been a PC user since there were PCs. My father is a computer database programmer, and we always had computers around the house as well as afternoons at his office playing on machines the size of the room. Once PCs became the mainstream, that was all that we ever had.

As my own Web design business started to expand, several of my clients had Macs, and I found that I needed to get one for browser testing. So I

Switcher Diary: HOWARD YERMISH

got myself an iMac DV Special Edition 400 MHz about two years ago. My biggest mistake was not anticipating how much I was going to like it.

After all, I was the official PC guru of my friends, the guy that you would call if you needed the system rebuilt or a new sound card or getting a cable modem set up. I was a PC snob to the bone. In my little home office, I had three PCs running on a network and a little iMac just for browser testing.

Within two months, I had switched almost all of my development onto the Mac. There were a few things that still were for PC only, but for the most part, there were either the same applications or equivalent applications for everything that I needed.

Later that year, I bought an iBook with AirPort so I could roam the house and work on the porch. Now that all of my Web development applications are available on Mac OS X, both of my Macs are running Jaguar.

Looking back on the whole transition, I've really begun to appreciate having a computer that just works. I remember countless weekends lost to rebuilding one of my Windows machines or trying to get a new video card to work or something that should only take a few minutes but wound up taking several days. On the Mac, I would just plug in the Compact Flash reader and it worked, or my Canon ZR30 or my extra FireWire hard drive or the CD burner.

I remember a specific incident this spring when my sister came to visit. She brought her digital camera and her IBM laptop down. After she had taken a bunch of pictures, my wife wanted to see them. So she started up her laptop and began to try to get the pictures transferred. After about an hour of her trying to get the pictures from the camera, I put her out of her misery by connecting her camera to my iBook. In under a minute, we were looking at a slide show through iPhoto. She was blown away. She asked me if it was usually like this, to which I replied that I usually don't spend the first hour trying to get it to work on my PC—I just go to the Mac.

David: Is your Mac a good value? How do you feel about Mac pricing?

Howard: My Macs are a great value. My iMac is almost three years old, and it is still running quite smoothly. I've upgraded the memory and hard drive in the machine, which cost about $250 total. So I've put about $2,100 into the iMac, which is still running strong, and with Mac OS X 10.2, I just got a performance boost. My iBook is a similar experience, although I haven't gotten a larger hard drive for it yet.

I think that Macs seem overpriced when you initially purchase one, but that doesn't factor in how consistently they will work without any effort. I used to buy or build a new PC every 12 to 18 months, but I've been running the same Macs since I switched. I want to get a new Power Mac but really just for a performance-speed increase, not for functionality.

Switcher Diary: HOWARD YERMISH

David: How do you feel about the look and feel of Mac hardware?

Howard: After working with Windows-based PCs and software for so long, it's refreshing to work with Apple products. I do design for a living, and what Apple does is beyond design for design's sake. Apple designs its software and hardware to be used every day. When I pick up a Sony laptop, it is thin and shiny but I feel like I'm going to break it if I did half of the things that I put my iBook through. My iMac is quiet, which may not seem like a big deal until I turn off the PC next to it. That Micron has three fans to keep it cool and that generates plenty of noise. I guess I would have to say that Apple commits to their designs and takes a stand for them. Because of this, they insist that everything coming out of Cupertino be awesome.

David: Is there something someone could have told you that would have made it easier for you to make the Switcher decision?

Howard: Not really. If you lived for 10 years and never had Belgian chocolate, no one could convince you that you would like it. But once you have experienced something that incredible, your entire context for living is changed, and plain chocolate just isn't as good as it once was.

I think that people fear the change for that reason alone. It is a change. But imagine if I told you that by using a different brand of gasoline, you could double your miles to the gallon with the same car. People would try it a couple of times because there is very little risk involved. If it doesn't live up to the hype, you just go back. When switching to a Mac, you have to be willing to make that commitment. If it doesn't work for you, you risk thousands of dollars in hardware and software as well as countless hours of lost time.

The key here is your brain and your productivity. I'm simply more productive and more creative with the Mac. It lets me do my job, which has nothing to do with configuring my computers. I never knew what I was missing until I got my own Mac, and now I wish I had switched sooner.

Viruses, Hackers, Backups, and Dealing with Emergencies

It's generally believed, and there seems to be ample justification for this, that Mac OS X is "safer" than Microsoft Windows. (I explain this in some detail below.) Even so, using a Mac is not without risks.

Here's the moral of this chapter: Back up your data, and never go on the Internet without protection, at least from an antivirus program and probably some sort of firewall. Do this, and you'll probably never run into a problem that you can't get out of. And did I remind you to back up your data?

General Information

Let's start with the basic stuff.

How do I avoid problems with my Mac?

Protect your data. Make backups daily, and save your files often. Make multiple copies of important files, and don't keep them all in one place—just in case you have a fire or theft. Never erase anything until you have created at least two backups. And never erase a backup and write a new version over it—what if the new version is corrupt?

It's useful to give these backups slightly different names (add a letter or number) and to keep each set of backups in its own folder with names like "backup docs a" and "backup docs b"— use whatever naming scheme works for you. Emailing copies of important files to a friend is also a good idea. (I'll talk about backup options later.)

As for hard-drive problems, the regular use of disk utilities can head off many kinds of problems before they become critical. One comes with your Mac and lives in your Utilities folder. It's called the Disk Utility, and you may find it useful to run its First Aid component every few weeks. It's most effective when you boot from your Mac OS X install disc by holding down the C key while booting with the CD in the drive. I also like Symantec's Norton SystemWorks ($69.95; www.symantec.com) (**Figure 9.1**), and a program called DiskWarrior from Alsoft has saved my life more than once. A "lite" version of Disk-Warrior comes with Norton SystemWorks.

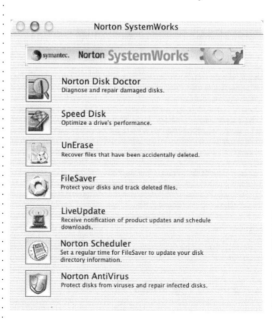

Figure 9.1
Norton SystemWorks is a collection of utilities that can play a big role in keeping your Mac healthy and out of trouble.

But if you run any of these utilities on a Mac that isn't backed up, you're flirting with danger, even though their stated goal is to set things right. On the other hand, if you've faithfully backed up your data every day, you won't have to worry even if things go horribly wrong.

How do I back up my Mac?

Here's how I do it:

- With your .Mac membership comes Backup, an application you can download for free (**Figure 9.2**). This software allows you to select various types of information on your Mac (as well as any files and folders you also care about) and automatically copy those files to a backup folder on your personal iDisk, which resides on an Apple server. Mine is set to back up all my important files every morning between 2 and 4 a.m., and it seems to work fine. The limitation with this is that you can only back up one machine per .Mac account. That bugs me because I have several Macs and want to back them all up every night. Seems like buying enough extra iDisk space should entitle me to do this. If you don't want to back up to an iDisk, the Backup program will also copy files to a CD or DVD, although a .Mac membership is still required. If you have more than one machine, a solution is to back up to a CD or merely copy your documents folder (with a new name) and drag it over to your iDisk. But that's a manual backup solution, and manual is a bad idea—an automated backup solution is much less prone to errors, such as forgetting to do it.

- CMS Peripherals (www.cmsperipheralsinc.com) sells a device called the ABSplus—ABS is short for "automatic backup system" (**Figure 9.3**). This external hard drive connects to your Mac with a FireWire cable. Included is software that automatically backs up your Mac to this external drive, creating a bootable hard drive that's a clone of your original. This means you can start up someone else's Mac from your ABS disk (press T while the machine is starting up) or use it to get your own machine restarted after a major hard-drive crash. The only thing I don't like about this product is the price: $300 to $600 for a typical unit (price based on capacity), and you'll need one for every Mac you want backed up.

Figure 9.2 Apple provides Backup as part of your .Mac membership. It automatically backs up important files, such as those selected here, to your online iDisk for safekeeping. My system backs up at 2 a.m. every day.

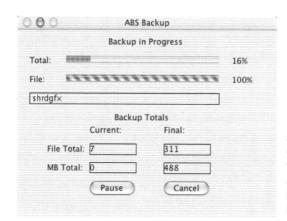

Figure 9.3 The ABS backup application shows you what's happening as it automatically backs up your hard disk.

- Less expensive and more flexible—but more work—is using Dantz Development's excellent Retrospect ($49–$799; www.dantz.com) to back up your Mac to an external FireWire hard drive (this is not an ABS system; **Figure 9.4**). Many external drives come with a free copy of Retrospect capable of backing up a single Mac, and the drives are less expensive (greater capacity for the money) than the ABS system. If you have several Macs to back up (or PCs and Macs, for that matter), check out the versions of Retrospect designed for multiple machines. I am not a big fan of backing up to tape drives, although relying on a single hard drive for backup can be iffy. One way around that is to back up each of your Macs onto the hard drive of another Mac on your network—that way a single crash won't result in large amounts of lost data.

Figure 9.4
Retrospect is a well-respected family of backup applications for everything from single PCs to entire networks. Originally developed for the Mac, the program comes in a Windows version.

One problem you will note in my strategy is that it's pretty short on off-site backups, necessary in case of fire or theft. Though limited, iDisk provides this capability for current important files, and a set of CD or DVD backups, left at a friend's house, provides an easy off-site storage place.

Any backup is better than no backup. My recommendation to a person with a single Mac is to use the iDisk backup daily and to occasionally make a CD backup to give to a friend for safekeeping. If you have the money, the ABS and Retrospect methods are great ways to increase your protection.

And while you are backing up: Make sure you have copies of all your applications and the Mac OS X discs that came with your computer. You do own the applications you use, right?

Make backup copies of the CDs. Also, always remember to keep copies of the various codes you have to enter to get your applications running, especially any you buy over the Internet.

Do I need a firewall for my Mac?

Maybe.

Your Mac comes with firewall software, which you can turn on from the Sharing Systems Preferences panel (**Figure 9.5**). I don't use this firewall, and can't tell you very much about it, other than that it's a Unix firewall built fairly deep into the guts of Mac OS X.

Figure 9.5 From the Sharing preferences panel you can access the Firewall tab to control Mac OS X's built-in protection against hackers.

When you start the built-in firewall, it will block all connections to your Mac except from Internet services—such as file sharing—you have specifically turned on. It may work just fine, but my experience (admittedly mostly in Windows) makes me distrustful of built-in programs, especially when there are many other options.

Personally, I'd prefer to see you using something such as Symantec's Norton Personal Firewall ($49.95; www.symantec.com; **Figure 9.6**), but that costs money. Also, it's likely that if your Mac is connected to a home network, then a firewall already exists in your gateway device. Apple's AirPort Base Station, a gateway for home networks, includes its own built-in firewall. A personal firewall, Norton's, or the one that Mac OS X has built in is really only required for Macs that are directly connected to the Internet via a cable or DSL modem.

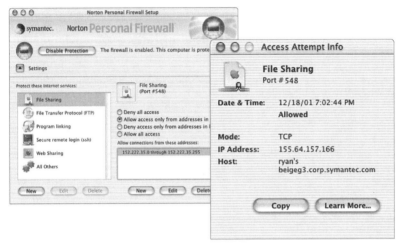

Figure 9.6 Another way to protect your Mac is with a software firewall, such as Norton Personal Firewall from Symantec.

But this protection exists only if the firewall, wherever it lives, is actually turned on. Check this to make sure, since the usual default setting is "off."

Although I wouldn't tell anyone not to have some form of firewall protection, you can probably get away without it if you are just connected to the Internet for short periods of time. For example, someone who uses a dial-up connection to AOL or another Internet service provider (ISP) is reasonably safe from attack.

If, however, you have a full-time Internet connection, typically using a DSL or cable modem, you ought to use a firewall. And if possible, turn your machine all the way off—I mean power it down—when you are not using it, thus reducing the time it is exposed to a potential external threat.

Do I need antivirus protection for my Mac?

Every time I think that only people with room-temperature IQs would ask this question, along comes someone whose intelligence I wouldn't otherwise question with a tale of woe about what some virus has done to him to her. Admittedly, these have also been people who were using Microsoft Windows.

Yes, every computer needs to have antivirus software installed on it. Mac users have two choices: McAfee's Virex ($49; www.mcafee.com), which comes with your .Mac membership (**Figure 9.7**), and Symantec's Norton AntiVirus (**Figure 9.8**), available separately ($69.95; www.symantec.com) or as part of Norton System-Works, which I consider a "must have" for Mac owners.

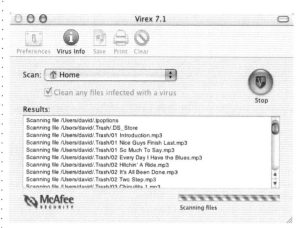

Figure 9.7
With your .Mac membership comes a copy of Virex, a well-respected antivirus application, shown here inspecting my hard drive.

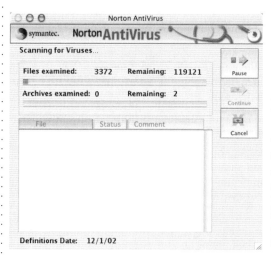

Figure 9.8
Another option for virus protection is Norton AntiVirus, which I have used for several years. Viruses aren't the threat to Macs that they pose to Windows systems, but since one virus can ruin your whole disk, why risk it?

This software is only as good as its last update, however, which means that you need to download the new virus-definition files when the program asks you to—usually once a month.

OK, but how dangerous is it for Mac users?

Now that I have (hopefully) frightened you enough to invest in some means of backing up important files and fighting viruses—the cheapest way to do this is a .Mac membership—I should tell you something: Macs aren't nearly as vulnerable as Windows machines.

The reason for this, as best I have been able to determine, is that the design of Mac OS X doesn't have as many vulnerabilities as that of Windows. Another reason seems to be that because Apple isn't Microsoft, coupled with the comparatively small size of the overall Macintosh installed base, virus writers and other miscreants don't worry about the Mac very much.

You may notice that those two reasons run in a circle—fewer virus writers because of fewer machines to attack and a less vulnerable OS also means that new vulnerabilities are less likely to be discovered and so on. Still, whatever the case may be, Macs are more secure than Windows and don't have nearly as many urgent security fixes to download and install.

I think I've caught a virus. What should I do?

I like bed rest, plenty of fluids, my mother's potato soup recipe, and the endless hours of reruns on TV Land or Food Network when I am feeling poorly. And since you took my advice about antivirus software, you must be talking about a medical problem, right?

But just in case some friend asks you for advice about computer viruses, here's what to do: Turn the computer off. Go buy a copy of Norton AntiVirus and follow the instructions for dealing with a possibly infected machine, which may include booting from the program's CD. Whenever you install the software, make sure you also download the most current virus definitions. I hope too much damage wasn't done, but now you should be protected against any future viruses.

How many security patches do Mac users receive?

You will receive occasional—once a month or less—security updates and other fixes for your Mac. The Software Update preferences panel determines how often your Mac checks for these and other updates from Apple. If you are using a broadband Internet connection, such as cable or DSL, your Mac may check for an update in the background, and the first time you're aware of it is when a window pops up asking you if it's OK to install the update. It's almost always a good idea to do so.

Are power spikes and lightning strikes really dangerous?

Yes. And while your insurance may or may not cover fried computers, the best offense is a good defense. This means plugging everything into high-quality surge suppressors, ideally including your network and telephone cables—power surges can travel through these, too. This can protect you from unexpected jolts—such as when a car hits the pole and brings down the transformer. But if you know a storm is brewing, just remove the power, network, and telephone cables from your Mac before heading down to the storm cellar.

How does a Mac automatically receive software updates?

Built in to Mac OS X is an automatic means of downloading patches, fixes, and other updates from Apple. Called Software Update, this feature has its own panel in your System Preferences (see Chapter 6 for more information; **Figure 9.9**). I set mine to check daily, thought if I were not using a DSL broadband connection, I would set it to weekly. Dial-up modem users should periodically visit this preferences panel and have it do an immediate check for updates, just in case your system hasn't had a chance to download while you were working.

When Software Update has downloaded something, you will be asked if you want to install it. You won't go wrong by accepting an update, although it may be nothing more important than a new set of menus in Italian. You can, however, refuse (or make inactive) a particular update.

Be aware that Software Update will *not* automatically update your applications or virus-definition files, though the latter would certainly be nice. Many applications, however, are capable of automatically checking for and downloading their own updates. Also, Software Update will not find new applications, so you need to check the Mac OS X Web site (from the Apple menu choose Get Mac OS X Software) to get this software.

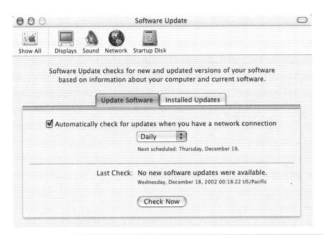

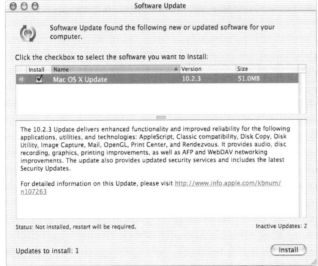

Figure 9.9 I have Software Update set to check for new software every day, so in the top figure, when I did this manual check for software, I was already current. When my system checked again later that week (in the bottom figure), Apple had posted an OS update. You don't have to set your system to check daily, but if you are on a broadband Internet connection, why not? Software Update makes sure you have the latest updates from Apple only, not your other software providers.

Is there another way to check for updates?

A service called VersionTracker (www.versiontracker.com) will watch over the software on your Mac, tell you when updates are available, and help you download them. The company also has an excellent catalog of shareware and freeware available for download. There are both paid and free services available at VersionTracker. You can also search the downloads page of Apple's Mac OS X site (www.apple.com/macosx) and find much of the same material.

Emergency Procedures

Now for the hard stuff.

My Mac won't start properly. What do I do?

If your Mac does something funny—or nothing at all—when you try to start it, first check for anything that might be wrong: stuck keys on the keyboard, stuck mouse buttons, cables that aren't plugged in all the way, that sort of thing.

The First Law of Computer Repair is all-important: It's always a cable until you have proved it can't be.

Once you prove it's not a cable, try booting from your Mac OS X installation CD and see if that works. To do this, hold down the C key while your machine attempts to start up. If it starts up, look to see if the hard drive appears on your desktop, and if all looks good, visit the Startup Disk preferences panel and see what your drive is trying to start up from. If your hard drive isn't selected for some reason, select it and try restarting from the hard drive.

If that doesn't work and the machine still just sits and spins (or doesn't), it's time to call for tech support and repairs. Check for a nearby Apple dealer with a service center, or ask around at your local Macintosh user group—fellow Mac users are usually eager to help.

My hard drive has crashed—now what?

Here's something you need to know—and this is why I hammered you so hard on backing up: The same disk utilities that can salvage your hard drive can also make the problem immeasurably worse.

In a dire situation, I trust Disk Warrior the most (**Figure 9.10**), but I always trust my backups even more. Unless you are a real technical genius with a masochistic streak, you will feel a lot better spending time making sure your automatic backups are really happening than you will about uncrashing a drive.

Figure 9.10 One of my favorite disk utilities is Disk-Warrior. It's saved me when nothing else would.

If you find yourself with a crash and no backups—and if the files are really important to you or expensive to re-create—I'd probably contact a drive-recovery expert (such as DriveSavers at www.drivesavers.com) before attempting a fix myself. If you have backups, of course, you are free to play with all the disk tools you have at your disposal, though only one at a time, please.

You might want to start up from your Mac OS X install disc by putting the disc into your CD and holding down the C key while your system restarts. Then run the Disk Utility program that comes with the installer (**Figure 9.11**). From the Installer menu choose Open Disk Utility. Once it's open, go to the First Aid tab, select your hard drive, and click Repair Disk (**Figure 9.12**). See what happens. When the repair is finished, exit the program without installing the operating system, and reboot. If you have really great Mac karma, your machine will restart and all will be well.

If not, well, I am not comfortable telling you how to do emergency hard-drive engineering—and you should be glad—at least not without being able to see the computer that is having problems and certainly not in the pages of a book. So my best advice: Seek professional help, and start making those backups.

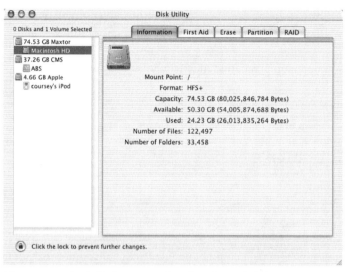

Figure 9.11 Disk Utility is Apple's first line of defense against hard-disk troubles. When you start your machine, it automatically checks your start-up disk, something it cannot do—as you see here—once the system is actually operating.

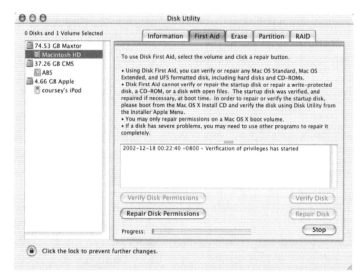

Figure 9.12 In an emergency, you can boot your Mac from the Mac OS X installation disc and then run Disk Utility to try to fix a badly fried hard drive.

What about preventive maintenance?

There is no Jiffy Lube for your Mac, but running a disk utility every month or so is a good idea—right after you've backed up the machine. Hopefully, you will find (and correct) minor problems before they become serious issues. I also like to defragment my hard drive, using Norton Speed Disk, to make sure that all my data is where it should be.

Microsoft Word crashed—where did my data go?

Word v. X will try to recover your data when you restart after a crash. (Yes, this does happen sometimes.) It will find your last saved version, which is why we save files early and often, and it can perform auto-recovery saves, holding on to data even if you haven't saved it yet (**Figure 9.13**). You can set Word to automatically save your document at regular intervals. Look in the Word help system for information on auto-save and -recovery. Do this now, before you need it.

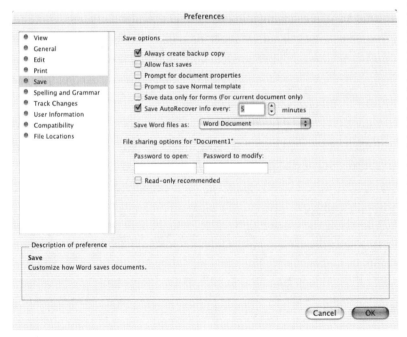

Figure 9.13 In Word's preferences, under the Save item, you will find the AutoRecover setting. Mine is set for 5 minutes, meaning that in case of a system crash I shouldn't lose more than 5 minutes of Word work.

My keyboard/mouse isn't working right—help!

First step is to make sure that something isn't stuck, such as a key or a switch. Or that one of the sticky keys—like that Num Lock key that sits with the Function keys—isn't on. Try unplugging and replugging in the keyboard or mouse USB cable to see if this helps. Or perhaps you have accidentally done something to the settings in the Keyboard, Mouse, or Universal Access preferences panels. That last one can be special fun—makes your keyboard behave in a way that only someone with a disability could truly appreciate—so check it before you call tech support.

Whoops! Something just spilled on my keyboard!

You are now in a place where your warranty won't help you. It is also one of the very rare occasions when I would just reach around and carefully (to avoid electrocution) yank the power cord out of the machine.

In the case of a portable, I'd yank both the power cord and the battery, being careful not to invert the machine until the power is off and the battery is out. Do not try to restart a laptop with a wet keyboard, on pain of frying its logic board. Next stop for you: the repair shop.

If you are using a desktop, hang the keyboard upside down for a day or two and see if it works once it has had a chance to dry. The more sugary and hotter the beverage in question, the lower your chances of success. Assuming that you need to use the computer in the interim, go buy yourself a new keyboard.

The new unit doesn't have to be from Apple, which may make a replacement easier to find. Most (if not all) of the Microsoft USB keyboards have Mac OS X drivers available—check the retail packaging or the Microsoft Mactopia Web site for specifics (www.microsoft.com/mac). In a pinch, a generic PC USB keyboard may be enough to get you temporarily back in business.

My Mac has frozen—what do I do?

Every so often, a Mac OS X application will freeze up, perhaps freezing the whole computer. This is not an operating system crash, and you can Force Quit the offending application without fear of crashing the operating system. But you probably won't be able to salvage unsaved data.

Sometimes an application that seems frozen is just thinking. It occasionally happens that a Mac will sit there with the little rainbow spinning, maybe with the hard drive chugging, maybe not, and if you just wait it out, everything will be fine. So my first step in dealing with a frozen Mac is to go make a cup of tea and see what things look like in 5 or 10 minutes. Then I unplug all the USB and FireWire cables and replace the keyboard and mouse connectors (but only those). People tell me this really works, just never for me.

Other times, I've already had too much caffeine and there is no unsaved data at stake, so I just do a Force Quit. Often the program will tell you that it's no longer responding (look next to the program's name on its window) but sometimes not. Pressing Command-Option-Escape simultaneously brings up a menu of the currently running programs (**Figure 9.14**). (You can also choose Force Quit from the Apple menu to bring up the same menu; **Figure 9.15**.) Often this will tell you which program is frozen, and you can click a button to force it to quit. Sometimes this needs to be done twice.

Figure 9.14 Here's how you quit a program that won't quit any other way: by selecting it from the Force Quit menu and then clicking the Force Quit button.

Figure 9.15 The Apple menu offers a shortcut to the Force Quit menu for those of us not wild about keyboard shortcuts.

Tip: *In Mac OS X 10.2, you can sometimes force-quit an application by Control-clicking its icon in the Dock and then choosing Force Quit in the menu that pops up. This same menu will show you a grayed-out item that says Application Not Responding, which is a good clue that something is wrong with it.*

If your Mac is unresponsive and all else fails, push and hold down the power button for 5 seconds or so, and your Mac will shut down. But only do this as a last resort.

Switcher Diary: PEGGY MILNE

Peggy Milne isn't a total switcher, because her job with a sales rep company requires her to use a Windows PC just like everyone else. And sometimes no matter that you can prove a Mac would be fine for your job, convincing the bosses may not even be worth the effort. But at home, Peg and her children are solidly in the Mac camp, as I found out during our interview.

Peggy: There were *so* many times that the system just crashed for no reason. Networking was such a hassle, and things seemed like they were changing overnight. One day the computer would work fine, and the next day, all my settings were wrong and I couldn't even access the Internet. I honestly could not explain why things kept happening to the computer; it made no sense to me.

David: Do you still use Windows?

Peggy: Yes, I have a PC that my kids use periodically, although they *greatly* prefer the iMac. Also, I have a PC at work.

David: Tell me about how you became a Mac user.

Peggy: My mom has always been a Mac user and has always told me to switch over, but I didn't like the way the old operating systems looked. I also thought that the pricing was prohibitive, and because I have other PCs in my life, I really had to have something that would let me share files seamlessly between the platforms. Until I saw the iMac and Mac OS X, I hadn't really seriously considered switching.

I sent the following email to a friend of mine at Apple who had worked with me on answering some questions about switching, like "Can it really do that?" and "Will it really work with my home network?"

The reason it's a good email to share with you is that it's the first email from my new iMac, and my enthusiasm for the experience was pretty clear:

"This was the greatest experience in my computing career. I got the iMac yesterday but didn't have the time to set it up, so when I woke up this morning I was stoked to get going. I pretty much had the day free, and figured I would keep track of the time, just to see how long it took.

"At 10:15 a.m., I started taking apart my PC, with its associated cables and various external components. It took me about 20 minutes just to get that out of the way. I opened the iMac box and took out the iMac. I know you've probably heard this a million times, but you have the best packaging of any product on the market. It is so clean and practical. I cannot imagine getting an "instruction manual" with a PC that is basically just a poster with a bunch of photos! Beautiful!

"It took me under 10 minutes to get the iMac plugged in and connected to my wireless network. What a total no-brainer! I kept thinking, "Well, this is probably where I'm going to get hung up on something," but there wasn't a single bizarre message. In fact, it was so easy, I started to laugh with euphoria!

Switcher Diary: PEGGY MILNE

"I cannot tell you how thrilled I am with the iMac. As the guy on one of your ads says, I only wish I'd switched sooner!

So, the gist of this is that the entire process of "switching" took me 30 minutes, of which 20 minutes was spent on getting rid of the PC!

David: Is your Mac a good value? How do you feel about Mac pricing?

Peggy: I think the iMac pricing was very good. For the beauty of the machine alone, it was worth it. Of course, that it's incredibly powerful and reliable helps a great deal. I was promised two $100 rebates (one for the software and one for the printer), and only one of them could be processed, so frankly that was the only thing that was a downer about the purchase.

I would not have purchased the printer if I'd known that I wouldn't get the money back for it as the guy promised. Maybe he just didn't know how the rebate program worked. Other than that, the value was good.

David: What do you consider to be the most important differences between using a Mac and using a PC?

Peggy: It works, there are no funny messages, and the physical machine is beautiful—no more ugly tower sitting beside my desk!

David: Any comments about Mac hardware?

Peggy: The keyboard clicking took a bit of getting used to, and I must say that I would really *love* to have a better mouse with a scroll feature in it. Maybe there is one and I just don't know about it. I have a Logitech mouse at my office that I love. Anyway, other than that, I love the hardware. Everything is so beautiful to look at, no nasty wires all over the place, and the white color is very appealing.

David: And the software?

Peggy: The Mac software that I mostly use is the Office suite for Mac, which is just like I was using on the PC. There are a couple of differences, but nothing too major. I *love* iPhoto and iTunes. There's *nothing* like those that I've seen on the PC. Absolutely wonderful! I'm finally saving my photos the way I wanted to but couldn't get to on the PC. I also have an iPod, which I love.

David: What was the most confusing part of using Mac OS?

Peggy: I had a hard time getting the printer set up. I accidentally deleted the printer setup and it took a while to get it loaded again properly. Other than that, I haven't really had to do much with the OS. It's pretty intuitive, though, so I'm sure I could figure it out if I had any problem.

My Annotated Top 10 Reasons to Switch

The Apple Web site includes the company's Top 10 reasons why Windows users should switch to the Macintosh. Seems worth repeating and commenting on, as a bit of a reality check. It can also serve as a reminder of why you bought this book and a little of what we've learned along the way.

1. The Mac … it just works.

Ask them—the millions of people who use and love their Macs— why it's become such an integral part of their lives, and most will tell you that it's because it just works. Letting them do what they want to do. How they want to do it. Intuitively. And there's good reason. Only with a Mac do you find absolutely flawless integration of hardware and software. Only with a Mac do you get an operating system built by the same people who built the computer it runs on. Take a Mac out of its box, and you experience that hand-in-glove fit from the get-go. Plug it in. Turn it on. And you're ready for anything. That's because with a Mac, you'll find all of the essentials built right in. USB. FireWire (IEEE 1394). Ethernet. Modem. Macs even come with built-in antennas for wireless networks. And every Mac comes with drivers for most of the printers, joysticks, DV camcorders, keyboards, storage devices, digital cameras, input devices, MP3 players, and game pads you'll be connecting to those ports. So when you plug them in for the first time, they'll just work, too.

Isn't it amazing what a monopoly can do? Since Apple builds the machines, develops the operating system, increasingly creates the applications, and even sells peripherals (such as the iPod), isn't it all supposed to fit together? It is, and with Apple it does.

I've talked to hundreds of Switchers, and the most common thing they tell me about their Mac is that, well, it does just work. They also say something closely related: It gets out of their way.

The problem with Windows is that nobody ever stopped it. I mean this in the sense that nobody ever said that Windows had simply gotten too big—was trying to do too much—and that stacking layer upon layer of new things on top of all the old isn't the solution, it's the problem.

The Mac does not try to do everything a computer can possibly do. It tries and mostly succeeds at being a computer that real people can use to accomplish real work. It's not intimidating, and like everyone says, it just works.

Of course, this is only possible because Apple is a small company. Imagine what Microsoft would do if it could control both Windows software and PC hardware as tightly as Apple does its operating system and hardware. Of course, we can only imagine, because the federal courts would never allow it. In fact, Microsoft's success (and Apple's failure to beat Windows) is largely because Microsoft tried to support everyone and every machine—while still managing to put competitors out of business. Neat trick.

Apple, meanwhile, has had the benefit of being able to stick to what it does really well, without the burden of being the overwhelming market leader. If Microsoft had failed and Apple had won, you can bet that Apple would be more messed up today than Microsoft.

Instead, Apple has had tremendous freedom to innovate, including a major rethinking of its operating system. And we are the happy beneficiaries.

So when Apple says the Mac "just works," it's not making it up—just listen to what its customers say. Add "and it gets out of my way," and you have the two best, if a tad nebulous, reasons to switch.

Nebulous because Windows users have to be so involved with the computer that it's hard for them to imagine life being different. Not having to worry, at least occasionally, about arcane control-panel settings. Not leaving the computer and coming back to find that it works differently than before you restarted.

As for the Mac, it really does, well, you know.

2. It doesn't crash.

Are you just a tad too well acquainted with the notorious "blue screen of death"? Bid it a fond farewell. With Mac OS X, you'll become accustomed instead to industry-leading stability. In this elegant new operating system, memory is fully protected and applications can't conflict with the OS or one another. And, oh yes, Mac OS X is built on the industrial strength of Unix. Most Fortune 500 companies, governments, and universities rely on Unix for their mission-critical applications. And now, so can you.

To be fair, Windows XP is pretty crash-proof, too. Both, however, are prone to a long moment of introspection when something goes wrong with an application. Crash-worthiness is almost as important in operating systems as it is in automobiles. Think of Mac OS X as a Volvo and Windows XP as, well, whatever is a close second to fine Swedish engineering.

If you are running Windows 98 and merely want an operating system that's pretty stable, you don't have to buy a Mac—unless, of course, your old PC is short the horsepower that Windows XP requires.

(I think a 500 MHz Pentium III with 512 MB of RAM is the slowest machine it makes sense to upgrade to Windows XP.

If your PC was purchased with Windows 95, even if you've upgraded to Windows 98 or the brain-dead Windows Me, you're out of luck. I would not upgrade such a machine to XP.)

One of the goals of this book is to help someone who is running Windows 98 and is ready to buy a new machine make a Mac versus PC decision. I think the Mac offers lots of things Windows doesn't that deserve consideration.

System stability is not one of them, however—at least when you compare Mac OS X with Windows XP. Sure, out at some decimal place, I am willing to bet the Mac is still more stable, but it's not something I've noticed in comparing the two systems.

3. Simply the best in digital music.

The critics all agree (and how often does that happen?)— not only does iTunes turn the Mac into an unequaled digital jukebox, but iPod has no peer among MP3 players on the market today. iTunes makes it easy to convert the music from your CD collection into MP3 files. Lets you make playlists to match your every mood. Offers one-button burning of audio CDs. And seamless integration with MP3 players. Like iPod. Which fits in your pocket, weighs as little as 6.5 ounces, holds up to 4,000 songs, features lightning-fast music transfers via FireWire, plays for up to 10 hours, and lets you bring your music wherever you go.

If you buy a Mac and listen to music, be sure to buy an iPod, too. It's the best MP3 player on the market, and less pricey than it used to be. I keep mine filled with old radio programs (*Dragnet*, Jack Benny shows, *The Great Gildersleeve*), Audible talking books, and a collection of, well, Abba music. Didn't I tell you Mac users tend toward eccentric?

What makes the iPod so great is that it takes advantage of all the things Apple is good at and brings them together in a great-looking package. Let's see, Apple designed the high-speed FireWire port that makes it possible for music to zip between the computer and iPod at a rate that makes having thousands of songs on a portable device practical. And through the FireWire cable, a Mac even recharges the iPod's battery, the sort of nice touch that Apple users expect but still love.

There's the very Mac-looking user interface on the iPod. Like the Mac itself, it doesn't overreach to provide more features than you are actually going to use. Could there be more to the iPod? Yes. Apple did add a calendar and contacts, and although I had a hard time imagining an MP3 player becoming a PDA, the company managed to pull it off. No, you can't enter information in the iPod, but all I really need is to be able to refer to my calendar and phone list, not rewrite it on the run.

iTunes is also a gem and was designed both to be a great stand-alone music player on the Mac and to serve as the front end for synchronizing your Desktop and mobile music libraries.

All this works so well because Apple's designers and engineers and, most important, sensibility were there every step of the way.

4. The missing link in digital photography.

Everyone loves iPhoto, which revolutionizes the way you save, organize, share, and enjoy digital photos. Included with every Mac, iPhoto lets you easily download, organize, find, and share your photos—as prints, in a slide show, or on a Web site it will even help you build. Simply drag your mouse, and iPhoto magically grows or shrinks your photo thumbnails. So you can view individual shots in detail or see hundreds of photos on the screen at once and quickly scroll through thousands to find the one you're looking for. iPhoto even lets you create your own custom coffee-table books. You may never go back to using a film camera again.

iPhoto is not the be all and end all of digital photography. It's a wonderful tool for downloading and managing huge collections of digital images. It also has some printing and publishing capabilities. And I love the coffee-table books that you can order using iPhoto.

But I have taken very few digital pictures that didn't benefit from the automatic adjustments in a good photo-editing package, which requires more than iPhoto can offer. Good thing there is Adobe's Photoshop Elements, a great editing program that fills in iPhoto's gaps. Although it's not Photoshop (the pro package that takes forever to learn), Elements is easy to learn and use—and much less expensive.

So try iPhoto first, but if you feel that something is missing—like the ability to get really creative or to solve problems in your images—then Photoshop Elements is an excellent way to spend less than $100.

5. Your own digital entertainment center.

Designed and built for today's digital lifestyle, the Mac offers a complete ensemble of digital tools. In addition to iTunes and iPhoto, Macs come with iMovie and, on all systems equipped with a SuperDrive, iDVD as well. Like the Mac itself, they're easy to use and work together flawlessly. You'll use iMovie to turn raw video footage into polished films—complete with sound tracks, titling, and effects—that friends will actually ask to watch over and over again. And iDVD will let you burn your photos and movies onto DVDs that can be played on most commercially available DVD players.

Digital photography and home videos are very good reasons to buy a Mac. iMovie is a great program, and iDVD is simply amazing. There is no comparison between raw video footage and an edited presentation, and iMovie makes it so easy. The Macs with SuperDrives are also very competitive—inexpensive even—compared with adding a DVD burner to a PC.

In fact, as I write this, the high-end iMac with the DVD burner and 17-inch display costs $2,000. Upgrading my current PC with a burner and big LCD-panel monitor would cost more than $1,000. Add the value of iMovie and iDVD, $200 or more, and it's almost as if Apple is giving the computer itself away. Tell *that* to people who say Macs are too expensive.

Further, because iMovie has a user interface that is built atop the Mac way of doing things—which Apple keeps a tight rein on—it works enough like the rest of the computer that you can concentrate on the video editing itself, rather than odd things about the user interface.

6. Goes everywhere you go.

We think computing on the go should always be a first-class experience. That's why we design our PowerBook and iBook computers the way we do. Light. Thin. Displays so bright and clear, you'd think you're working on a desktop system. And they come standard with what some other laptops consider "extras": capacious hard drives, built-in optical drives, USB, FireWire, Ethernet, modem, video out, audio in, Wi-Fi. Consider this: Can your PC laptop go coast to coast with just one battery? Can you put the system to sleep just by closing the lid? Does it wake up instantly? Can your PC laptop automatically switch between Ethernet, dial-up, and wireless connections on the fly? Without a restart? Ours can.

iBooks are reasonably priced, and PowerBooks, while not overpriced, cost more than most people want to spend. You probably won't confuse working on a portable Mac with working on a desktop Mac. And I generally wish laptop Macs had more memory and larger hard drives, and were less expensive. But I say that about Windows notebooks, too.

People who aren't ready to replace their Windows desktop PC with a Mac would do well to buy a Mac laptop. iBooks really are great machines and wonderful traveling companions. If you mostly use Microsoft Office and don't have to connect directly to an Exchange server, an iBook or PowerBook is perfect.

(As I discussed in an earlier chapter, Microsoft has, it seems rather intentionally, not built an Exchange client for Mac OS X. Instead it created Entourage, a possible sign that Microsoft doesn't want Macintosh to be considered a "serious" computer. Here's a workaround: If you need to use an Exchange server, ask your mail administrator about using Outlook Web Access to get into your account from any Web browser. Or have your email automatically forwarded to your .Mac email or some other account.)

7. It's built for the Internet.

When did you last configure a PC for the Internet? Take you long? It won't on a Mac. Fact is, most of our customers are up and surfing within 15 minutes. And that includes people who never touched a computer before in their lives. What will your experience be like? You'll find moving your favorites, email contacts, and email messages to the Mac mere child's play. And wait till you try the software. Microsoft built features into Explorer

*and Entourage found nowhere else, features that make brows-
ing and email on a Mac an absolute joy. Feel like chatting?
AOL Instant Messenger, Yahoo Messenger, MSN Messenger—
all your favorites are available. In fact, you'll find tons of Internet tool options. That includes QuickTime. When it comes to
world-class streaming video, no product offers a better digital
media experience. (And with QuickTime 6, we just upped the
ante.) Of course on a Mac, it's just as easy to stream video,
chat, read email, and surf wirelessly. That's because every
Mac is ready for Wi-Fi (802.11)—we call it AirPort—right out
of the box.*

Experienced Windows users are amazed at how easy Windows
XP makes setting up a network, especially a wireless one. But
the Mac makes this even easier, and AirPort wireless networking
is a dream. Those looking for an easy Internet experience
should buy a Mac—with one caveat: If you need all sorts of
special network or VPN settings (and if you do, you probably
already know), you may not find what you need on a Mac.
As I write this, I am not clear on which of the third-party VPN
software clients will solve this problem or whether Apple will
step up and solve it, saving us all some money.

If you positively have to use your corporate network from
your Mac, make sure it works with the network before you
buy it. Your system administrator should know, or check with
Apple support for information more current than I am able to
provide here. However, 99 percent of users will never notice
the VPN issue.

Know an Internet virgin? Get him or her a Mac.

8. Office is Office, and then some.

*The transition to a Mac is easy in part because you'll continue
using the same applications you already know. Microsoft Office
v. X for Mac OS X gives you Word, PowerPoint and Excel, all
with the same familiar features and shortcut commands. And
thanks to exclusive features, the Mac versions improve on their
Windows counterparts. Office documents are all fully compatible between Mac and Windows, so you can share everything
from spreadsheets to presentations. Beyond Office, you'll find*

you can run more than 3,000 applications designed specifically for Apple's new operating system, Mac OS X. You can do anything you'd dream of doing on the Mac—from CAD to databases to finance.

Microsoft Office is a very different set of applications on Mac than on Windows. There's no Access, for starters, and Outlook is replaced by an OK-but-not-great program called Entourage.

Despite significant differences, Word on Mac OS X feels very much like Word on Windows. All the features most people actually use are there, without all the stuff Microsoft keeps adding in hopes of persuading people to upgrade every two years.

As for the 3,000 applications available on the Mac, many of them are shareware and freeware, so don't think you really have that many commercial-grade apps to choose from.

A whole section of this book is dedicated to the "Is there enough software?" question. In general, there's at least one application for all the major categories, and it's often excellent. But very specific software probably doesn't exist—things such as Quicken's cool point-of-sale system or the applications we use in search and rescue.

The answer to the "software question" is sometimes just to purchase a copy of Connectix's Virtual PC, which allows Windows to run on your PC. For the couple of "must-have" Windows apps in my life, Virtual PC is a good answer.

9. Works effortlessly with PCs.

Standards let everyone work together harmoniously. That's why Apple has adopted so many of them. Take networking. Networking on a Mac is built on the same technologies used by PCs. As a result, the Mac is at home on PC networks (or just about any other kind), making the business of sharing files and printers with PCs entirely painless. And in Mac OS X you don't have to be a network administrator to make it all work. What's more, Gigabit Ethernet is built in. As is support for 802.11 wireless, so you can network without cables inside your house using AirPort or another wireless access point. Of course, you can also swap files via data CD, floppies, or Zip disks. And most new peripherals connect via USB or FireWire (two other industry standards), so you can use them with either PCs or Macs.

Apple's AirPort is the easiest way to set up an 802.11b/Wi-Fi wireless network, and USB and FireWire are both standards. Gigabit Ethernet sounds impressive but requires special hardware that most of us don't have. Not to worry—Apple's Ethernet works just fine at the commonly used speeds of 100 Mbps and 10 Mbps.

However, Apple hasn't said if or when it will support the new, faster USB 2.0 protocol, and FireWire (also known as IEEE 1394) is widely used only with digital video cameras and external hard drives. I don't see a reason for Apple users to purchase USB 2.0 peripherals right away. If you already own some, you might purchase one of the USB 2.0 add-in cards for the desktop Power Mac G4s offered by such companies as Orange Micro.

As for effortlessly working together, Mac OS X 10.2 Jaguar makes it fairly easy to connect Windows machines and Macs together for file sharing. "Entirely painless" probably stretches it a bit.

Connecting a Mac to a PC network (or vice versa) is quite easy. Power network users should consider a third-party add-on called Dave, from Thursby Software (www.thursby.com) that turns a Mac into a better client for corporate networks.

Home network users can save the extra $149—the Windows networking built into Mac OS X should be fine.

10. It's beautiful.

Our designers and engineers agonize over every millimeter of every new Macintosh model and every pixel of the user interface. The result: ergonomic products that are the toast of the design world. iMac. PowerBook. iPod. iBook. You can see obsession with design and detail wherever you look: the spring-loaded screws that secure the bottom plate of the new iMac, laser-etched text where others would put a sticker, the tough colorfast polycarbonate cases of the iMac and eMac, the swing-away door on the Power Mac G4, the elegant optical mouse included with all desktop Macs, the instructions on the back of the door you open to add memory to an iBook or PowerBook. They're objects that would be striking even if they weren't computers. Tools that are, at every level, a pleasure to use.

This is another way of saying, "Life's too short to use an ugly computer." And while all those manufacturing details cost money, I have never seen a PC built as well as a Mac. Or one that looks as nice.

Is there a real benefit to good looks and fit and finish? Depends on whether you find joy in using a really great tool. If you do and appreciate the attention that serious designers put into minute details, then you're already a Mac person, whether you know it or not.

If you don't notice these things, maybe it's time you started. You may not be able to afford one of the world's truly great automobiles or regularly dine at Michelin three-star restaurants, but you can afford a Mac. And that's a pretty good start.

So there you have Apple's official "Top 10 Reasons to Switch," along with some comments that I hope will bring some perspective to the advertising copy. Although Apple certainly spared no sunshine—reduce the brightness by half to avoid damaging your eyes—the gist of the 10 reasons the company gives is true. And these are the things Mac users love about their machines.

Thank You for Reading My Book

Thank you so much for reading my book. I hope you found it interesting and perhaps even entertaining. But mostly, I hope it either helped you decide whether a Mac is right for you or, if you'd already made that decision, got you started successfully.

I am sorry for all the things I did not put in this book. I apologize if I led you astray at any point. And I should be whipped for assuming you know either too much or too little about Windows. Or Macintosh.

Mea culpa.

Since you read my book, the least I can do is read your email. I would love to read your comments, including corrections, clarifications, and things you'd like put in or left out if I do another edition. Please write me at book@coursey.com or visit www.coursey.com. I cannot promise to answer all your emails, but I will do my best, and I will read and consider each one.

You can also visit me at www.anchordesk.com and at www. cnetradio.com.

Switcher Diary: GREGORY PIERCE

Ex-Microsoft programmer "used to be a big fan" of Windows

A former Microsoft employee, Gregory Pierce liked Windows so much that he once coauthored a book about a piece of its technology called Direct3D. But today he only uses Windows to play games (a common knock against Macintosh) and for a few programming tools that aren't available for Mac.

Gregory: I am extremely proficient in using and coding for Windows. There aren't too many things I can't do with Windows, including hopping into regedit to hack some nVidia drivers or setting up a Web server.

I still like Windows, but only really because that's where the games are. As Microsoft pushes the Xbox more and more and as other vendors satisfy my gaming needs without the need for a PC, this becomes less and less important.

David: What did/do you like least about Windows?

Gregory: Well, there is a lot not to like about Windows. Windows is hard to keep configured a specific way because everyone and their mother installs things all over the place and corrupts the registry.

Getting an application to be the default application for a type of file became easier over time but is still a pain. Then there are hardware blue screens. There would be times that you'd drop in a piece of hardware and the machine just wouldn't boot and you'd spend a few hours trying to find out what didn't work and cobble Windows together enough so you could get to the Internet to download a driver.

Then there are the driver models for Windows that people just seem to ignore. To me, every driver should have to pass certification tests or the OS should just reject it. But that's just me—I favor stability more than having a million different versions of crappy sub-$100 hardware selections.

David: How did you become a Mac user?

Gregory: I became a Mac user because I needed a single OS that let me do everything that I needed to do (whereas games are more a want than a need). I grew tired of fighting with Linux and its arcane application suite and configuration process that only a programmer could love.

But I needed to operate more in the Unix world. I needed more practical experience with an OS that for years I had avoided because to me it made less sense and was harder to use than Windows. So I figured I'd give this new Mac OS X thing a run. So I had to swallow my pride (I've mocked and hated Macs for *so* long) and experiment.

Here at the office there was one of those nasty "Grape" iMacs, so I installed a copy of Mac OS X on it and was pleasantly surprised with how much it didn't absolutely disgust me. So I took a few more steps. I acquired the

Switcher Diary: GREGORY PIERCE

Mac by trading away a Solaris terminal that I rarely used, and determined that I was going to actually try to do work on the thing.

Since I work with Java for a living, the migration was painless, and within a few days I was actually doing all my work on the iMac. Then I figured I'd try my hand at that newfangled version of Office for the Mac, and lo and behold, it was excellent—somehow a lot cleaner and less bloated than the Windows version. But it was slow. Since folks here still think of Macs mostly as toys (except for a group of us on a crazy-ones mailing list), getting another one through the office was likely out of the question. And since I really wanted to do a lot of coding at home, I figured I'd pick up a new Mac and purchased a PowerBook G4.

David: Is your Mac a good value? How do you feel about Mac pricing?

Gregory: Absolutely. Except for those rare instances where I have something that must run in Windows, I just seem to get a lot more done on the Mac (which does occasionally crash despite the ads, though that would be twice since I've owned the Mac as opposed to three to five times a week with Windows 2000).

David: What are the most important differences between using a Mac and using a PC?

Gregory: Well, as much as I hate restating marketing stuff, the Mac "just works." I plug stuff in, and standard applications or applications that I can configure open up and I do work. It's just that easy. I don't have a piece of hardware in my repository that won't work with it—easily. I was incredibly impressed when my brand-new Olympus camera was plugged in and it worked. I didn't even have to install a driver or software.

David: Is there anything you want to do on your Mac that you cannot do because the software is Windows-only?

Gregory: Games.

David: Did you make any changes in the applications you use or how you use them when you switched?

Gregory: I take a lot more photos now because it's easier to get them onto my Web site, and I've started to look more at programming in Perl and PHP now that I have an environment that more cleanly supports it.

Keyboard Shortcuts

Probably the first thing you'll notice after you set up your Mac is that you don't have a two-button mouse. (If you really miss your two-button mouse, however, you can pick up one from a handful of third-party companies that do make them for the Mac.) You can still get to an item's shortcut menu (called a *contextual menu* on the Mac), however, through a keyboard shortcut: Hold down the Control key while clicking an item, and a contextual menu pops up next to it (**Figure A.1**).

The second thing you may notice is that your Mac's keyboard doesn't have an Alt key. Instead, you see a key with a clover-leaf-like symbol and the Apple logo. Apple calls this the Command key, and it behaves like Windows' Ctlr key. You'll also find an Option key, which performs similar functions to Windows' Alt key, and a Ctrl key, which helps compensate for the lack of a second button on your mouse.

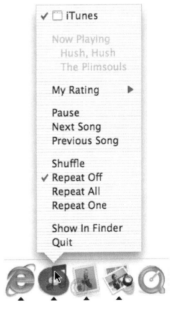

Figure A.1 By clicking an item while holding down the Control key (here, I'm Control-clicking iTunes in the Dock), you can select from handy commands associated with the item.

But like Windows, Mac OS X has a bunch of useful keyboard shortcuts. This list isn't comprehensive (by working your way through the various menus, you can find many of the shortcuts), but after you get used to the one-button mouse and new keys, these shortcuts can save you a lot of time.

General Shortcuts

To do this action	Use this shortcut
Move highlighted item to Trash	Command-Delete
Empty Trash	Command-Shift-Delete
Empty Trash with no warning dialog	Option-Empty Trash
Create a new Finder window	Command-N
Create a new folder	Command-Shift-N
Go to your Home directory	Command-H
Go to your Applications folder	Command-Shift-A
Duplicate an item	Command-D
Create an alias	Command-L
Add to Favorites	Command-T
Find	Command-F
Get help	Command-?
Log out	Command-Shift-Q
Turn off your computer	Power key

Menu Shortcuts

To do this action	Use this shortcut
Undo	Command-Z
Cut	Command-X
Copy	Command-C
Paste	Command-V
View as icons	Command-1
View as List	Command-2
View as Columns	Command-3

Window Shortcuts

To do this action	Use this shortcut
Close a window	Command-W
Close all open windows	Option-click close button
Minimize a window	Command-M
Minimize all open windows	Option-click minimize button
Hide all application windows except the one you're in	Command-Option-H
Move a window without making it active	Command-drag window
Choose a folder that contains the current folder	Command-click window title

Dock Shortcuts

To do this action	Use this shortcut
Hide or show the Dock	Command-Option-D
Change the size of the Dock	Drag the dividing line
See the contextual menu	Control-click an icon in the Dock
Quit an open application	Click its icon, and choose Quit
Force-quit an application	Hold down the Option key, click its icon, and then choose Force Quit
Switch from one open application to the next	Press Command and Tab
	To reverse the order, hold down the Command and Shift keys and press Tab
Hide the active application	Command-H
Quit the selected application	Command-Q
Force an application to open when you drag a document onto it	Command-Option

Dialog Shortcuts

To do this action	Use this shortcut
Select the next area of the dialog	Tab
Click the default button	Return or Enter
Click the Cancel button	Esc
Close the dialog	Escape or Command-period (.)
Select folders above or below the current item (Save and Open dialogs)	Up arrow and down arrow
Scroll list up	Page up
Scroll list down	Page down

Icon Shortcuts

To do this action	Use this shortcut
Select an icon by the first letter of its name	Letter key
Select the next icon	Arrow keys
Select the next icon alphabetically	Tab
Add an icon to the selection	Shift-click
Select adjacent icons in a list	Shift-click
Select or deselect nonadjacent icons in a list	Command-click
Select all icons	Command-A
Select the name of the icon	Return
See the contextual menu	Control-click icon

Startup Shortcuts

To do this action	Use this shortcut
Start up from a CD	C
Select a startup disk (on some computers)	Option
Prevent startup items from opening	Shift key
Start up from an external drive	Command-Option-Shift-Delete
Eject a stuck CD or DVD	Press mouse button down
Reset Parameter RAM	Command-Option-P-R

Screen-Capture Shortcuts

To do this action	Use this shortcut
Take a picture of the whole screen	Command-Shift-3
Take a picture of part of the screen to select the area you want in the picture	Command-Shift-4, and then drag
Take a picture of a window, menu bar, the Dock, or other area	Command-Shift-4, and then press the Space bar. Move the pointer over the area you want so that it's highlighted and then click.

Troubleshooting Shortcuts

To do this action	Use this shortcut
Stop a process	Command-period (.)
Force an application to quit	Command-Option-Escape
Force some computers to shut down or restart	Command-Option-Shift-Power key
Force the computer to restart	Command-Control-Power button

Resources

Like some things in life—having kids, for example, or rooting for the Red Sox—owning a Mac makes you part of a tight-knit community you barely knew existed before.

Mac users are a welcoming bunch, full of useful advice they gladly share.

Apple's Safari and the version of Microsoft Internet Explorer that comes with Mac OS X is preloaded with plenty of Macintosh-related links. They are a good start, but we have our own set of Web sites we check frequently—and some daily.

News and Troubleshooting

MacCentral *http://maccentral.macworld.com*
Look here for no-nonsense, timely Apple industry news.

MacFixIt *www.macfixit.com*
If your Mac is acting funny, check here. If someone else is having the same problem, chances are you can learn about it—and learn how to fix it—at MacFixIt.

MacInTouch *www.macintouch.com*
Great site for Mac news, information, and analysis. At times, MacInTouch is almost an advocacy group for Mac users.

MacSlash *www.macslash.com*
Similar to Slashdot, the popular programmers' discussion site, this Macintosh news and discussion forum is updated daily. Good for finding out what loyal Mac users *really* think.

MacNN *www.macnn.com*

Good, prompt news coverage with analysis.

MacWindows *www.macwindows.com*

Focuses on making Macs and Windows machines work together.

Tidbits *www.tidbits.com*

A wonderful online publication full of useful news and insights.

Magazines

MacAddict *www.macaddict.com*

News, reviews, and how-tos with attitude.

MacHome *www.machome.com*

Magazine written for the personal—as opposed to professional—user.

Macworld *www.macworld.com*

The first Mac magazine and still the best.

Apple Sites

AppleCare Support *www.info.apple.com*

First stop for Apple's news, discussion groups, and software downloads.

Mac OS X *www.apple.com/macosx*

Apple's home base for Mac OS X.

.Mac *www.mac.com*

If you have a .Mac account, here's where you can get the latest software, participate in discussion groups, get support, access your Web mail, and more.

Switching *www.apple.com/switch*

Apple helps you make the switch here. Plus, all the commercials.

Third-Party Software and Other Sites

dealmac *www.dealmac.com*
Provides useful information on buying Apple and third-party products.

Detto *www.detto.com*
Software for making the switch.

The Mac Orchard *www.macorchard.com*
Clearinghouse for Internet-related applications for the Mac.

MacUpdate *www.macupdate.com*
A comprehensive site for software updates.

Making the Macintosh *http://library.stanford.edu/mac*
A tremendous online resource that documents the history of the Macintosh.

Mactopia *www.mactopia.com*
News, updates, and support for Microsoft's Mac applications from Microsoft's Mac software division.

Small Dog Electronics *www.smalldog.com*
The online Apple Store is a fine place to buy Mac products, but many swear by this site, too.

VersionTracker *www.versiontracker.com*
Look here for an exhaustive list of Mac OS X software updates.

Transition Glossary

This glossary contains definitions for some common Mac OS X terms and functions. The corresponding Windows terminology cross-references to the Mac terms. If a common Windows term or function is not listed, then it is similar to the Mac version.

A

About The command that tells you the version of the software you're using can be found in the application menu (the one with the name of the program), not in the Help menu, as in Windows.

Accessibility Options See *Universal Access*.

Accounts The System Preferences panel that allows you to add or delete users and determine their privileges on the Mac. The Windows Control Panel counterpart is Users.

active window The topmost window; the window that is currently receiving mouse and keyboard input. In Mac OS X, this window is identified by the colored buttons in the upper left (inactive windows have clear buttons). In Windows, the active window has color in its title bar; inactive windows have gray bars.

Add New Hardware There is no equivalent on the Mac. Most hardware comes with its own installers, as in Windows.

Add/Remove Programs There is no Mac equivalent. Most program removal is handled in a straightforward manner, by dragging the application to the Trash.

AirPort and **AirPort Extreme** Apple's wireless networking technologies. There are AirPort cards, which fit into Macs, and AirPort Base Stations, which communicate with the cards. Apple's version of wireless networking comes in two flavors: The first, which Apple calls AirPort (and which is also known as 802.11b in PC circles), runs as fast as 11 Mbps; the second, AirPort Extreme (also called 802.11g) can communicate as fast as 54 Mbps. The two are compatible, so an AirPort device can talk with AirPort Extreme device, although at the lower 11-Mbps transfer rate.

alias A file that points to another item, such as a file, folder, or application. When you double-click the alias, the item it points to is opened. Aliases can be identified by the small arrow at the bottom left of the icon. Aliases are equivalent to shortcuts in Windows.

Alt key See *Option key*.

Alt-Tab See *program switching*.

Alt-Z See *undo*.

anti-aliasing The blurring of certain pixels to smooth out an image. Usually used to make onscreen fonts easier to read.

Apple menu The menu on the far left of the menu bar, marked by the Apple icon. It contains the main commands for the entire system. It is somewhat similar to Windows's Start menu.

AppleScript A simple programming language you can use to automate your Mac. There is no built-in equivalent on Windows.

application menu The menu bearing the name of the currently active program. It usually contains general commands such as Preferences and Hide.

Applications folder The folder on your hard disk displaying an "A" holds your Mac OS X applications.

Aqua The name of the interface in Mac OS X. So called because of its translucent blue highlights.

C

Carbon A developer's tool to write programs that run in Mac OS X as well as older versions of the Mac OS. Such applications are often referred to as "Carbonized."

Clipboard A special section of memory dedicated to items you cut and paste. When you use the Cut command, the selection is placed in the Clipboard. Paste places what is in the Clipboard at the insertion point. This is basically the same in Windows.

Classic environment A component of Mac OS X that allows you to run older Mac programs not designed for Apple's latest OS. It is basically a way to run Mac OS 9 along with Mac OS X. Applications not updated for Carbon run in the Classic environment; applications updated for Carbon run natively in Mac OS X.

command-line interface An interface where the user types in commands after a prompt, such as C:>, to give the computer instructions. Unix uses a command-line interface. Compare with *graphical user interface.*

Command-Option-Escape The command to open the Force Quit window. The Windows counterpart is Ctrl-Alt-Delete.

Computer A Finder window that shows local disks and computers that the Mac is connected to. Anything attached to the Mac shows up here.

Ctrl-Alt-Delete See *Command-Option-Escape.*

control panel See *System Preferences.*

cross-platform An adjective describing something compatible with more than one type of computer system. For example, Microsoft Word files are cross-platform because they can be opened and edited on both Macintosh and Windows computers.

cursor A graphic symbol that indicates where a user-initiated action will take place. On the Mac, the cursor is often a pointer. The cursor often changes appearance depending on what is happening. For example, if the computer is busy, the Mac cursor changes to a spinning ball; when this happens in Windows, the cursor becomes an hourglass.

D

Darwin The Unix underpinnings of Mac OS X. Darwin is available to open-source developers.

Desktop The main area of the Mac OS screen; the part that contains icons for drives, files, folders, and the Trash.

Desktop picture An image displayed as the background to your Desktop. It's basically the same thing as wallpaper in Windows.

disk letters There are no letters to denote drives (such as C: for the main hard drive) on the Mac. Each disk has a name, such as "Macintosh HD" or "Spot."

Dock The Dock is a strip of icons representing running applications and frequently used items. Open or launch items by clicking them in the Dock. If you seek functionality similar to that of the Windows Start menu, you can place the Applications folder in the Dock. Click and hold the folder icon in the Dock, and a list of applications pops up. Select an application to launch it. The Dock performs some of the functions of the Start menu and taskbar.

Documents folder The default folder where most programs store a user's documents. You don't have to store your documents there, however. Because Mac OS X is designed to support multiple users on a single machine, there may be more than one Documents folder—one for each user.

E

emulation Mimicking another program or hardware device in software. For example, the Macintosh program Virtual PC emulates the Windows environment, allowing you to run Windows programs on your Mac.

Energy Saver The System Preferences panel that controls when your monitor, drives, and computer are turned off after a period of inactivity. It's similar to the Power Management control panel in Windows.

F

Finder The main application of the Mac OS. The Finder manages the Mac's files and folders. It's always running (except when using certain advanced troubleshooting techniques).

FireWire and **FireWire 800** Communications standards developed by Apple. They transmit data, video, audio, and power over a single line. FireWire can transfer data at up to 400 MBps (more than 30 times faster than USB 1.2) and FireWire 800 has a data-transfer speed of 800 MBps (nearly double USB 2.0). FireWire is a popular choice for digital audio and video professionals. How popular? In 2001, Apple won an Emmy Award for FireWire's impact on the TV industry.

G

Go menu A navigational menu in Mac OS X. You can open specific folders or connect to servers from this menu.

graphical user interface A graphical user interface, or GUI, uses a computer's graphical capabilities to make the computer easier to use. A GUI usually features menus and icons, which represent disks, folders, and files. Commands are sent to the computer via mouse-clicks. The antithesis of a GUI is a command-line interface, where the user types commands after a prompt, such as C:>. DOS and Unix use command-line interfaces.

GUI See *graphical user interface.*

I

icon A graphic representation of a file, application, or folder.

insertion point The place where items are placed in documents when you type or paste. It's usually a blinking vertical bar.

interface The means by which a user communicates with the computer. Mac OS X and Windows use a graphical user interface. Unix, Mac OS X's core system, uses a command-line interface.

International The System Preferences panel that sets what language the Mac uses and how it displays dates, time, and numbers. Similar to the Regional Settings control panel in Windows.

J

Java A cross-platform programming language developed by Sun Microsystems. The theory behind Java is that a developer can write a program in Java and have it work on Windows machines and Macs without altering it.

M

Mac Help Mac OS X's built-in help system.

maximize button While the maximize button in Windows expands the current window to fill the screen, the Mac's button (the green one in the upper left) makes the window resize to enclose its contents.

menu A list of commands from which the user can choose which one will be performed.

minimize button The Mac's minimize button (the yellow one in the upper left) does approximately the same thing as its Windows counterpart, collapsing the window into the Dock.

modifier key A key that is held down in combination with another key, thereby changing the function of that key. The Shift key is a simple example of a modifier key, but the term is usually reserved for the Command, Control, and Option keys on the Mac. (Portable Macs may also have a function, or Fn, key.)

mouse The Mac's pointing device—a peripheral that controls the movement of the cursor on the screen. The main difference you will find when switching to the Mac is that the standard Mac mouse has only one button (actually, the latest Apple mice have no buttons, since the entire mouse is used to send clicks to the Mac). The right-click in Windows is replaced by a keyboard-mouse combination, Control-click. It doesn't have to be that way, though. Mac OS X does support multibutton mice. If you use a multibutton mouse, it will behave similarly to its Windows counterpart.

My Computer See *Computer.*

My Documents See *Documents folder.*

N

Network Neighborhood There is no direct analog to the Network Neighborhood on the Mac. You can find machines to connect to using the Connect to Server command in the Finder's Go menu.

O

Option key A modifier key on the Mac, whose function changes depending on what application is running.

P

Power Management See *Energy Saver.*

Program Files folder See *Applications folder.*

program switching The act of changing the active (frontmost) program. On the Mac you can switch programs by clicking the appropriate icon in the Dock or by using the Command-Tab keyboard combination. The two Windows equivalents are using the taskbar or pressing Alt-Tab.

protected memory A memory scheme that sets aside unique space for each application so that if one program crashes, it will not affect the others. This is a feature of Mac OS X.

Q

Quick Launch See *Dock.*

QuickTime Apple's software for playing audio and video on a computer. It's actually more complicated than that; it's also a media-authoring platform and a file format. But if you're like most of us—a regular old computer user—it's just a media player. Windows Media Player is the basic counterpart to Quick-Time on Windows.

R

Recycle Bin See *Trash.*

Regional Settings See *International.*

S

scheduled tasks The capability to schedule specific tasks isn't directly included in Mac OS X but instead is found in the Unix foundation of Mac OS X. The utility is called cron. If you don't want to work in the command line to use cron, a number of third-party utilities can handle this task.

scroll bar The bar on the side or bottom of a window that controls what part of a document is displayed.

shortcut See *alias.*

Sherlock Apple's Internet search-and-retrieval utility.

Start menu There is no direct equivalent in Mac OS X, but the functions can be replicated by placing the Applications folder in the Dock. Some functions are also duplicated in the Apple menu. See *Apple menu* and *Dock.*

System There is no one System Preferences panel in Mac OS X that parallels the System control panel in Windows, but most functions are covered by the panels in the Hardware section of System Preferences.

System folder This can be a bit confusing, as there is a folder named System right alongside a folder called System Folder. The former holds files crucial to the running of Mac OS X, while the latter holds files for Mac OS 9—which is needed for the Classic environment.

System Preferences An application that serves the same purpose as the control panels folder in Windows. Individual settings are handled through panels in the System Preferences application, rather than via individual applets in the control panel. Most basic Windows applets, such as Keyboard, Sounds, and Date/Time, have similarly named counterparts in Mac OS X's System Preferences. Other not-so-clear cases are cross-referenced here.

T

taskbar See *Dock.*

Terminal A program for accessing Mac OS X's Unix underpinnings.

title bar The top border of a window, which contains the name of the window.

Trash The holding area for things you want to delete from your computer. Like items in the Windows Recycle Bin, items in the Trash aren't actually deleted from your computer until you empty it.

U

Universal Serial Bus (USB) USB is a technology for connecting peripherals—such as pointing devices and printers—to your computer. Mac OS X supports USB, so many of your Windows peripherals will work on the Mac.

Undo A command that takes back the previous command, "undoing" it. For example, if you deleted a word from a sentence, Undo would put it back. Undo is usually Command-Z on the Mac.

Universal Access A System Preferences panel that allows users with hearing or seeing problems or users who have trouble using the mouse or keyboard to adjust the way they interact with the Mac.

USB See *Universal Serial Bus.*

Users See *Accounts.*

W

wallpaper See *Desktop picture.*

Windows Media Player See *QuickTime.*

wizard A wizard is a help program that guides a user step-by-step through a task, such as the creation of a document or the setting of Internet preferences. Wizards basically work the same on the Mac as they do in Windows.

AnchorDesk Columns

In January 2002, I decided to see if a Windows-dependent technology columnist could happily live as a Macintosh user. What follows are my ZDNet AnchorDesk columns, from January to April 2002, documenting my answer to that question. These columns are still timely, although many of the concerns I raised in them have since been addressed.

These columns appear as published originally on ZDNet AnchorDesk (www.anchordesk.com) and are used with permission of CNET Networks Inc. (www.cnet.com).

Column 1
The challenge: If I go Mac, will I ever go back?

David Coursey,
Executive Editor, AnchorDesk
Wednesday, January 16, 2002

Can a Windows-dependent technology columnist live happily as a Mac user? That's the question I am about to spend a month of my life trying to answer.

In theory, a Windows user ought to be able to get along quite well with a Mac. But will it prove true in real life? And how much will I have to give up or find workarounds for because the Mac doesn't go there?

It's been half a decade since I used a Mac as my primary, day-in/day-out computer. I left Mac because I found it hard to organize my conferences using a mostly Mac solution. Today, FileMaker—the ease-of-use winner among databases for both Windows and Mac—has grown up enough that it wouldn't be a problem. (Of course, I am no longer organizing conferences, so that problem solved itself, anyway.)

SO BEGINNING NEXT MONDAY, subject to a couple of technical qualifiers I'll outline in a minute, I am going to go all Mac for a month. At the end of the process I'll write a detailed report, and between now and then I'll write an occasional log of my experiences.

Some things I know already. For example, Microsoft Office is available in a very nice version for Mac OS X. But it is also very different from the Office XP version I have become used to. Many XP features don't exist in the Mac version, but the Mac suite has a few tricks of its own I'll check out.

During the workday, I pretty much live in three instant-messaging programs—Microsoft Messenger, AOL Instant Messenger, and Yahoo Messenger. I need all three, and fortunately they're available for Mac. On the other hand, PalTalk, a conferencing program I also use at least semiregularly, isn't available in a Mac version, so I could end up losing some friends over this.

OR, MORE LIKELY, I'll add a Windows emulator to the Mac. In some ways that's signaling defeat, and I will try to stay away from that option as much as I can. But if I have to work on my personal Web site, which is built with Microsoft FrontPage (and uses the FrontPage server extensions), and FrontPage won't run on the emulator, I have a problem. I'd pretty much rather die than build all the buttons and links that FrontPage does for me.

Networking won't be an issue, however, because the desktop Mac has an AirPort 802.11b card installed, and I know it works. The LCD panel display is also gorgeous, and I know the machine works with my digital cameras. Actually, using a Mac is probably a good thing for my growing interest in digital photography. But what about a nice audio-editing program to use for the AnchorDesk radio show?

I need to return my iBook to Apple (both my Macs are loaners) and get it replaced, as I have broken the power connector at the machine end. I am hoping to get one of the new iBooks with the 14-inch screen, introduced last week but lost in the glare cast by the new iMacs with the Luxo-lamp screen attachment. If, however, I don't get a replacement, my portable— I am sitting in a comfortable chair writing this on a laptop using a wireless network connection—will remain a Windows machine.

WHY AM I DOING THIS? First, to see if I can really take my own medicine. I've been saying that many more people should have Macs than actually do—while accepting the inevitability that comes with living in a Windows world—so now I am going to walk that walk for a while.

Yesterday, I was also trying to do a comparative review of the media features included with Windows XP versus the equivalent Mac software. After a few hours of mucking around with the different programs on the Mac, I noticed something: What I was looking at, more than anything, was the philosophical differences between the operating systems rather than actual differences in the feature sets. I kept expecting Mac apps to behave like Windows apps, and they didn't. But they were consistent in what they did do and how they performed.

The other reason I am doing this—and watch out, desktop Linux might be next—is to get my Mac skills closer to what they used to be. Why do I want to do this? Because future Microsoft operating systems and PC hardware are much more likely to borrow from the Mac than vice versa.

Like everything in the world today, this project comes with some fine print attached, and here's mine:

- I am replacing my Windows desktop with a Mac; specifically a G3 Mac loaded with the most current versions of OS X and OS 9 (for compatibility). To avoid temptation, I will actually move the PC off my desk, but I will need to do something about using it as a file server for the Mac, since lots of important documents will still reside there.

- I will run OS X whenever possible, but won't hesitate to use applications only available in OS 9.x.

- While I won't do my writing, e-mail, browsing, listening, or photography in anything but Mac OS, I will go back to the Windows machine for a couple of projects I am working on that are specifically Win XP-related. Also, if it turns out that an application I just can't live without won't run on the Windows-emulation software, then I may go back to XP for that app only, but will note it in the log for this project.

- If I were more dependent on my PDA, the biggest issue might be the lack of Mac support for Pocket PC (thanks, Microsoft!), so I need to round up some cables and get everything running on a Palm device of some sort. Of course, I will try Pocket PC with the emulator, but that would really be almost cheating. So I will give preference to solutions that don't require a copy of Windows running atop Mac OS, as that seems to miss the point of the whole exercise.

- FusionOne never seems to have gotten its Mac act together—Macs are not a high priority for start-ups these days—so synchronization of e-mail, calendars, and such could be a problem. Or maybe not. It's something I'll deal with when it comes up.

- And, of course, if I find myself needing to review software or do something else that's required to write my daily column or do the AnchorDesk radio show that can only be done on a PC, then I will. But I will also note it in the log.

So there you have it—my plan to find out how using today's Mac stacks up to using Windows. I have some ideas about what I will learn, but I also know I'm in for some surprises, some frustrations, and perhaps some changes in attitude. We'll see.

Meanwhile, you can join me for this adventure here at AnchorDesk and on the daily radio program, where I usually work out my angst before turning it into a column. But you can start out by taking my usual role and making a prediction: Take the QuickPoll below and offer your opinion on how I'll feel about Mac and Windows at the end of the 30 days. Or give me your feedback by posting a TalkBack.

How will I feel about Mac and Windows after 30 days?

- I'll be frustrated with the Mac's quirks and will eagerly rush back to Windows. 764 (4 percent)
- I'll appreciate the Mac's benefits but will still return to Windows as my full-time environment. 8,601 (50 percent)
- I'll become a diehard Mac convert, and never give Windows another look. 7,877 (46 percent)

Column 2

How living on a Mac nearly made me change careers

David Coursey,
Executive Editor, AnchorDesk
Friday, January 25, 2002

> **Editor's note:** *Starting on Monday, Jan. 21, David took up a challenge. A longtime and loyal Microsoft user, he decided to make a big switch—and spend a month with the Mac at the center of his computing universe. What follows is the first of several periodic reports about his grand experiment.*

On the first day of my month as a Mac user, I made a momentous decision. I made up my mind to change careers.

Here's the scene: I am sitting at Apple's headquarters in Cupertino, the fourth-floor boardroom, and I mean *the* boardroom. And I'm looking at software demos.

We're done with iTunes, Apple's MP3 music program, and we're into iPhoto, iMovie, iDVD, and Final Cut Pro 3—all photography and digital movie programs. Three of these come free with every Mac, and the Pro software is only $999—quite inexpensive for that sort of thing.

THE APPLE GUYS had brought in a $4,000 digital video camera/recorder and a PowerBook G4 notebook—a titanium-encased model just like the one they loaned me for the month. And damn if they aren't doing pro video editing, with real-time effects, on the notebook.

The same machine I use for writing this column is displaying really great video, and we're rearranging it about as simply as Word lets me fix a badly structured sentence.

Watching Mac-based video editing—at about one-tenth the cost of only a few years ago—brought me to a revelation: It made me realize that what I was really meant to do was produce documentaries for public television. Or news. Or even my favorite, "Good Eats," for the Food Network.

I want to work with pictures and sound, not just words.

IF THERE IS a creative bone in your body, it's hard not to look at the Macintosh and not feel something tingle—which is precisely what Apple is counting on. Because while Windows is good at many things, if what you do is create something visual—be it digital photography, Web pages, magazines, television, film, or anything else—the Mac is your platform.

By the time I'd gotten home, better sense had prevailed—so I will remain your faithful columnist.

But this is a warning to Candy, Jackie, Hari, and Melissa at CNET Broadband: I want to learn how to do this stuff. The Mac makes it so cool and so approachable.

* * *

I AM WRITING this on Wednesday night, three whole days into the Mac odyssey. I have replaced my Windows desktop almost totally. I am still using Windows during my daily radio program because I have developed a system for that and I'm not yet facile enough with the OS X user interface to do a radio program, scan the news, and watch two instant-messaging windows simultaneously. But I am getting there.

There have been a few snags along the way, which I will document in separate short essays on various days as the Mac project continues.

The short version is that Mac OS X is a wonderful operating system that's about six months away from having the networking features and third-party applications support it needs. That doesn't affect someone with a single Mac, but it is a challenge—though even today a surmountable one—for someone like me, with Macs and Windows machines on one network.

Like I said, stay tuned for the technical details on another day sometime soon.

THE OTHER THING I've noticed is that despite the propaganda about how many applications have been created for the Mac—Apple says 2,500 are now available for OS X—there don't seem to be that many compelling ones. Apple stores, for example, carry only about 20 OS X titles. And if you delve through the list on Apple's Web site, many of the titles sound more like shareware than real commercial products.

There is a world of creative applications for visual artists and designers. Microsoft Office is available for OS X and works very nicely, although I can't get data out of my Pocket PC device (which I had expected I couldn't do) or out of a Palm device (rats!) and into Office for Mac OS X.

Connectix Virtual PC, which runs very nicely under Mac OS 9.2, is clunky under OS X. So clunky that it crashed the new iMac—to the extent that Unix error messages appeared on the screen. That is, however, the only thing even close to a crash I have experienced, and it could be something I did wrong in the setup. Or perhaps it's a sign from God that 9.2—the predecessor to X—still has a place in my life.

I AM NOT LOOKING forward to running Windows apps atop Mac OS, but it's nice to know I can. For the record, on the Titanium PowerBook—nicknamed the TiBook after the elemental symbol for Titanium—Virtual PC runs Windows 2000 very nicely, if slowly.

Apple has pretty much perfected what the industry calls the "out-of-box experience"—what you experience when you first open the box and power up the machine. Even getting the AirPort wireless networking up and running was as close to brain-dead simple as anything I've seen. While the various Windows hardware companies have made great strides in this area, Apple is the master.

So after three days of Mac-dom, I am still feeling some transition pains. I naturally try to do things the Windows way first, which isn't always the Mac way. Sometimes I try to do things the way I used to do them a long time ago on earlier Mac operating systems, but OS X changes many of those things.

IF I WEREN'T such a computer junkie, this probably wouldn't be such a problem—and it's less of a problem now than it was when I started first thing Monday. But I would be lying to you if I didn't say it is taking a little getting used to.

On the other hand, I'd expected Microsoft Office, which looks very different on the Mac than the Office XP I've gotten used to on the PC, to be more of a pain than it has been. The core functions and menus work virtually the same on both Windows and Mac, even if the feature sets are different. So my writing productivity hasn't suffered at all.

Overall, the experience is a positive one. I'm having a good time and learning things—including my real calling in life.

Note: Since many have asked, I am now running OS X on two G4-based machines, a new iMac, and a Titanium PowerBook. I am using AirPort cards in the machines to connect to Linksys and Agere-based wireless networks. I have also installed a utility called Dave—more on this later—that allows the Macs and Windows machines to see one another.

What do you think of my initial experiences on the Mac? Are they pretty much what you expected? Got any advice? TalkBack to me!

Column 3

Will Microsoft pull the plug on Apple?

David Coursey,
Executive Editor, AnchorDesk
Tuesday, January 29, 2002

Is Microsoft going to kill Apple Computer? Some may say it's already happened, at least from looking at the relative dominance of Windows over Apple's Mac OS. But I'm talking about Microsoft pulling the plug on Office and Internet Explorer for Mac OS.

Is this actually going to happen? I don't think so. Apple CEO Steve Jobs doesn't think it will happen, or so he said during a meeting I had with him last week to discuss this and other topics. I've heard the same from the people at Microsoft who develop the Mac applications.

BECAUSE OF A CONTRACT between Microsoft and Apple that runs out this summer, I think it's very important for Microsoft to make a clear statement about its commitment to Apple products. And since Microsoft's support of Mac OS is sometimes viewed as an extension of its antitrust defense, a formal commitment becomes even more essential. If Microsoft is going to continue to support Mac OS, going on the record shouldn't be a problem, right?

Microsoft also needs to promise—and this is what I am really hoping for—to do a better job of supporting core technologies such as .Net, as well as the user experience across the two platforms.

The current arrangement between Microsoft and Apple dates back to 1997. As part of what amounted to the settlement of lawsuits Apple had filed against Microsoft—and was winning—Microsoft invested $150 million in Apple and promised to continue developing Microsoft Office, Internet Explorer, and development tools for Mac OS until August 2002.

MICROSOFT SHOULD NOW SAY—in writing and ideally in the form of a contract—that this support will continue over the next five years. This is important, because many people—myself included—believe Microsoft Office is an essential application, one that drives Macintosh sales.

And this time, Microsoft needs to go even further and expand its Mac OS support, because aside from Office, Microsoft's Mac support, well, sucks.

Here's my list of areas where Microsoft should improve.

> **Media player.** Yes, there is a Windows Media Player for Mac OS X. And I can even get over that it's little more than a player and lacks much of the functionality of the XP version. But could Microsoft at least provide all the codecs? Right now, only some are available—meaning I can listen to some Windows Media streams, but not terribly many.

Pocket PC compatibility. Currently there is no way to synchronize Pocket PC devices with anything on a Mac. A third-party developer is working on such an application, but if Microsoft really cares about the Mac, it'll create a Mac version of ActiveSync on its own.

Palm compatibility. Microsoft is also taking its time in building a new conduit that will allow Palms to sync with its Mac products. At this moment, I know of no way whatsoever to sync a Palm device with Microsoft products operating on Mac OS X. Even importing a file doesn't work from Palm Desktop.

Web authoring. No Web authoring tool for the Mac supports Microsoft FrontPage extensions. While I appreciate that there isn't a market for FrontPage for Mac, perhaps Microsoft could persuade some other developer to support its extensions.

.Net. If Microsoft is developing a .Net client for Macintosh, they are keeping it very hush-hush.

Messenger. Microsoft Messenger for the Mac lacks the multimedia features in the newest Windows versions. How long will it be until they arrive on the Mac? Or will they ever? Mac users ought to be able to video and audio conference with Windows users.

Exchange. Accessing a Microsoft Exchange server from Mac OS is best done using a Web browser (if your server supports Outlook Web Access). The Mac-only version of Outlook runs on Mac OS 9.x and supports only Exchange servers, which means that people with Exchange and non-Exchange accounts have to run multiple email clients. There's nothing especially bad about using Outlook Web Access—actually, it's quite pleasant—but being forced to do so keeps Mac users second-class citizens.

Microsoft has taken the attitude that its Mac Office programs should share file formats and many features with the Windows programs. Yet the Mac team often goes off in its own direction when it comes to designing the user interface and specific features. I have not found this to be a problem—even if it means that Mac's major email/calendar/contact-management application is called Entourage and not Outlook.

THERE ARE MOST DEFINITELY some function and feature differences between Mac Office and Office XP (no task panes on Mac, for example), but the Mac version is still a first-class product. In some ways, I've grown to prefer Mac Office to Office XP, although it's hard to say why. In general, I find it difficult to compare my experiences with Mac OS to Windows XP. It's like trying to explain why some people like redheads more than blondes—it's just personal preference.

Still, Microsoft should commit to providing all its core functionality and features on a cross-platform basis. That doesn't mean Microsoft needs to create a bunch of new Mac versions of its applications—although that would be nice. Rather, Microsoft should promise that Mac users of .Net and Microsoft's calendars, email, contact managers, Web browsers, media players, instant messaging, media authoring, and other core technologies will have the same functionality as their Windows kin.

The reason Microsoft should put this on paper is because of legitimate concerns that its interest in Macintosh is more a ploy in its antitrust battles ("Look, we support multiple platforms!") than a real interest in serving Mac users. And the sooner Microsoft reaffirms this commitment—and expands it as I've outlined above—the better for Mac users, both present and future.

Column 4

Why I just love the new iMac (and why you might, too)

David Coursey,
Executive Editor, AnchorDesk
Monday, February 4, 2002

It's been a week since I started using a new iMac as my full-time desktop computer and a PowerBook G4 as my portable PC, all as part of my monthlong challenge to see if I, long a loyal Windows user, could make Apple the center of my computing universe. There are still a few problems—specifically related to getting PDA data in and out of Microsoft Office.

But besides that, I've made a very smooth transition. I have even started using the Apple key instead of the Control key when cutting and pasting.

None of the photos I've seen do the new iMac justice. It's hard to take a picture of a white computer with a clear frame around the screen and make it look good. It is especially difficult to do this against a white background, as Apple is prone to do. They had the same problem with the iPod, which people thought was much larger than it is because they had seen it only on a billboard. Now, they didn't think it was *that* big, but …

If you are trying to show off the iMac base—about the size of a big salad bowl turned upside-down—it's hard to have the monitor in a normal position. This is probably why the best pictures of the new iMac, such as they are, have been taken from the side. That shows off the arm that connects the screen to the base rather nicely.

IN USE, the base of the iMac, which contains the computer itself, essentially disappears from view, hidden by the screen. The screen—a 15-inch flat panel—has all the predictable benefits of LCD displays, but the mounting mechanism is really special. This is the first time I've been able to position a screen precisely where I want it.

Mac OS X also does an excellent job of driving the screen, with great graphics performance. I am not quite so wild about the characters that show up while I am typing using Word or the other Microsoft Office apps. Microsoft has yet to fully implement the features of OS X that put great-looking fonts onto the screen.

This was likely lost in the rush to get a version of OS X to market and will be resolved in a future release. The "poor" quality of the Microsoft fonts is noticeable because the rest of the computer looks so great, not because it's putting my eyes out or anything.

The iMac has no fan—actually it has a fan, but I've never heard it—meaning my office is quieter than it used to be. The fan is thermally controlled, so it turns on only if the machine heats up. The iMac also has a very small footprint, leaving me with a lot of free desk space.

If I were making any changes to the iMac, I'd increase the screen resolution (1024x768 is standard) or go to a 17-inch screen. The higher resolution is a personal preference (I need more open windows sometimes), and boosting the screen size would make the machines too expensive. To think of it, so would the increased resolution.

I'VE DISPENSED with the Apple one-button mouse that came with the machine. I replaced it with a Microsoft optical mouse with all the buttons and a thumbwheel. I just plugged it in, and it worked immediately. While the stock Apple mouse— with its single button—doesn't support right-clicking, all the iMac apps seem to. This gives me access to a wide range of shortcuts I've grown used to under Windows. "Real" Apple users know you can Control-click the one-button mouse to access the right-button features, but I still like my extra buttons and the thumbwheel.

The transition to the Mac way of doing things has been pretty easy, once I got the hang of the docking bar that is the OS X equivalent of the Windows start menu. Now that I have all my frequently used apps in the Dock, I am a pretty happy camper.

Based on my experience, I have no reservations whatsoever recommending an iMac as a family's new or next home computer. Only really hard-core gamers would have trouble with a Mac, and those people should be looking at the new gaming consoles, anyway.

I'M TEMPTED to say that Apple should have waited to make OS X the standard operating system for its consumer Macs, at least until there was better support for things such as Palm PDAs, media players for Windows Media, and RealNetworks file formats. But as Steve Jobs told me on Day 1 of my Mac odyssey, there are some things that simply won't happen until the OS becomes the Apple standard.

I can't really disagree with that logic, so this is more a warning that you may find yourself working in Classic mode from time to time. I am doing my very best to remain totally in OS X, so I have to admit that my concerns about this issue may be inflated.

As for working from the iMac, I can only hit the corporate Exchange mail server using a POP client or a Web browser. This isn't a problem for me, but it may be for a few of you. I also have not tried to find a VPN client, so I need to call our IS department and inquire.

The lack of OS X support for both Palm and Pocket PC devices is, however, troublesome. I think this will be worked out, at least for Pocket PC (and only with the help of a third-party developer) in a few weeks. Palm OS support will doubtless come, though I cannot today tell you when with any level of confidence. Six months seems likely.

I'VE HAD NO trouble exchanging files with colleagues, sending and receiving email, or browsing the Web. And the free mail client Apple provides, though lacking a calendar function, works very well. Actually, it's a better pure mail client than Microsoft's Entourage, its office productivity suite for the Macintosh platform.

It's for this reason that so many Mac users have separate calendar, contact-management, and email programs. The single-solution approach, à la Outlook and Entourage, is very attractive, but I am looking at other options as well.

The iPod is a fantastic MP3 player, and iTunes does a good job of managing my music. I want to find a "disco" software package, which I believe exists, to do some mixing, but the basic dubbing of music from CD (or Internet) to computer to iPod works very well.

THE MORE I USE IPHOTO, the more useful I find it. The program is not a photo editor, although it will allow you to crop a photo, correct red-eye, and convert color images to black and white.

But iPhoto really shines in managing a large photo collection, thanks to its ability to vary thumbnails of the photos from very tiny to full-screen. This means you can zoom back and easily scroll through hundreds or, more likely, thousands of photos and then zoom in to pick the one you want.

iPhoto is also great for sharing your images. While the program does not have an easy way to resize and email an image, it does a very nice job of collecting photos into books, which you can print at home or have commercially printed by Apple ($30 for 10 pages, and the books are really quite nice). iPhoto can also be used to create slide shows and HTML photo pages, and, of course, to order prints.

OVERALL, I'D RATE the Macintosh photo "experience" significantly superior to Windows XP, although XP has the basics covered.

I have not played with iMovie, but finally have an idea for a home movie project (lacking kids, I have no ready players), so I am planning to compare the Mac and XP cinematic experiences this weekend.

Another area in which OS X has a little maturing to do is support for streaming media. Microsoft Media Player doesn't support all its formats on the new OS, meaning I can't listen to a number of online radio stations. Real doesn't seem to have announced an OS X version of RealPlayer, though I suspect one will appear.

So that's where things stand after the first week of "Mac Month" here in my office. About the only thing I am still using the XP box for is some instant messaging (especially during the radio program) and to keep the Outlook telephone directory open when I need to make a quick phone call.

Based on what you're hearing and reading, are you more tempted these days to try—or buy—a Mac?

- Yes. It doesn't matter as much anymore that it's a Windows-dominated world. 17,906 (86 percent)
- No. I don't have the time or patience to convert to an entirely different platform. 3,003 (14 percent)

Column 5

Mac voyeurs: All talk, no action

David Coursey,
Executive Editor, AnchorDesk
Tuesday, February 19, 2002

Have you heard about the Mac voyeurs? I've been running into them in spades lately. Maybe you've met them, too. Or perhaps you, yourself, are a Mac voyeur, and don't even know it.

Mac voyeurs are people who want to know all about my Macintosh project. They are intensely interested in knowing everything about how the Mac works. That's innocent enough, but it grows from there.

THESE PEOPLE tell me—almost emotionally—how important they think Macintosh is. They usually say something like, "It keeps Microsoft honest" or "Bill Gates stole all his good ideas from Apple."

They speculate about what a genius Steve Jobs must be. "You've really met him?" they ask in awe. "Yes, but only recently," I tell them. I suspect they'd buy me dinner just to hear my Steve story. I should probably thank him for all the free meals I'll be getting. (Did I also mention that I have a story about how my radio producer's wife walks her dog with Steve Wozniak every morning without recognizing the other Apple founder?)

And there's one other thing about Mac voyeurs, and this explains the voyeur part: They absolutely, positively, under any circumstances wouldn't ever buy a Mac. I suspect that for these people, the Apple Store would be adult entertainment.

FRANKLY, I AM getting a bit tired of telling these Windows bigots—people who don't even know why they use Windows except that everyone else does—about the wonders of Macintosh. Hell, Windows is just fine for them, so I'd hate to push them into a nonconformity they just couldn't handle.

Now, I am not here to tell these people to shut up and go buy a Mac if they love them so much. OK, maybe I am. But despite the month (due to illness it's going to turn out to be six weeks) that I've promised to use a Mac as my primary work machine, I haven't become a Mac zealot.

But I have developed a very healthy respect for the Mac as a home computer and, with some networking improvements, as a player on a Windows-based network. All the things the Mac voyeurs like about the computer they'll never own are right there. And I'll keep saying that if more people were exposed to Macintosh, more people would buy one.

SO WHY DON'T the Mac voyeurs buy in? They are absolutely, positively convinced that buying a Mac means losing something important. I understand this point of view. And if someone is really convinced, I can't make him or her think otherwise. Truth be told, there really are many fewer Mac apps than Windows apps.

But the real question is whether the apps you need—or acceptable alternatives—are available on Macintosh. And in most cases, for your typical home or office user, I think the answer is yes. And the apps are generally nice ones, too.

Be that as it may, it probably won't convince any of the looky-loos to make the leap from voyeur to owner. Perhaps more extreme measures might work; maybe the next time I run into some of these Mac voyeurs I'll just load them into the car, drive them down to the Apple Store, and tell 'em it's time to put up or shut up.

And then either I'll have created a new Mac user or maybe get some peace and quiet. Either way, I win.

Are you a Mac voyeur?

- Yes. 1,703 (24 percent)
- No. 4,950 (70 percent)
- I won't say. 438 (6 percent)

Column 6

Try a Mac? Why it won't hurt as much as you think

David Coursey,
Executive Editor, AnchorDesk
Monday, February 25, 2002

What does it take to turn a Mac voyeur into a Mac user?

Last week I wrote about people who are very interested in Macs but remain firmly wedded (welded?) to Windows. In response to that column, I received email from a reader (whose identity I won't reveal, since he works for Sun) challenging me to present the Mac's case and convince him that it's worth making the switch.

It occurred to me that this reader's concerns might be yours, too. So let's take a look at his questions and see if my answers will change you from cautious fan to convert.

1. Convince me that on a Mac I'll be able to share and swap files (word processing, spreadsheets, presentations) with my Win colleagues.

This is old hat. Microsoft Office for Macintosh (in either Mac OS 9.x or 10.1) is absolutely file-compatible with the Windows version. Despite some feature differences, the core functionalities are close enough that I can make the switch from Office XP to Mac Office without thinking about it.

Having said that, I need to mention that Microsoft Access does not exist on the Mac. However, FileMaker, available for both Mac and Windows, is to my thinking a much better database. There is also no FrontPage for the Mac, nor any Web tool that supports the FrontPage server extensions. This is a big deal for me, but most people don't care.

I am not a power Excel user. Nor do I use Word macros. I get some spreadsheets with scripts in them and they all work fine, but if you are a big Excel buff, you'll want to visit the Microsoft Web site or ask someone who knows more than I do about how complete the scripting and other programmatic elements are across the two platforms.

All this file swapping is easily possible on either Mac OS 9.x or OS X 10.1. The easiest way to move files from a PC to a Mac is to email them. Also, Apple provides a free online storage service called iDisk—which can be accessed from a Windows machine—that you can use to store commonly used files. An add-on Mac disk drive (about $50) will also read and write PC-formatted floppy disks. And, of course, you can always burn a CD or use a Zip drive.

One more compatibility point: Out of the box, OS X can create Adobe Acrobat .pdf files of any document you can print. This makes it easy to send people copies of your Mac treasures, even if they don't have the app you used to create them.

On the email front, Microsoft offers a version of Outlook that supports Exchange servers on the Mac, though only for OS 9.x. It will, of course, run in Classic mode under OS X 10.1. Classic mode is a compatibility feature that allows older Mac apps to bring up OS 9.2 on the OS X 10.1 desktop.

Apple provides an excellent email client on OS X. Microsoft Outlook Express works great, as does a new Microsoft email/calendar/contact manager called Entourage, which comes with Office X. There are also a number of other email, calendar, and contact managers for the Mac. One thing: Some of them come as separate, though tightly integrated, applications. That's not a problem, but it's different from the all-in-one approach of Outlook (not the Express version) and Entourage.

2. Convince me that after the initial changeover period, using the Mac will be easy for a nontechnical person.

I think Macs are, for the average user, much easier to use and manage than Windows machines. True, the Mac—especially OS X—is different from Windows, so it takes some getting used to. But if you have a computer-phobic friend, the best thing to give him or her is a Mac. No one who I have ever persuaded to buy a Mac, or given one to, has ever called and complained.

3. I'm in the market for a new machine for my son, who goes to university in the summer. He is quite happy to use either Windows or Mac, as long as it will work for him and he doesn't have to get techie when he creates and submits assignments or wants to connect to the university WAN.

Which machine to suggest depends on a few factors—for example, your son's major. Why does this matter? Well, if he's majoring in graphic design or photography and you buy him a Windows machine, you're a borderline bad father. Likewise, if your son is pursuing an MBA in hopes of becoming a finance guy, that's a reason to buy Windows.

Computer science major? I'd probably get both—Windows because it's the standard, and Mac OS X because it's a cool Unix box that offers a lot for programmers.

Another major? I think the compatibility questions I answered earlier apply here. For surfing the Web, doing papers, downloading music, and those sorts of things, the Mac is fine. Hard-core gamers, however, probably need a high-end PC or a game console.

As for connecting to the WAN, Macs have wonderful wireless and built-in Ethernet capabilities and are easy to network. That said, you might want to buy some third-party software, perhaps something like Dave (no relation) or one of the other utilities from Thursby so your Mac becomes a full citizen on a Windows network. Unix network or the Internet? No problem—no new software is required.

The new iMac is easy to set up, easy to connect to the Internet, easy to network wirelessly, has a great screen, doesn't take up much space, and your son's friends will think it's really cool. Splurge for the $1,799 model with the DVD burner. An iBook is a good notebook choice as well. An absolutely equivalent desktop would cost more than the Mac, thanks to the DVD burner. At the same time, Macs remain, overall, a tad more expensive than Windows machines. But with the original iMacs now priced well under $1,000, cost should not be a barrier.

4. You're a technical maven. But can you step back and say, hand on heart, that for someone who isn't a tech star the switch to Mac will be pretty painless? THAT'S what we need to know.

It is doubtless more difficult to move from a Mac to Windows than vice versa. Switching from Windows to Mac (which for most people isn't so much switching as gaining Mac skills) requires an open mind and about a week of regular use. The hardest thing in my reacquaintance with Mac has been that file/edit/view/etc. choices at the top of Microsoft apps have shifted one place to the right, so I had to get used to actually looking at the word to hit the right choice for a few days.

On OS X, it also took a little time to get used to managing the Dock, which is the OS X equivalent to Windows's Start Menu. I do recommend replacing the one-button standard Mac mouse with a two-button mouse because right-clicking makes life easier, but that is true on either platform.

If you are planning to use this Mac at the office, I would probably use OS 9.2 for the time being. If connecting to Windows machines or a corporate network (perhaps over a VPN) is key, then I'd probably start with OS X and backtrack to OS 9.2 if there are problems that Thursby's Dave won't solve. Remember, since OS 9.2 is a standard feature of OS X-based systems, moving to the earlier OS isn't a hassle.

As a single computer at home, a Mac is fine. Talking to your Windows machines is, again, easiest with something like Dave. A Mac will work fine on your Windows-based wireless or hard-wired local area network, as will a Windows box on a Mac AirPort network. I really like the Agere Orinoco wireless products for this—it's the same stuff Apple uses in AirPort, but a Wi-Fi–compliant 802.11b wireless device can talk to an Airport access point. Plug that into your DSL or cable modem, and you're on the Internet.

There is still one important question:

5. Can you do what you need to do using a Mac? Another way of asking this is: Are the apps I need available on the Mac?

I won't lie to you: There are not nearly as many Mac apps as Windows apps. On the other hand, how many apps do you use? And if there is a Windows-only app that you absolutely need—mine are some ham radio programs—will it run on a Windows emulator running on your Mac, or can you find a Windows machine to use occasionally? The emulation option actually works quite well (on OS 9.x, that is), but adds expense. Using a friend's Windows machine for an hour is an almost universally available option.

Are you a convert yet? If not, feel free to TalkBack to me below and let me know about your additional concerns. Am I a convert yet? That remains to be seen. I'm reaching the end of what was supposed to be my monthlong Mac odyssey; however, I spent three weeks of it with the flu so I'm sticking with it another two weeks to finish all my testing and investigating.

So what, as Regis would say, is my final answer? I don't know yet—but I will in a couple of weeks. Stay tuned.

Column 7

How Apple's iMovie made me a Spielberg— in just one hour

David Coursey,
Executive Editor, AnchorDesk
Wednesday, March 20, 2002

As I've already told you, if you're buying a computer mostly to do digital photography, buy a Mac. Well, here's another recommendation, based on my own recent hands-on efforts: If you're buying a computer to make digital home movies, buy a Mac.

Both Windows XP and Mac OS X include video-editing apps. Apple's iMovie stands up as a powerful, full-fledged application. By comparison, XP's Windows Movie Maker comes off as an afterthought.

YES, THERE ARE commercial Windows video editors simple enough for home users. Over the next few weeks I'll be testing a few of them. But iMovie represents the same remarkable combination that has kept Macintosh in business since 1984: It's powerful and it's easy to use. And better yet, it's free with every new Mac.

Using iMovie, I turned 20 minutes of raw video into a snappy presentation just under 6 minutes long. My minimasterpiece includes 11 edits, 8 transitions, a fade-in with titles at the beginning, and a fade-out with credits at the end. And all this took about an hour to create—the very first time I ever used the program.

Regular AnchorDesk readers will remember that last week we bade farewell to our colleague C. C. Holland, who left us to go write a novel. On Thursday we had a going-away party. Since I don't have kids, this is about as close as I get to a Kodak moment. So I brought along a Canon ZR25 MC digital video camcorder to preserve the event for C. C.'s keepsake file.

AT LEAST, that's what I told everyone. The real reason was to collect some raw material for this column (the next-to-last in my "Month with Mac" series).

Home from the party, I connected the camcorder to the iMac using a FireWire cable. FireWire is so fast (400 Mbps, which feels like the speed of light compared with USB 1.1 connections) that you can capture video on the computer directly from the camera in real time.

The iMovie application allows you to control the camcorder directly from the iMac—a real help when deciding which sequences to include. As I played the video from the camcorder into iMovie, I was able to fast-forward or rewind as necessary and then hit the import button to capture the video as an iMovie clip. Each time I did this, iMovie added a thumbnail of the clip to the onscreen window.

ONCE I'D IMPORTED all the clips I wanted, I sequenced them by dragging and dropping their thumbnails along a timeline.

Note that I'd gotten this far without reading any documentation or watching the video tutorial. But once I'd assembled the clips in the correct order on the timeline, I couldn't figure out how to trim away the bits I didn't want. Turns out it's easy, and the online help file showed me how.

Pretty soon, I had the video edited down just the way I wanted it. But the final product still looked jerky. So, again dragging and dropping, I added transitions—wipes, dissolves, fades—

to the edit points. Adding titles was just as easy. I could have added video and audio effects and narration the same way, but chose not to.

WHEN I WAS FINISHED, I saved the file. First, I saved it as a 6 MB QuickTime suitable for emailing to C. C. That took about 6 minutes.

Saving it as a DVD-quality file took the better part of an hour. I am not sure of the exact time, however, because after checking my email and sending C. C. the QuickTime file, I walked away from the computer.

When I came back, the DVD file had been created, and I was ready to use another Apple application—iDVD, free with all Macs that include a DVD burner—to burn it onto a disc. The software allows you to create a professional-looking disc that can be shown on most home DVD players and on PCs equipped with DVD-ROM drives.

AT THE END of the project, I have a QuickTime movie file consisting of my C. C. moment and a DVD to send her as a farewell gift. Lacking extra lighting and a better microphone (along with a sound mixer and other goodies), my iMovie is by no means professional in quality. But it's way, way better than all those home movies my parents took. The 90 minutes it took me to shoot and assemble was time well spent.

I'd like to tell you how to do all this on a Windows XP machine, but I can't. Windows Movie Maker just doesn't do what iMovie does. Together, iMovie and iDVD allowed me to share my world in a way I'd never tried before. The various Windows systems I've seen were just too complex.

Which is why I say, if you want to make home—or even simple business—movies, you need a Mac.

Column 8

Can a Windows guy learn to love the Mac? You bet!

David Coursey,
Executive Editor, AnchorDesk
Thursday, April 18, 2002

"Can a Windows-dependent technology columnist live happily as a Mac user? That's the question I am about to spend a month of my life trying to answer."

That's how I started my "month on Mac" series, which now runs to eight columns. Yes, it's been three months rather than one, but I had my reasons for stretching it out.

First, I spent February in the clutches of a nasty flu. Then I started worrying that I was writing about Apple too much, which makes some of my readers antsy, and decided I should spread out the columns a bit.

And when I'd used up all my other excuses, I finally came to the real reason I'd extended the experiment: I like this little iMac and don't want to give it up. It's a whole lot more fun than my Windows machine, and a great creative tool for whacking out these daily columns.

AT ONE POINT, I even took a G4 PowerBook up to Microsoft for a few days. Everyone ogled the cool titanium exterior and gave me only a little guff over the operating system. As I said to one (but only one) MS product manager, "See, I'm running Office—and here's Windows 2000 running on the Mac—you have a problem with that?"

As promised, I pretty much divorced myself from the PC for the past three months. Over the course of these three months, most of my computing has migrated away from it. My entire world—documents, spreadsheets, photographs, email—is now on the iMac—and I'm pretty happy with things the way they are. More specifically:

- On the Mac, the computer just doesn't get in the way of my work as much a PC does. Doubtless this is due, in part, to OS X's spare user interface. The ergonomics of the iMac—jokes about its looking like a table lamp aside—are excellent.

- Compatibility between Office XP and Mac Office is very good to excellent, and will improve even more when the Office for Mac service pack comes out later this spring.

- OS X is only so-so for sharing files with PCs over a network. Setting up the necessary connections could be much easier—but in the grand scheme of things, it isn't that difficult, either. If you want to spend $149, a copy of Thursby's Dave network utility makes the Mac an excellent Windows network machine.

- Macs and PCs share my wireless home network, and the Macs have been less trouble than the PCs. This is a reflection of Apple's being able to control the entire system, hardware and software, and making sure it all works together.

- I love my iPod.

- Mac is a vastly superior platform for digital movies and photography than stock Windows XP. Yes, you can buy additional software for the PC, but if creating anything—movies, photographs, books, Web sites—is driving your decision, Mac is better.

- That said, it's too bad there's no easy-to-use low-end Web building program for the Mac. That's a problem.

- Good thing that FrontPage 2002 and the rest of Office XP, and every other Windows app I tried, run very nicely on Virtual PC. I used the version with Windows 2000 and had excellent results. Sure, Virtual PC is slow, but it works.

- I did not get my Pocket PC to work with the Mac—largely because a little company called PocketMac, which supposedly has a solution for this, wouldn't send me their beta code. Palms and OS X ought to work fine together, but check the specifics first.

- Instant messaging, including video conferencing, works better on Windows XP than on Mac OS X. Media players work better on Windows. For example, there's no version of the latest RealPlayer for OS X, and nothing I've seen makes me sure there ever will be. Windows Media Player, meanwhile, doesn't work the same on Mac OS X as on Windows. Good thing Apple made things so that OS 9.2 opens whenever an application—like one of the older, Mac-compatible versions of RealPlayer—needs it. This is more a problem in concept (why am I having to run two operating systems on one computer?) than in practice, where it works fine.

As you can see, I don't think the iMac is perfect. But with the improvements I know are coming for Office and suspect are coming for OS X, I can live with its limitations.

Wanting to keep my Mac doesn't mean divorcing from Windows entirely. I still like Windows XP a whole lot. I still use a Windows machine during the radio show as a second computer. I do this partially because the PC is handy and partially because it has a larger screen than the iMac, the better to have four or five instant-messaging windows open simultaneously.

But if I just want to sit down and write—and use a computer that doesn't get in the way—Microsoft Office for Mac and OS X are a powerful combination. A Mac is a perfectly creditable desktop or portable system for me, even if sometimes I run Windows on it. The Mac, enhanced by OS X, has a level of simplicity and transparency in operation that allows it to get out of the way and just let me work. That's something Windows never does.

Would you ever switch platforms?

- Sure, why not? A computer's a computer—as long as it runs my software. 8,002 (61 percent)
- No! I'll never switch. They'll have to pry my PC/Mac from my cold, dead fingers. 5,056 (39 percent)

Index

A

About This Mac option
  Apple menu, 92
  definition, 241
ABS (automatic backup system), CMS
    Peripherals, 201–202
Access (Microsoft)
  migration process, 29
  replacing with FileMaker Pro, 131–132
accessing contextual menus, 233
Accounts panel, System preferences,
    System Preferences pane, 114–115, 241
Acrobat PDF files, manual migration
    process, 59–60
active windows, definition, 241
Adams, Aaron (Switcher), 44–47
Add New Hardware option (Windows),
    242
Add/Remove Programs option (Windows),
    242
adders. *See* Switchers
Address Book, 152–153
  Dock, applications running, 28
  Mac OS X with iSync, 54
  migration process from Outlook
      Express, 53–55
  position on Dock, 93

Adobe
  Acrobat PDF files, manual migration
      process, 59–60
  cross-platform applications, migration
      process, 29
  Photoshop Elements, reasons for
      switching, 223–224
AirPort Admin Utility, 180, 182, 184
AirPort Setup Assistant, 180–181
AirPort wireless networks
  AirPort Extreme, 172
  Base Stations
    configuring, 180–185
    home networks, 172–173
  connection process, 178
  definition, 172–173, 242
  desktop icon, 91
  help from Knowledge Base, 188
  installing cards, 82
  range, 179–180
  security, 186, 187
  use by others, 186–187
aliases, definition, 242
Alt key (Windows), 234
AnchorDesk, author's position, 6
antialiasing, definition, 242
antivirus protection, 206–207